Housing Policy in Scotland

HOUSING POLICY IN SCOTLAND

By
TOM BEGG

FOREWORD BY MICHAEL FORSYTH

JOHN DONALD PUBLISHERS LTD
EDINBURGH

A catalogue record for this book is available
from the British Library.

ISBN 0 85976 433 8

Phototypeset by WestKey Limited, Falmouth, Cornwall.
Printed and bound in Great Britain by Bell & Bain Ltd., Glasgow

Foreword

WE can learn a great deal about a society from an examination of its housing. Our homes form a fundamental part of our environment, but they can also teach us about our social, political and economic history.

In this book, Tom Begg has attempted to supply an authoritative answer to the question of why, in the period following the second world war, Scotland developed what was proportionately the largest state housing system of any non-communist country. He has also considered where the responsibility for this development lies, and what the consequences were of creating such places as Castlemilk, Easterhouse or Whitfield and the host of smaller but not dissimilar contemporary schemes in many of our other towns and cities. Dr Begg has also examined the price paid, both by the residents of such places, and by Scotland as a whole for creating these estates and has attempted to assess how much has been achieved in retrieving the situation as a result of the policies pursued by this Conservative Government since 1979.

Dr Begg has used his skills as an academic economist and historian to examine the development of housing policy in Scotland during the twentieth century. He has also had the great advantage of having been personally involved in some of the key developments in Scottish housing in recent years. In 1980 he was appointed to the Council of Management of the Scottish Special Housing Association, and he served on the Board of Scottish Homes from its creation in 1988 until March of 1995. He has therefore had a unique opportunity to observe and analyse Scottish housing policies.

I am sure that anyone who has an interest in housing policy will want to read this account of its development. More generally I suspect that many Scots who wish to know more of how Scotland came to be as it is today will find much here on which to reflect. I know that not everyone will necessarily agree with Dr Begg's conclusions or recommendations, but I believe that few people will set aside this book without having added considerably to their understanding of modern Scotland.

The Scottish Office, 1996   *Michael Forsyth*

Acknowledgements

*T*HIS book was written at the end of a period of fifteen years during which time I had enjoyed the privilege of serving first with the Scottish Special Housing Association and then latterly on the Board of Scottish Homes. My main intention was, of course, to contribute constructively to the work of each organisation and to that end it was necessary to extend and develop my knowledge of housing. Many colleagues, members of staff, civil servants, tenants, councillors, local government officers, members of housing associations and their professional employees, contributed to my education. Included in this list must also be the un-named authors of hundreds of briefing papers on housing and related topics. In addition, I am extremely grateful for the many opportunities which I was given to visit and examine a host of different locations and sites, both at home and abroad, to discuss and debate housing matters with knowledgeable and experienced people and to learn of their circumstances and of the problems which they were attempting to address.

Over these years I was also fortunate to be able to work with many excellent students. Fresh, challenging ideas delivered at an enthusiastic seminar go to form the best type of encouragement and stimulus which an academic can have, and I freely acknowledge my debt to past and present students.

With the approach of the S.S.H.A.'s fiftieth anniversary in 1987, I was invited to set out its history and *Fifty Special Years* was duly published in that year. This exercise drew my attention to the magnificent archive which the organisation possessed and at the same time heightened my interest in the modern history of Scottish housing. Subsequent involvement in Scottish Homes commanded consideration of the development of the housing system across all sectors and encouraged the wish to offer readers a more comprehensive and, perhaps more mature, study which examined the subject in the context of the economic and social progress of modern Scotland. The conclusion of my term of appointment in March 1995 seemed to be the appropriate time to complete this task.

Various people have assisted in the process of producing the book in its final form. My thanks go to those individuals and organisations who gave me permission to make use of photographs, including, T. & R. Annan & Sons Ltd; Clackmannan District Library; the Smith Art Gallery and Museum; Bill Spalding; The Herald and Evening Times; and Wester Hailes Community Housing Association. I am particularly grateful for permission to draw on the photographic library of Scottish Homes and I very much appreciate the help of Donald Ross of the P.R. Department.

Books of this nature are notoriously expensive to produce and thanks are therefore due to Scottish Homes for the financial support which has enabled it to be made available to readers at a reasonable price. I should emphasise, however, that the book is an entirely independent work and Scottish Homes cannot in any sense be held accountable for the views and judgements expressed throughout the text.

Authors are inevitably enormously dependent on their publishers and I wish to place on record my gratitude for the unfailing courtesy and professional skills of Donald Morrison and his colleagues at John Donald Publishers Ltd.

Finally, I am grateful to Michael Forsyth for contributing his kind and thoughtful Foreword and I am delighted to have this expression of his interest. Again, however, I must make clear that, as with all the other individuals and organisations mentioned above, he shares no part of my responsibility for this book.

Queen Margaret College, Edinburgh   *Tom Begg*

Contents

CHAPTER ONE

State Intervention in Housing

*T*HE 1991 *Scottish House Condition Survey*, organised by Scottish Homes on behalf of the Secretary of State, was probably the most comprehensive investigation of the condition of Scottish housing which has ever been conducted. Among the mass of information which was revealed the Survey illustrated that Scotland is currently adding to its housing stock at a rate of a little less than one per cent per annum; that Scottish housing is generally modern, with about sixty per cent of the dwellings having been built since 1945; but that more than twenty per cent of the houses pre-date 1919.[1] Clearly, therefore, housing is a subject which requires to be considered over a reasonable time period. To understand contemporary Scotland, and to recognise why our buildings, villages, towns and cities are shaped and formed as they are, it is necessary to examine the modern history of housing. In particular, it is essential to consider the more important turns and twists of housing policies as these have developed throughout the present century, since so much of the fabric of the built environment in Scotland has resulted from decisions made by politicians.

The industrial revolution in Scotland was both more concentrated in geographic terms and in time than was the case in much of the rest of the U.K.. By comparison with typical English experience, the processes of industrialisation and city and town formation in Scotland perhaps more definitely merited the use of the word revolution, since they affected an economy and a people which were initially, far less prepared. By any measure of wealth, personal income, standard of living, level of agricultural development, scale of capital formation, experience of international trade, or management of urban concentration, in general terms eighteenth-century Scotland lagged far behind England.[2] It is not, therefore, surprising that the upheavals of the next century and a half affected a population which was both less demanding of good standards of habitation and less able to obtain and organise the resources with which rapid improvements could be accomplished. The Highlanders and Irish migrants who crowded into Glasgow and other Scottish urban communities in the nineteenth century, propelled by the realities of rural poverty and drawn by the lure of employment for cash, brought with them an all too ready acceptance of low standards and, by their ever growing numbers, collectively ensured that rapid improvement through better wage levels remained an elusive

A Stirlingshire Toll-house c1865. (Smith Art Gallery and Museum)

prospect for the majority. (Any reader with an eye for the slums and shanty towns which surround so many of the great cities of the contemporary developing world will have some sense of many of the influences at work.)

The story of the appalling housing and consequent social evils associated with the slums of nineteenth-century Glasgow has been well recorded.[3] What is perhaps less generally understood is that, although rarely compounded by the high population densities associated with Glasgow, housing conditions were typically at least as poor in many of the older villages, towns and burghs throughout the country. It has to be remembered that those migrants flooding into Glasgow or Dundee or Edinburgh, or fleeing to England or North America, were in the main trying to escape from the poverty of old Scotland. As rates of population increase began to accelerate so the local economies of many ancient communities proved incapable of supporting the additional mouths, hence flight to the perceived areas of economic growth was often the only viable answer for many families and individuals. Not surprisingly, in these circumstances, vile housing conditions could have been found in almost every corner of nineteenth century Scotland, from the 'black' turf-roofed houses of the Western Isles, or 'pits' of decaying terraced village cottages, to the slums of the many closes or vennels of small venerable burghs.

Low walled cottages around the village pump; Tullibody, late 19th Century. (Clackmannan District Library)

As the century progressed inevitably politicians, local and national, were forced to confront the problems of the emerging industrial cities. As far as housing specifically is concerned many commentators regard the Torrens Act of 1868 as a starting point in the evolution of subsequent policy. This Act gave local authorities the power to pull down insanitary dwellings and improve slum areas and, as with other contemporary measures, it was largely the result of concerns that the grim living conditions of the urban poor were the breeding grounds for a host of lethal infectious diseases from which wealthier citizens were not immune. The 1868 Act, the subsequent Artisans' Dwellings Act of 1875, which widened the powers of local authorities to clear whole districts and to build new houses for the displaced citizens, and the great Public Health Act, also of 1875, giving local councils the power to control house-building through local bye-laws, do indeed seem to mark out the mid-Victorian period as a significant point of departure.[4] However, it is also true that these measures were themselves founded on earlier initiatives through private legislation made by a few progressive cities including Liverpool and Glasgow, both of which were under particular pressure from Irish immigration.

Glasgow (1866), was followed by Edinburgh (1867), Dundee (1871), Greenock

Old High Street, Alloa, showing the type of housing found in Scottish burghs c1880. (Clackmannan District Library)

(1877), Leith (1880), and Aberdeen (1884) in taking powers to initiate improvement schemes and to get rid of the worst slums. But knocking down slums did not remove the problem; rather it intensified it – particularly since 19th century property owning electors were far from willing to allow local rates to be used to finance the provision of replacement houses for the displaced slum dwellers. The policy of destroying the worst dwellings, but not providing alternative housing was 'self-defeating. The poor were pressed into even smaller areas of greater densities, and any house suitable for subdivision was 'made down' (partitioned).[5]

Indeed, it has been argued by some historians that the intervention of municipal authorities may initially have had particularly unfortunate consequences for some of the poorest urban dwellers. The destruction of slums not only displaced residents, but other controls designed to curtail slum nuisances and enhance housing standards may actually have added significantly to the costs involved in erecting and maintaining houses for the poor and it has been suggested that this helped to precipitate something of a crisis in housing in the years around 1900.[6]

It is true that Glasgow's City Improvement Trust, set up under the 1866 Act, did

4

65 High Street, Glasgow (1868) illustrating the close proximity of the tenements of the backlands in the heart of the 19th Century city. (Annan)

provide some houses as well as demolish the worst slums.[7] However, it was not typical and in any case its achievement, though interesting, was on a very modest scale. 'Thus the Corporation, through its Improvement Trust, probably housed about 10,000 people, one per cent of a total population of over one million and fewer in total than were housed in any one year by private builders in the periods 1867–1878 or 1893–1902'.[8] In 1902 there was a total of 162,721 dwellings in Glasgow, of which 'only 2,488 had been provided by the Corporation and of these only 257 were new'.[9]

Municipal efforts elsewhere were similarly limited in their scale of accomplishment. For example, in her impressive study of the development of housing in Dundee, Jean Kay Young points out that in 1911 Dundee Council owned a mere 112 tenancies, and, far from being purpose built, these were properties taken over from landlords who had failed to take action to abate a slum nuisance or who had not responded to a closure notice.[10] Richard Rodger concluded that in 1913 only

Slum housing in Edinburgh's 'Old Town'.

about one per cent of the families in the largest burghs of Scotland were housed in municipal properties, and similarly at the U.K. level, R.L. Reiss estimated that at about the same time council dwellings represented no more than a half per cent of the total housing stock.[11]

Before the First World War, therefore, Scotland, in common with the other parts of Great Britain, had a housing stock which was almost entirely provided by private builders. Moreover, again as with most of the rest of the country, the pre-eminent tenure form was renting from a private landlord.

By the turn of the century several philanthropic housing associations or trusts were making a useful contribution to the provision of houses for working people, but their activities were mainly in England and concentrated in the greater London area. By 1905, the nine largest associations were accommodating about 123,000 Londoners.[12]

Elsewhere, however, renting from a private landlord meant obtaining the tenancy of a house owned by a private individual and, typically in Scotland, managed by a house factor.[13] Reviewing the literature on the ownership of domestic properties in Scotland in the years around 1900, Young concluded that 'Dundee, like Glasgow and Edinburgh, was owned by small investors from the middle class, predominantly shopkeepers and small businessmen. The amounts of property they owned were quite small'.[14] These individuals usually borrowed

A terrace of miners' dwellings at Fallin, Stirlingshire c1900. The large number of children indicates the probability of the overcrowding which characterised much Scottish working class housing of the day. (Smith Art Gallery and Museum)

money from bondholders[15] with which they purchased their properties, often from speculative builders.[16] Thereafter the houses were usually managed by factors, some of whom had considerable quantities of stock under their control. In 1907 80 per cent of working class housing in Glasgow was reported to be privately factored and in 1911 the equivalent figure for Dundee was 60 per cent. In the latter city the five largest factors between them evidently controlled no less than 23.6 per cent of tenancies.[17]

Up to 1914 then, with a few minor exceptions, the provision of housing was largely in the hands of private landlords who obtained their properties from speculative builders or acquired older properties which were modified for the purposes of renting. Unfortunately, however, the incomes of a proportion of working people were insufficient to permit them to pay rent levels which would have provided a reasonable return for good quality premises. Butt argues that 'the inability of most Scottish workers to live in better conditions rested mainly upon the fact that their incomes were inadequate to pay the rents which would have been demanded for improved accommodation'.[18] Others have drawn attention to the perceived reluctance of many Scots to allocate a greater proportion of their incomes to housing in order to obtain better dwellings and in that case the low expectations of the early generations of Scottish urban workers may be a significant underlying determinant contributing to their poor housing standards.[19]

Miners' houses at Stanburn c1880. These were owned by Sir James Nimmo and Partners, Coalmasters, Glasgow. (Smith Art Gallery and Museum.)

Traditional 'black' houses of the Western Isles.

It is interesting to speculate as to why a low rent tradition took such a strong hold, particularly in the Glasgow area. R. H. Campbell points out that in the 19th Century Scottish coal miners were especially badly housed in tiny cottages and that low rents were typical in such places. As things happened, the first destinations of many of the earliest Irish immigrants were coal-mining villages and the large families of the incomers led almost inevitably to overcrowding. Both culturally and traditionally this huddling together was probably considered to be a fairly normal way of life. Moreover, there is no doubt that the accommodation which had been left behind by both rural Irishman or Scottish Highlander had usually been little more than a one-roomed dwelling of dry stone and wattle with a turf or thatched roof, its useful life-span often being very short. It seems likely that the migrants did not traditionally regard their houses as having any great economic value. The idea of paying a greater rent in order to secure an improved residence, therefore, was not particularly meaningful and it is probable that many considered their rent to be little more than a form of roof tax. As increasing numbers of Irishmen and Highlanders were drawn to the developing urban communities in and around Glasgow so this view of rent seems to have hardened into something approaching a customary belief and the resistance to higher rents became very strong in certain neighbourhoods.

Another factor to be kept in mind is the nature of the developing regional economy. In Clydeside in particular, where so many of the early generations of urban workers were dependent on shipbuilding and related industries, industries which were often disrupted by cyclical depression, periodic unemployment frequently engendered a sense of insecurity of income.[20] In the early part of the 19th Century frequent fluctuations in trade meant that people quickly learned to both fear economic downturn and to regard such an event as inevitable. Consequently households with small cash margins at the best of times were often both unable and unwilling to expend their resources on anything other than the most miserable of accommodation. As a result they huddled into the oldest parts of the city

> where buildings were oldest and rents cheapest. To take advantage of this wretched market and the lack of legislation to safeguard health, tenements of the poorest description were built in what had been garden ground belonging to the street buildings – These *back lands* ... were reached only by narrow lanes or closes..[21]

It was to a great extent the legacy of this housing stock which gave Glasgow its particularly villainous reputation for slum housing. But the fact is that up to the outbreak of the First War there was an almost inexhaustible demand for the cheapest possible accommodation: hence small, sub-standard dwellings were the normal habitations for thousands of Scottish working people, while many men avoided or postponed marriage and settled instead for a bed in a lodging house. Thus it was that by the beginning of the present century slum conditions were normal rather than exceptional in many parts of the city of Glasgow and it was reported in 1903 that population densities in some districts ranged between 508 and 876 persons per acre.[22]

Before continuing with the discussion of working class housing, however, it is perhaps important to point out that it is a grave error to assume that all Scottish urban housing in the pre-First War period was of a low standard. While it is true that the conditions confronting many working class citizens were often appalling, it is equally the case that many of the Victorian and Edwardian dwellings in Scotland's towns and cities were excellent. The stone tenements and terraces of Edinburgh's 'new town' or of the King's Park area of Stirling, for example, still splendidly illustrate the grace and style of the homes of many urban Scots in the 19th and early 20th Centuries; and, as late as the 1960s, Glasgow was still being identified as perhaps the finest Victorian city in Britain. The stone tenements of urban Scotland undoubtedly resulted in many magnificent buildings and the large rooms and elegant plaster work of interiors indicate that many people of even quite modest means enjoyed the life style afforded by fine apartments and town-houses. Indeed, it is worth stressing that through the filtering down process as well as new building, urban working class Scots were by no means all badly housed before the 1914–18 War. Unfortunately the very solidity and enduring qualities of tenements meant that through the process of sub-division they could readily be turned into slums.

Our understanding of housing conditions in Scotland prior to the First War is obviously greatly influenced and informed by the 1917 report of the Royal

Not such a 'mean city'! The suburb of Partick was absorbed into Glasgow in 1912, but these views of Merkland Street, Fielden Drive and Partick Cross, showing the area around 1905, clearly illustrate the quality of the tenements of the period. (Bill Spalding)

Commission on the housing of the industrial population of Scotland, with its vitriolic description:

> These are the broad results of our survey: unsatisfactory sites of houses and villages, insufficient supplies of water, unsatisfactory provision for drainage, grossly inadequate provision for the removal of refuse, widespread absence of decent sanitary conveniences ....

It stigmatized the rotten, damp, poorly built rural housing of Scotland and protested at

> congested industrial villages and towns, occupation of one-room houses by large families, groups of lightless and unventilated houses in the older burghs, clotted masses of slums in the great cities.[23]

The Report and the census of 1911 also focused attention on the remarkably small size of Scottish dwellings. In 1911 the housing stock of Scotland was shown to be as follows[24] –

12.8 per cent – 1 room
40.4 per cent – 2 rooms
20.3 per cent – 3 rooms
26.5 per cent – 4 or more rooms

In effect this meant that almost three quarters of the population lived in houses with three rooms or less and almost half were in houses with only one or two rooms. Professor Butt found the contrast between conditions in Scotland and England and Wales 'startling'. South of the border in 1911

> only 3.2 per cent of the houses had only one room and only 8.3 per cent two rooms, while only 7.1 per cent of the population lived in these abnormally small houses; the great majority of the (English and Welsh) houses, 73.8 per cent, had four or more rooms.[25]

Similarly, Richard Rodger points out that on the basis of the 1911 figures inhabitants of Clydebank, Cowdenbeath, Airdrie, Govan, Hamilton, Motherwell, Barrhead, Johnstone, Port Glasgow and Renfrew 'with 60–69 per cent living more than two per room were ten times more overcrowded than in Hull or Manchester'.[26]

On a standard of more than three persons per room, just over one million people – about a quarter of the Scottish population – were living in overcrowded conditions. On the contemporary English standard of two persons per room, 2,077,000 Scots (45.1 per cent) suffered from overcrowding. But even these figures do not fully reveal the extent of the problem since it has to be remembered that typical Scottish urban tenements multiplied the evils of interior congestion by adding extreme densities of population per acre.[27]

In order to replace houses which were totally unfit for human habitation and to ease overcrowding the Commission estimated in 1917 that 121,000 houses were needed immediately. In addition, half of the one-roomed houses and 15 per cent of the two-roomed houses needed to be replaced in an effort to bring some modest improvement in standards; hence, according to the Commission, a total of 236,000 new houses was required at once, and this made no allowance for the lack of building throughout the war.[28] Marion Bowley suggested that the shortage of houses in Scotland in 1921 as a direct result of the First War was 95,000.[29] It would, therefore, seem that if one adds to the Commission's calculations the additional requirement caused by the lack of building between 1914 and 1918, not less than 300,000 houses were urgently required at the end of the war. This was, of course, in addition to the normal annual requirement for new houses as a consequence of household formation.

In setting out the qualitative and quantitative nature of the Scottish housing problem the majority of the members of the Royal Commission also rejected the possibility of the remedy being provided by traditional methods.

> Private enterprise was practically the only agency that undertook the building of houses, and most of the troubles we have been investigating are due to the failure of private enterprise to provide and maintain the necessary houses sufficient in quantity and quality[30]

If the task of producing the required number of reasonable houses could not be left to private enterprise, the alternative favoured by the majority on the Commission was for the state to hand the responsibility to local government. Central government should also provide subsidies which would make up the difference between economic rents for the houses and the actual rents which the local authorities would be able to obtain from their low income tenants.

In fact, however, even before the Commission had reported, the State had already intervened in a manner which was to bedevil housing for many years to come. In 1915, in response to industrial unrest and what was perceived to be a potentially explosive situation in Glasgow, the government introduced the Increase of Rent and Mortgage Interest Act which effectively limited rents to the levels obtaining at the outbreak of the war.[31] Given wartime rates of inflation this was perhaps a reasonable, even necessary, emergency measure. But subsequently no government had the political courage to remove these restrictions; hence for decades the private sector for rented accommodation lost all responsiveness, and the rents of local authority houses – which were normally fixed in relation to house size and neighbourhood rent levels – became at times wildly divorced from economic reality. It may be argued that these controls also helped to condition the British in general, and the Scots in particular, to expect housing subsidies of one kind or another and thereby to be even less willing to allocate a realistic proportion of their incomes to housing. Rent control was not partially removed until 1957.

In many ways the First World War represents a key watershed for housing policy as, indeed, it does in respect of other political developments, particularly as these relate to the role of the State and its relationship to the individual citizen.[32] That the war should have been a major catalyst for political change is not, of course, surprising, given the traumatic and catastrophic nature of the experience of the first modern war on a society which had little by way of previous example on which to establish forewarning or preparation. What is more surprising, however, is the inclination of contemporary social and economic historians to refer to the war in landmark, almost incidental terms, without conveying any real sense of its force in precipitating political, social and economic upheaval.[33] Modern historians tend to seek out and identify continuities in the development of policy and to trace the roots of post-war events deep into the pre-war era. This is, of course, absolutely correct if a realistic and accurate picture of sequence and causation is to be constructed. However, the danger occurs if continuities are so emphasised as to imply that – war or no war – events were bound inevitably to have unfolded along the identified lines. There is a clear risk of ignoring or undervaluing the significance of the war, for example, in terms of its emotional effect on the attitudes and priorities of politicians and electorate alike from about 1915 onwards. Following the destruction of the cream of the first volunteer army at Loos in 1915, and increasingly through the introduction of conscription and as one devastating battle casualty list succeeded another over the next three years, the relationship between the State and the citizen was transformed. It is very difficult to believe that, without the war, the tenets of classic liberalism would have been so thoroughly eclipsed, or that the administrative power of all levels of government would have developed so swiftly.

Be that as it may, there can be little doubt that by the 1920s a fundamental shift had taken place in housing policy and that the State, by a mixture of planning and force of circumstance had assumed a central role. Whereas prior to the war private renting had been the pre-eminent method by means of which accommodation was obtained by the bulk of the community, from 1919 onwards a growing proportion of housing was provided with the assistance of State subsidies of one form or another and there was an increasing trend for housing for the working classes to be supplied directly by the State via the local authorities.

The development of housing policy in the years around and during the First War has been admirably described in detail elsewhere[34] and there is no need for the ground to be retraced here in more than summary form. Briefly, however, there seem to be two inter-linked elements which require to be considered, the one concerning the quality and nature of working class housing, and the other the methods by which such housing was to be produced.

The origin of the drive towards qualitative improvement has two stems and the first of these extends back to the publication in 1898 of Ebenezer Howard's little volume *Tomorrow* (renamed *Garden Cities of Tomorrow* in 1902) in which he set out his vision of planned balanced communities of 50,000 people who would live in cottages with gardens, surrounded by extensive open spaces and protected green belts.[35] Although it was highly unlikely that such ideas would have an immediate impact on the lives of the great mass of urban dwellers of the period, Howard's ideas were enormously influential in shaping not only notions of town planning, but also of house design. They were taken up vigorously by architects like Raymond Unwin and Barry Parker and by the planner, Thomas Adams, and some tentative first steps were made in the design and construction of the earliest parts of Letchworth between 1904 and 1906. Thereafter, the garden city 'movement' continued to grow in strength and its influence was developed through the National Housing Reform Council and, within government, following the appointment of Adams to the Local Government Board in 1909.[36]

> The various elements represented in the garden city movement had one central belief which was a rejection of the city as it then existed and a search for some kind of better alternative based on the countryside and the village.[37]

By bringing a romanticised notion of the countryside into the town in developments of no more than twelve houses to the acre, Howard and the others hoped to replace older forms of urbanism.

In some ways opposed to these romantic dreams was the second stem to the campaign in favour of better standards and this was represented by the formal school of urban design associated with the American City Beautiful movement. The focus in this case was on the Beaux Arts tradition of straight roads, formal approaches and symmetrical layout and such ideas were taken forward in the U.K. particularly by the Department of Civic Design at Liverpool University and led by C.H. Reilly, Stanley Adshead and Patrick Abercrombie.[38]

Especially after the appointment of Adams, the influence of the garden city advocates within the Local Government Board was considerable and the pre-war climax to their activities was perhaps the passing of the 1909 Housing and Town Planning Act, which has been categorised as an attempt 'to promote garden city development *without* increasing the State's expenditure on housing provision'.[39] This Act gave local authorities optional powers to lay down plans for new developments, to design street layouts, to restrict building densities, to set aside land for public uses, to obtain land for development purposes and to restrict other building activities while a scheme was being prepared. In addition, as the Act became law it was given administrative reinforcement by the establishment of a Housing and Town Planning Department within the Local Government Board.[40]

In its passage through Parliament the original bill was severely modified and, to some extent, weakened. However, Thomas Adams and his Minister, John Burns, both believed that despite being impaired the Act was important because the urgent need was 'to secure the acceptance of the principle of statutory planning; experience in working it would bring about improvements.'[41]

One of the features of the Act was that it did finally oblige local authorities to rehouse people displaced by the destruction of slums in the course of planned development. Initially councils seem to have been unwilling to accept the potential new responsibilities involved and there were, perhaps in consequence, few proposals submitted for government approval before the war. A Local Government Board for Scotland memorandum of 1914 recognised 'that the provision of more houses is the key to the whole position'. However great the powers of local authorities to clear slums or demolish houses, their activities would continue to be 'restricted unless there is other proper accommodation for the persons displaced.'[42]

Whatever the cause, the local authority response to the 1909 Act was disappointing. Out of the 1500 local councils in England and Wales 'only one-tenth' had shown any interest prior to the outbreak of war, and the reaction in Scotland was no better. A few councils had sought advice and some had been given authority to prepare plans. But only seven schemes had either been approved or were awaiting approval by August 1914, and three of these were in one city, Birmingham.

> The poor response was due to indifference to environmental conditions, ignorance of planning as an instrument of improvement, the absence of local reformist pressure, the fear of heavy expense and the lack of sufficient or competent staff. Few councils had councillors or officials committed to planning.[43]

There can be little doubt, therefore, that before the war councils up and down the country had neither the enthusiasm nor the ability required to provide houses directly for the working classes, still less to construct them to garden city specifications. For example, as Young noted, in 1914 Dundee councillors could see no reason at all for the council to build houses for the working people displaced from the Greenmarket and Overgate areas of the city.[44]

Whether or not local authority attitudes would rapidly have changed, whether or not central government would have decided to provide the key ingredient of central finance, and whether or not the drive to secure improvement in the quality of working class housing would have lost momentum, had not the war intervened, must now, of course, be matters purely for conjecture. What is clear, however, is that it did not take burgeoning military requirements long to provide the campaigners with the opportunity to further their cause. At Crombie, Rosyth, Gretna, Chepstow, Crayford and elsewhere the need for housing in support of military and naval establishments opened the way for demonstrations of what might be achieved by direct State involvement. Moreover, this was from the outset apparent even within so staid a Department as the Admiralty where the opportunity for the government to demonstrate the principles of housing policy at Rosyth was rapidly identified. Such a policy involved the 'recognition by the State of the duty of seeing that a relative standard of comfort and convenience is secured in the housing of the working classes'. The object was, therefore, to develop Rosyth 'in a manner that shall secure to the future community at reasonable rentals ... model standards of health and comfort'.[45] (An additional important departure in the case of Rosyth was the decision to construct the town via a public utility society, the Scottish National Housing Company, especially created for the specific purpose.)

At Rosyth, to some degree in consequence of Raymond Unwin's influence, the garden city derivation is obvious in terms both of layout and variety of cottage designs.[46] At Gretna, by contrast, the more formal notions favoured by the Liverpool group seem to have been preferred. In both cases, however, ideas of what might be achieved after the war had been given a practical demonstration. In 1917 the National Housing and Town Planning Council indicated an assumption that post-war 'assistance by the State ... will be on the lines of the housing that had been done for munitions workers'.[47]

Houses in the 'garden village' of Rosyth.

From July 1917 a committee was established jointly by the President of the Local Government Board and the Secretary for Scotland to consider building construction in the provision of houses for the working classes after the war. Under the chairmanship of Sir John Tudor Walters, this committee, which included in its membership both Raymond Unwin and John Walker Smith, Chief Engineer at the Scottish Local Government Board, in its Report of 1918 powerfully carried forward the notion of a major qualitative improvement in housing standards after the war. The munitions villages were certainly the 'models for the designs in the Tudor Walters Report'[48], but the proposals were also firmly supported by the contention that the standards demanded by the working classes were likely to rise in the long term. Designing and constructing cottages to a high standard, therefore, made sense, even if the outcome was expensive buildings the rents of which might only be afforded by better off workers.[49]

The Report was so influential that as late as 1935 Lord Simon could conclude that 'it is safe to assume that the Tudor Walters cottage may be regarded by town planners as a permanent standard'.[50] If not exactly 'permanent' certainly the standard set was high and at least in the short term it chimed in well with the intention to build houses which were 'fit for heroes'. But as was pointed out by Swenarton in his excellent account

> It was from the munitions programme that the 1919 campaign derived its subsidy system, its chief administrators and architects, and its doctrines on housing design. These were essentially the same as the principles and techniques of low-density layout and house design developed by the garden city movement before the war ..[51]

The second key issue determined at the end of the war concerned the extent to which central government would become directly responsible for housing and how such responsibility would be exercised. By the mid years of the war it was clear that there would be no rapid reversion to the *status quo ante bellum*. In response to the bitter sufferings and low morale of the community in the context of the terrible struggles of the years 1915 to 1917 the government turned increasingly to thoughts and words of reconstruction.[52] Hence, by '1917 reconstruction meant far more than a set of administrative rearrangements after the war ended; it meant a new spirit and outlook'.[53]

Following Lloyd George's reformation of the government's Reconstruction Committees in 1917, Panel Four, under the chairmanship of Lord Salisbury, was given the task of considering post-war housing needs. Throughout its deliberations its intention was to devise a major effort to address the problems of working class housing[54] and Seebohm Rowntree was the formidable author of a particularly influential report for the panel. One scholar who examined the relevant Reconstruction Committee documents concluded that Rowntree's report was not decisive and argued that the near simultaneous publication of the Royal Commission Report on Scottish housing was at least as important.[55] However, the key point is that both reports accepted the need for State intervention into the market for working class housing, a position which was ultimately endorsed in the final report of the Housing Panel and adopted as policy by the Ministry of Reconstruction.[56]

For much of the remainder of the war there was considerable tension between the Ministry of Reconstruction and the Local Government Board.[57] Broadly, the Ministry favoured direct State intervention in the housing market in the immediate post-war years because price levels were then likely to be abnormally high. The Ministry position was that local authorities should initially merely act as its agents and managers although after a seven year period, by which time it was expected that conditions should have returned to something like normality, the houses could be sold to the councils. By contrast, the Local Government Board, typically with support from the Treasury, argued that the local authorities should from the outset be responsible for building and managing the houses, and the role of central government should merely be to give such financial and other aid as was required.[58] It had all the hallmarks of a classic inter-departmental dispute over respective spheres of influence.

Swenarton and other historians have argued that as the war drew to an end the government was forced to accept responsibility for funding a housing drive as an ad hoc response to a political crisis. Essentially, from this point of view, the decision to State-fund housing is regarded as something designed to abate some of the dangers of a potential revolution.[59] Certainly, there were serious political risks at the time. Moreover, high prices and severe shortages of materials and skilled labour immediately after the war were almost bound to produce at least a short-term crisis in housing, a situation, indeed, made worse by the government's own decision to remove war-time controls from building materials as soon as peace was declared.[60]

It is, of course, easy to be cynical about political behaviour, and to assume that the government was merely doing what was required to defuse a potentially critical situation. The Ministry of Reconstruction had seen housing in the context of its main task of smoothing the transition from war to peace. The need for a dynamic housing policy was at least partly to absorb returning servicemen into employment. After the Armistice in 1918

> the government found itself faced with the emergency foreseen by the Ministry of Reconstruction – the demobilisation of five million men from the services and the release of a similar number of men and women from munitions production and other war industries ... there is no doubt that at the time the Cabinet took the threat of revolution very seriously.[61]

With contemporary events in Russia and Germany in mind, ministers could scarcely have failed to be alert to the dangers.

On the other hand, it is important to keep this kind of argument in proportion. On the day after the Armistice Lloyd George called a General Election and repeated his promise to obtain 'habitations fit for the heroes who have won the war'.[62] By the end of the year the Coalition Government had been returned commanding 478 seats in the Commons and enjoying a huge majority of 259 over all other parties. The authority which was bound to adhere to such a government – at least in the short term – does not sit easily with the theory of near revolution in 1919. Indeed, perhaps this episode actually provides one of the classic demonstrations of the capacity of an elected government to use the democratic processes to confront and defuse a potential major social and economic crisis.

In a speech in Dundee on November 28, 1918, during the election campaign, Winston Churchill called for a continuation of the wartime unity in order to produce prosperity in peacetime.

> All the arts and science that we used in war are standing by us now ready to help us in peace. All the organised power which moved the fleets and armies ... which made

us victors in the air, which produced unlimited munitions of every intricate kind – all the clever brains, true hearts, strong unwearied hands – all are available ... Five years of concerted effort by all classes ... would create an abundance and prosperity in this land ...[63]

Churchill himself was returned with an 'immense majority' of 15,365. While industrial unrest was a matter for concern, it seems at least as likely that, buoyed up and relieved at the successful conclusion of the war and in the context of an election campaign, policy was impelled for a time by a genuine desire to turn the apparent political, administrative and technical power of the community, revealed in war, to produce a major enhancement of living standards including housing. In particular, the returning troops had more than earned the right to an improvement with minimal delay. To put it another way, at least some of the political rhetoric of the day simply has to be accepted at face value.

Other historians have also rejected the more extreme position. 'State housing was not intended to prevent an imminent revolution, it had a more mundane purpose of easing the adjustment of rents to a market level'.[64] In other words, it would take time to remove the rent controls introduced in 1915 and allow the rented market to recover, and throughout the necessary period some government provision of housing would be required to make up the deficiency in supply. As another writer expressed it, 'the government was trapped ... It had pledged itself to provide homes for heroes but, if it continued control of rents, private enterprise would be totally unwilling to build the homes'.[65] In these circumstances, and to navigate through the transition from war to peace, the housing programme was required as 'an extension of the war effort, and therefore war-time measures and solutions were quite acceptable'.[66]

Thus it was that the drive to enhance standards in housing quality and the acceptance by government (albeit temporarily) of the task of shouldering a major share of the burden of funding, came together in the 1919 House and Town Planning Act.

As far as Scotland is concerned it is interesting to note the way in which the climate of opinion swung during the war years.[67] Fundamental to the shift in favour of council houses provided with the assistance of central government finance, were the war-time activities of officials at the Local Government Board for Scotland, which has been categorised as an 'embryonic Scottish power-base'.[68] Board officials consistently campaigned for such policies as being particularly appropriate to the requirements of Scotland. However, it is also clear that many Scottish local councillors remained convinced that the 1919 Act was a temporary measure and that it was only a matter of time before private renting recovered.[69]

The House and Town Planning (Scotland) Act of 1919 – sometimes known as the Addison Act after Dr Christopher Addison, the then President of the Local Government Board – gave local authorities the specific task of determining the housing needs of their districts and of then submitting plans to the Scottish Board of Health to provide appropriate numbers of houses for the working classes. Advice and administrative assistance were to be provided to the councils and, most crucially, the general taxpayer through central government, rather than local ratepayers, would accept responsibility for almost all of the cost of the losses incurred on these houses. Local rates could be increased by four-fifths of a penny (one penny in England) as a nominal contribution, but beyond that token level all of the difference between the expected income from rents and the cost of borrowing the funds to build the houses would be borne by the government. Moreover, as far as the house designs were concerned, these had to conform to the Board's minimum standards before loans were approved, hence the form living space took in the first state-built houses was dictated by central government.[70]

At first building seemed to get under way extremely slowly. Obviously few councils had much experience of organising house building, but other serious problems were the shortages of materials and men, particularly as there was also a heavy demand on the resources of the building industry to undertake repairs to property neglected during the war.[71] As a consequence, by the autumn of 1919 it was being alleged that the policy was a failure and in the year following the Armistice only a handful of houses had been built and less than 10,000 had been progressed to an approved tender stage.[72] As a result, the private sector was called to assist the programme by the Housing (Additional Powers) Act of December 1919, which empowered the Minister of Health to make grants to any organisation engaged in providing houses for the working classes.

In the event, only 176,000 houses were built under the Addison Act and 25,129 of these were in Scotland. Dundee apparently produced the first Scottish development in a scheme of 262 houses at Logie[73] and built a total of 886 houses under the Act[74]. In Glasgow activity was held up, evidently because the building unions, fearful of dilution of labour, were opposed to the employment of ex-servicemen,[75] but in time the city produced 4,856 Addison houses,[76] including fine estates at Riddrie, Craigton and Mosspark.

As early as 1921 the government was forced to the decision to terminate the 1919 Act because of the fear that the expenditure involved was becoming insupportable. The Chancellor warned his Cabinet colleagues that as the building programme speeded up they would be committed to providing an increasing annual subsidy which, by August 1922, would have reached £25 millions and they would be confronted with financing a further half million expensive houses at a cost of £75,000,000.[77] In these circumstances the government took the decision to limit to 176,000 the total number of houses to be built under the Act and this brought the programme to a gradual halt, more or less completed by 1923.

In 1933 Sir Ernest (later Lord) Simon wrote dismissively of the 1919 Act, complaining that 'housing had become a political stunt of the first magnitude. People thought and talked about a million 'homes for heroes', and did not trouble themselves about details of contracts and building methods and costs'. He argued that the Act helped to force prices up to an unprecedented level so that a house which might have been bought pre-war for £250 could not now be built for less than £1,250.

Under the Addison grant the local authority was divested of every shred of financial responsibility for good management; the most efficient and the most extravagant local authorities would each pay exactly the product of a penny rate, neither more nor less.[78]

Clearly, given the guarantee of unlimited central government subsidy, councils had no reason whatsoever to adopt a restrictive attitude to house designs and costs, hence the houses constructed at this time were built to very high specifications and with little restraint on expense.

Nevertheless, from a more distant perspective, a different and equally accurate conclusion may be reached about the first post-war housing campaign. In important ways it validated the concept of municipal housing as well as setting the standard by which such accommodation would be justified (and would rarely ever reach) far into the future. Swenarton argues that all

> over the country there were municipal estates that were of a far higher standard than anything provided for the working class by private enterprise. Moreover, in the years 1918–21 the notion of high quality public housing, particularly as set out by the Tudor Walters report, acquired an authority that subsequent attacks and smears could not entirely obliterate.[79]

In essence, this argument is correct, although one might reasonably point out that "the far higher standard" is something of an exaggeration since the pre-war Edwardian terraced housing was also excellent and has, for example, stood up well to the test of time. In 1923 Neville Chamberlain, the Minister of Health in the new Conservative Government secured a replacement Housing Act in which his main

The first Addison Act houses built in Stirling at Shiphaugh, Riverside.

First generation council houses on the left and a terrace of Edwardian houses (completed c1914) on the right.

intention was to shift the responsibility for house provision back to the private sector. Bearing in mind the Royal Commission findings in respect of Scottish house conditions, and that an objective of the Addison measure in making local authorities into house providers and giving them national funding support had been precisely 'to bring the Scottish standard up to a level approximating to that already achieved in England by private enterprise before the Great War',[80] it would have been not unreasonable to have expected some variation in public policy north and south of the border. However, in Chamberlain's haste to curb the levels of local government expenditure the Scottish problem was quietly returned to the shelf.

The Chamberlain Act provided a modest subsidy of £6 per house for a maximum of twenty years. Today the sum appears derisory, but it should be seen in the context of the low and rapidly falling house prices of the day, when a good three-bedroomed home could be purchased for around £400 (the same house might have cost more than £900 just three years earlier).[81] The subsidy could be paid in a lump sum of up to £100 and its effect was to provide a moderate boost to private construction. Falling prices and the wider availability of mortgages also stimulated private building, but, by contrast, local authority activity contracted.

In the years in which the Chamberlain subsidies were available (in England they were reduced to £4 per house from 1927) it is estimated that they yielded 438,000 houses in England and Wales, of which 363,000 were built by private enterprise, hence it is clear that Chamberlain's main objective was achieved.[82] It is equally clear, however, that the needs of low income working people generally, and of the Scottish problem specifically, were given little priority under the measure. Not surprisingly, Scottish public sector house completions in 1924 and 1925 fell back to the lowest levels recorded in the inter-war years.

Again, however, it has to be suggested that the 1923 Act had a crucial long-term impact all over the country. Quite simply the Chamberlain subsidies succeeded in stimulating and validating the concept of owner occupation to a completely unprecedented degree. Under their influence little bungalows appeared on the suburban fringes of cities throughout the land and rapidly encouraged millions of lower middle class and better off working class families to aspire to the ownership of their own homes, ideally set in well defined gardens.

In 1924 the Labour Party came to power for the first time as a short-lived minority government tacitly supported by the Liberals and under the premiership of Ramsay Macdonald. The only significant piece of legislation which was enacted was the Housing Act which takes its popular name from John Wheatley, the Minister of Health and a member of the Glasgow I.L.P..

The influence of Wheatley on the development of housing policy, particularly in Scotland, can scarcely by overstated. Not only was he identified as 'the one conspicuous success'[83] in the 1924 government, but he successfully imposed his attitude to housing on a generation of Scottish socialist politicians. In 1913, as a witness to the Royal Commission, he passionately asserted the need for council housing.[84] His own experience as a member of Glasgow Corporation coloured much of his attitude to policy.

> Indeed his council work drew him to the belief that energetic municipal action by socialists could, if widely enough diffused, make the role of the State redundant. He would write with eloquence of a civic, decentralised socialist future, in the attainment of which Glasgow would lead the way.[85]

Such was the outlook which was to make its mark on many of the politicians from the West of Scotland who were subsequently to be concerned with housing matters and, in so far as he was the major voice articulating and disseminating such a point of view, Wheatley can be said to have exercised a crucial influence on the pattern to which housing in Scotland was to develop over the next forty years. Meanwhile, council housing was at the head of the 1924 government's agenda.

By the nature of the government, Wheatley's room for manoeuvre was constrained, but realistically he attempted to encourage the local authorities to tackle the shortage of working-class houses without any undue inhibition or conflict with the private sector. The Chamberlain assistance to private builders was maintained. However, there was to be no return to the blank cheque centrally provided subsidy of the Addison measure. Instead the burden was to be limited and shared between central and local government. Wheatley's moderation in this instance was rewarded, for when the Conservatives returned to office within the year their codifying Housing Act of 1925 left the main elements of the Wheatley Act in place and thus accepted the necessary involvement of local authorities as main house providers.

Having struck a deal with the building unions to allow an increase in the numbers of apprentices to the skilled trades, Wheatley hoped to bring about a long-term plan to stimulate the production of houses to a U.K. output in excess of 150,000 per annum by the mid 1930s. The subsidy to local authorities was fixed at £9 per annum (£12 10s in rural areas) for forty years. Although rent controls were not removed, local authorities fixing new rents could now use average rent levels for similar houses as a guide and could charge a higher rent if such was required to cover costs in excess of a rate contribution equivalent to £4.10s per house for forty years. The effect of this was that local authority losses per house were restricted to a maximum of £4.10s per annum and the maximum subsidy was limited to £13 10s (£17 in rural parishes). If losses exceeded that level average rents could be increased accordingly.[86]

The scheme was ingenious, particularly since it appeared to give both local and national government the confidence that the problems of working-class housing could be tackled realistically without allowing public expenditure to get out of control.

The result of the Wheatley Act was a steady increase in building by the local authorities. The Exchequer subsidy was reduced to £7 10s in 1926, but the Act remained operative until 1933, by which time 508,000 council houses had been erected under its influence in England and Wales, while in the same period in Scotland just over 100,000 council houses were built.

In operation the financial controls of the Wheatley Act gradually gave rise to a problem which was to have a depressing long-term consequence. What had formerly been minimum standards of housing design and layout became progressively to be regarded as maximum standards. The result was a significant qualitative decline from the garden city specifications promoted by the Tudor Walters Committee. Douglas Niven pointed out that the

> Board of Health was compelled by the government of the day to reduce the costs of houses submitted to it for approval under the Act. Design standards were reduced to a minimum and builderwork specifications severely curtailed.[87]

He went on to complain about the severe, unimaginative and plain houses which resulted for much of the period between the wars. 'Collectively they marred the approaches to all urban areas and completely destroyed the continuity of domestic architectural design in Scotland.'

As Niven conceded, not all of the developments were of an unreasonably low standard and, for example, he exempts the Glasgow Corporation estates at Knightswood and Carntyne from the most severe of his strictures. What is clear, however, is that as increasing numbers of houses were built under the terms of the Wheatley Act, so a sharper distinction began to emerge in the appearance of houses constructed for the council on the one hand and for the private consumer on the other. Increasingly council houses became more and more clearly recognisable as council houses and in the longer term this was bound to be deeply socially divisive.

Wheatley Act houses at Milldamhead, Dumfries. Note the lack of detail in the design.

At first such problems were masked because in the 1920s the four-roomed local authority houses were considered to be better (certainly in terms of size) than many of the existing older middle-class houses. Not surprisingly, therefore, many people who were by no means amongst the lowest paid scrambled to obtain a council house. One scholar who investigated this question in the context of parts of Glasgow is clear that, for example, in Govanhill,

> the vast majority of Corporation tenants ... between the wars were, in fact, drawn from the more prosperous skilled and white-collar strata of society. At no time during the period did these groups account for less than 67 per cent of all known tenancies.[88]

The difference in the nature of the inter-war housing problems in Scotland and England was well illustrated by the operation of the Chamberlain and Wheatley Acts. Up to 1934 of all the mainstream houses built in Scotland '83.9 per cent were built with the aid of a subsidy, including 61.1 per cent provided by the local authorities. In England and Wales the corresponding figures were 48.8 per cent and 31 per cent'.[89] The significance of these figures is that the private sector in England was now well into its stride in the creation of middle-class suburbia; hence the overwhelming bulk of the houses being constructed by private builders were of a standard which precluded subsidy. By comparison the smaller subsidised private dwellings (supported under the Chamberlain measure) were more suited to even the better-off Scotsman's purse. Similarly, while council housing represented less than one-third of the English output the equivalent figure for Scotland was approaching two-thirds. Nothing could more clearly indicate the variation between the problems and affordable standards north and south of the border.

Indeed, the difficulty in Scotland was even more intractable than the above comparison might suggest. Initially the Department of Health for Scotland had repeatedly sought to encourage local authorities to maintain a standard of three or more rooms to a dwelling.[90] The codifying Housing (Scotland) Act of 1925 had also laid down that plans for private houses with less than three rooms should only be approved in 'exceptional' circumstances. However, the pressure to meet the requirements of the low Scottish levels of income made it an uphill struggle to raise standards even with the help of the various subsidies. Eventually, in 1929, the Department of Health was forced to agree that 25 per cent of the local authority houses might have only two rooms.[91]

In the same year progress in Scotland under the various state assisted schemes was announced as shown below.

		Completed	*Building*
1919 Act	Local Authorities	25,129	–
	Public Utility Schemes	421	–
	Additional Powers Act	2,324	–
1923 Act	Local Authorities	4,028	2
	Slum Clearance	11,022	1,782
	Private Enterprise Assisted	17,574	1,243
1924 Act	Local Authorities	41,672	5,200
	Private Enterprise	1,558	1,498
	Demonstration Steel Houses	17	–
	Government Steel Houses	2,552	–
Total		*106,297*	*9,725*

Source: 1st Annual Report Department of Health for Scotland 1929, p3

Of the total shown, some 78,609 houses had been completed in burghs and 27,688 in county council areas.

From these figures the comparative success of the Wheatley Act in stimulating local authority construction can easily be seen, even if the houses being produced were typically not yet available to the poorest working class people. Even in England the

fundamental problem was the level of rents in relation to earnings. Although the heavy Wheatley subsidies had been specifically designed to reduce the level of rents, they could not bring council housing within the reach of the mass of poorer workers who everywhere continued to live in old, rent-restricted property, much of it turning into slums.[92]

The problem was acknowledged by the Department of Health in 1931[93] and a little later Simon wrote that while 'the Wheatley Act succeeded in stimulating local authorities to build a greatly increased number of houses for letting, it failed to produce the low-rented houses which Mr Wheatley hoped for', although a few of the 'more economical' councils were getting rents down to levels 'very near the original aim' by the early 1930s.[94]

Despite such problems, however, and even in retrospect, the Wheatley Act itself must be regarded, from a Scottish point of view, as successful, since it enabled the local government agencies to draw on national resources in the first prolonged attempt to improve housing conditions for the mass of the people of Scotland. Had it been seen by all concerned purely as an approach dictated by short-run circumstances, as a pragmatic means of addressing some of the worst housing problems in the context of the immediate post First War period, Wheatley's Act would deserve little other than unqualified praise. However, Wheatley, together with those who shared his views, regarded council housing as the flagship of a particular concept of municipal socialism, an approach which was ultimately to prove little short of disastrous for thousands of Scots. Middlemas claims that the Act 'can fairly be said to be the basis of all modern local authority house-building ... (and) the first substantial measure of legislative socialism'.[95] However, with equal accuracy Alan Massie commented that the

> extension of municipal socialism, a logical development of the municipalism policies of the old Glasgow Corporation, made town councils landlords on a scale, and with a power over their tenants, such as no private landlord could have dreamed of. It was Wheatley's major achievement.[96]

CHAPTER TWO

Inter-War Controversies

*T*HE inter-war years are frequently recalled as a period of severe economic depression with record levels of male unemployment and widespread poverty, not just in the U.K., but in many other countries. They were also, of course, years during which many new products and technologies were developed and turned into the essential output of future mass-consumption. Motor vehicles, the aircraft industry, electrical supply and related goods, chemicals and synthetic fibres were all sources of growth throughout the period.[1] These were not, therefore, economically bad years for citizens in every part of the country. Low prices and low interest rates in the 1930s meant rising real incomes and living standards for those in work, hence to some extent the popular memory of the period needs to be treated with caution, especially if England from the Midlands south is under discussion. Regional and sectoral variations in economic performance need to be kept firmly in mind.

As far as Scotland is concerned, however, the events of the preceding decades had conspired to make this part of the country particularly vulnerable between the wars. The U.K. economy as a whole was significantly distorted as a result of the demands of military production in the years leading up to and during the First World War and to some extent the inter-war economic problems can be seen as the recoil to that distortion. The Scottish economy was especially stimulated by the naval arms race which preceded the outbreak of war and Hugh Peebles, for example, estimated that 'warshipbuilding firms were responsible for upwards of 40% of the total value of all the work undertaken by the Clyde shipbuilding industry between 1889 and 1939'.[2] A single firm such as Beardmore's, for instance, employed no less than 42,000 men at the height of the First War, and clearly it and similar firms had attracted many workers into the region in the three decades up to 1918. Moreover, a host of small businesses developed to service the component and subcontracting needs of the great shipbuilding companies.

With the return to peace in 1918 many ships were cancelled or broken up on the stocks and there was obviously little high value naval shipbuilding to be expected for a time, but a predictable recession was turned into something more severe by the Washington Conference of 1922 which restricted the Royal Navy to just two new battleships in the next ten years. (Neither of these ships was built on the Clyde.) Moreover, first the Labour Government of 1924 and thereafter the following government (ironically with Winston Churchill as its Chancellor of the Exchequer) bitterly resisted the Admiralty's plans for new cruisers under the

1925–26 estimates. Only one ship came to the Clyde, to Fairfields, and although in the next year John Brown's secured an order for two ships for the Australian government, it is easy to see why this was such a difficult period for the region.[3] Indeed some grasp of the scale of the problem may be gleaned when it is realised that from 1900 until 1918 Clyde shipyards had constructed no less than eighteen major battleships and battlecruisers in addition to the machinery for other similar vessels as well as a host of lesser warships. However, for the seventeen years from the completion of the *Hood* in 1920 until the commencement of *Duke of York* and *Howe* in 1937 not a single capital ship was under construction on the Clyde.[4] Moreover, the slack could not be taken up by the building of merchant ships since the international trading position was very poor throughout the period and U.K. exports, for example, never regained the levels reached in 1913. In any case, merchant vessels were generally far less complex and represented much lower value work than warship construction.

The significance for the regional economy of the situation described above was that with a grossly over expanded ship-building industry in deep recession, other related sectors, notably the steel and coal industries, but also engineering and similar trades, which existed largely to service the requirements of the yards, were all severely depressed. Small wonder that west central Scotland, in particular, was one of the regions of the U.K. which was most disadvantaged during the inter-war years.

Inevitably in this period the eyes of businessmen and government ministers turned to housing policy as a potential instrument of economic strategy and it is worth giving some attention to this subject, not least because it was eventually to lead to a sharp debate, the outcome of which was significant to the future shape of many Scottish towns and cities.

House construction in the U.K. in the years up to the First War was almost exclusively in the hands of contracting builders who employed skilled tradesmen to undertake the various crafts involved. Given that the tradesmen concerned – bricklayers, joiners, plumbers etc – had typically to serve lengthy apprenticeships as teenagers, so long as house-building was restricted to conventional methods there was a limit to the industry's capacity to create jobs for the existing generation of the unemployed. To provide work for the latter other methods of construction, perhaps using different materials, would be required.

During the war the Tudor Walters Committee had considered alternative non-traditional methods of building and suggested that these could be helpful in some parts of the country where a scarcity of bricks was probable in the years immediately after the return to peace. The Committee indicated that building methods which involved concrete slabs and blocks had been successfully and widely used for emergency war-time work, and argued that more information was required about the various projected house construction systems involving pouring concrete *in situ*.[5]

In fact, after the war in some parts of the U.K., attempts were made to use non-traditional systems and Swenarton established that 'of the 160,000 houses for which contracts had been signed in April 1921, 20,000 involved the use of new methods'.[6] However, because of lack of capital at the time, these methods evidently proved to be of little help in speeding progress. In Leeds 'to offset the shortage of bricklayers, experimental concrete houses were tried out, but progress was slower than expected' and those few houses which were built cost about £1000 each instead of the then 'normal' price of less than £500.[7]

In 1924 and 1925 others, such as J.M.Keynes[8] and Harold Macmillan[9], both attempting to devise means to help the unemployed, took up the advocacy of alternative methods of house construction, and it can be seen, therefore, that the Scottish developments shortly to be discussed had at least some of their roots in ideas which were being debated and considered from the war years onwards.

As was noted in the previous chapter, during the war there was some tension between government departments as to the best methods of organising direct State participation in the provision of houses. In the case of Rosyth for example, a public utility company, the Scottish National Housing Company, had been established in 1914 and given the specific task of constructing the town. The majority of the company's shares were held by Dunfermline Burgh Council, but 90 per cent of the funds were loaned by the Local Government Board.[10] The name of the company is particularly interesting because, although in outcome its activities were actually confined to Rosyth, the word Scottish in the title implies that its founders had in mind the possibility of operations on a rather wider scale.

Between 1916 and 1919 the company completed the first 1,872 houses in Rosyth. 3,000 houses had originally been planned, but under the Housing Acts of 1919 and 1924 the Burgh Council was able to take over the task and it continued to build council houses in the town over the next decade.

The first S.N.H.C., therefore, built no houses after 1919. Indeed, at that point – with the 'Addison Act' providing subsidies to enable local authorities to build their own houses – there were moves to dissolve the S.N.H.C., but these were rejected by the Local Government Board on the striking grounds that 'we may need such bodies as the company in the event of the local authorities failing to undertake housing schemes'.[11] Clearly there were still official doubts about local authorities as house providers and, as a result, this novel organisation survived, maintaining its houses at Rosyth until they were taken under S.S.H.A. management in 1963.

From a financial point of view the S.N.H.C. was not a success and it consistently failed to achieve its targeted maximum annual dividend of 5 per cent. (Perhaps the relatively high cost of building during and immediately after the war and, in particular, of having had to borrow at war-time interest rates, may have saddled the company with a burden which was to become progressively more onerous throughout the inter-war years.[12]) In terms of the evolution of housing policy, however, the interesting points are that the establishment of the S.N.H.C may be said to mark the first attempt at direct central Government intervention in house provision in Scotland through a centrally funded organisation; and that, even after it ceased building operations in 1919, a section of opinion within the Local

Government Board remained favourably disposed to initiatives of this kind. More-over, such a viewpoint was in keeping with notions which had been advocated elsewhere within government.

As noted previously, the Housing Advisory Panel of the Ministry of Reconstruc-tion had argued in its 1918 report, *Housing in England and Wales*, that in the transition years after the war central government subsidies should be used to under-pin a statutory duty placed on local authorities to build the required houses. If the local authorities failed to discharge the task effectively then government should not hesitate to act directly. This 'was not an empty threat in view of the house building carried out by the Ministry of Munitions during the war, and that Ministry's apparent ability to organise the production of almost anything'.[13] Clearly, in both England and Scotland, the possibility of centrally organised house provision as an alternative or supplement to local authority activity was a valid proposition so far as the appropriate government departments were concerned. Moreover, as has been explained, it was estates such as those constructed by the S.N.H.C. at Rosyth during the war that set much of the style and tone for housebuilding by the public sector in the early 1920s.

The second Scottish venture of this type occurred in 1926. By this period it was becoming abundantly clear that the recession in shipbuilding was deep-seated and likely to last for several years.[14] The outlook, therefore, not only for the shipyards of Clydeside, but also for the Scottish engineering, steel and coal industries was, in the medium term, bleak. In these circumstances it is not surprising that many of the industrialists of the region became keen to use steel and unemployed steel and shipbuilding workers to attack Scotland's housing problem.[15] To attain such an objective via the private sector proved virtually impossible,[16] partly because of the novel nature of the proposed houses, but perhaps also because of the current relative cheapness of traditional housing for the private market. Confronted with this situation the industrialists concerned turned to the public authorities for assistance. But many local councillors reacted unsympathetically to the notion, arguing that the attempt was being made to foist inferior housing on working-class tenants.[17]

Walter Elliot, the then Parliamentary Under-Secretary of State at the Scottish Office, now intervened in the matter. As a Glasgow MP, Elliot was under no illusions as to the serious nature of both the unemployment and housing problems. Moreover, his experience as Parliamentary Secretary for Health at the Scottish Office during the passage of the 1923 Housing Act had convinced him of the need for Scotland to be given special treatment in respect of housing policy.[18] This opinion was not shared by the Minister of Health, Neville Chamberlain; hence Elliot and the Scottish Secretary, Sir John Gilmour, contrived to enlist the support of the Prime Minister, Stanley Baldwin, by inviting him to undertake a private visit to view for himself the slums of Cowcaddens and the Gorbals.

Elliot accompanied the Prime Minister on his visit to Glasgow on 1st October, 1925 and, although it was supposed to be informal, did not hesitate to keep the press informed as to his purpose. The *Glasgow Herald* reported Elliot as saying that the Prime Minister and Secretary of State were giving close attention to housing and that

> he hoped it might be possible, especially after Mr Baldwin's visit to Glasgow, to get the justice of the Scottish claim admitted, namely that we in Scotland had a special problem and should, if necessary, be allowed special consideration in dealing with it.[19]

The plan worked perfectly and that evening Baldwin announced an offer of a subsidy of £40 per house to Scottish local authorities which agreed to erect steel houses prefabricated by local firms normally active in the shipbuilding and engineering industries and using labour of which only 10 per cent would be conventional building trade workers.[20]

When the news broke Chamberlain was furious. 'The Scottish Office', he wrote to his sister, 'will always make a bungle of it, if it is possible to do so ...', and he went on to berate Elliot outrageously.[21] A fortnight later he came himself to inspect the slums of Dundee, to 'extol the virtues of owner occupation, and at the City Chambers that evening (to) speak not at all playfully of the need of his Department to be 'exceedingly watchful' that the Scottish Office got no more out of government than its due share'.[22]

If it was hard to persuade some of his colleagues of the merits of support for steel housing, Elliot found the response of most of the local authorities to the offer of the special subsidy equally unenthusiastic, for few councils declared an immediate interest. The Under-Secretary of State, however, was not prepared to let the project languish. In the view of his Department there was a current shortage of some 80,000 working-class houses in Scotland.[23] Accordingly, if the local authorities were not interested in building steel houses, the government would find another way. Thus the offer of the additional subsidy was withdrawn and Baldwin announced on 18th December 1925 that the government would itself build 2,000 prefabricated steel houses.[24]

First thoughts seem to have been to use the original Scottish National Housing Company as the government's agent in building the houses, and such a proposal was actually made to the company. In the event, however, it was decided to operate by means of a separate subsidiary, although the S.N.H.C. did provide its new partner with office accommodation and administrative and technical back-up.[25] Thus it was that in January 1926, the Second Scottish National Housing Company was incorporated. Its activities were funded by a loan from the Public Works Loans Board equivalent to 50 per cent of the cost of the houses and repayable over forty years at a fixed rate of interest. The remainder of the required money was to be contributed by the Scottish Board of Health by a loan to which 5 per cent annual interest was attached.[26]

The original purpose of the Second S.N.H.C. was to erect, finish, maintain and let 2,000 houses in several parts of the country.[27] Later an additional 500 houses were added to the programme and, between 1926 and 1928, a total of 2,552 steel houses were constructed in a variety of industrial locations. Specifically, as a letter to the Treasury explained, the purposes of the venture were to assist in relieving the housing shortage, to alleviate unemployment in the steel and kindred (ship-building) trades and to induce local authorities to follow suit, thus enhancing the impact of the effort.[28] The latter hope was regrettably not fulfilled since few councils responded and the effect on unemployment was, therefore, not sustained.

The three firms involved in the provision of the houses were Messrs Cowieson, Atholl Steel Houses Limited and G. & J. Weir (Cardonald). In the case of the Atholl houses the management of the operation appears to have been in the hands of the naval shipbuilding company, Wm Beardmore and Company Limited.[29] The contracting firms provided the foundations and superstructures while the Housing Company arranged for all services such as gas, water, drainage, fencing, footpaths, and clothes poles. Costs proved to be competitive with traditional building costs and it was argued that the introduction of these houses would help to keep general house prices down.[30]

The houses themselves were built mainly in Glasgow at Springboig (540), Shettleston (470), Robroyston (184), Cambuslang (100) and Garngad (86). The remainder were erected elsewhere in the west of Scotland (522) and in Edinburgh (350) and Dundee (300). In terms of external appearance the houses did not look especially unusual. The majority were two-storey, either semi-detached or terraced, and usually topped with a pitched roof. In general, the external walls consisted of large steel plates with turned flanges which were bolted together on the bottom, over which a U-sectioned steel stiffener was welded to provide additional strength.

Lord Weir concluded that his company's houses were 'extraordinarily good houses – much better houses than I had anticipated',[31] and time seems to have vindicated that judgement. Their original predicted life was assumed to be forty years and almost all easily reached that target. Sixteen, located in Greenock, were flattened by enemy bombs during the Second War and a handful of the remainder succumbed to the normal risks of destruction by fire. Otherwise, they are all still in use and most have been extensively modernised and are, therefore, likely to be occupied for many years to come. (Indeed, in recent years these houses have been the subject of a considerable dispute. Following the 1980 Tenants Rights etc Act, many of the houses were bought by their tenants, which is perhaps the best indication of their utility as dwellings. However, later in the 1980s major corrosion appeared in some of the buildings – typically those which were not provided with external cladding at the time of their modernisation in the period 1978–83. A dispute, therefore, followed concerning the liability for the costs of restoring the latter to a fully sound condition and to determine whether or not the houses still available for rent should be repaired or replaced. Remarkably, tenants who had not yet purchased campaigned to have the houses renovated so that their rights to buy would be restored and the existing communities preserved. Moreover, invariably there is a sizeable waiting-list for any of the houses that become available for let. Not withstanding the delays and uncertainties resulting from such problems, by the end of 1993 700 of the houses had been bought by tenants, while many of the others – for example, those at Shettleston – were about to be acquired by local housing associations. Given the circumstances of their

Steel houses built c1926 for the Second Scottish National Housing Company at Garngad, Glasgow.

design and construction, by almost any yardstick time has proved them to be successful and relatively attractive dwellings.)

Meanwhile, in 1926, Walter Elliot was reasonably pleased with his achievement. Addressing a by-election meeting in Kirkintilloch he hammered home the point that Baldwin's had been the 'first government to admit the justice of the claim that Scotland had a special case in the matter of housing, and to make special provision for it'.[32] As has already been explained, however, the local authorities declined to follow the example which had been set, hence the eventual outcome of the project was considerably less than Elliot had intended. Nevertheless, it is interesting to note that Elliot himself had won favourable opinions. In September 1928, no less a judge than Winston Churchill told the Prime Minister in a private letter that Elliot was 'by far the best' of the government's junior ministers.[33] This was a sentiment echoed by Harold Macmillan who included Elliot in a list of members of the government who 'had comprehensive and receptive minds', and he also identified Elliot as being 'specially favourable to the views' that he and his colleagues in the Young Conservative Group were trying to develop throughout the 1920s.[34] (In these years, of course, Macmillan and his friends were evolving economic thinking along lines later to be identified as Keynesianism.)

Elliot's biographer summed up the episode thus. Elliot, drawing on his short experience as a doctor in the Gorbals of Glasgow, was keenly aware of the damage to health caused by life in the city slums and, therefore, constantly agitated on the

Scottish housing question. He 'strongly pushed the Weir steel house both as an instrument of social policy and as a truly productive means of relieving unemployment'.[35]

Moreover, he was aware that lack of skilled building craftsmen was a major cause of the slow pace of house construction in Scotland and, therefore, he fully welcomed Weir's idea of a prefabricated steel house. It seemed a fine method of enabling the unemployed metal workers, engineers, plumbers, electricians and woodworkers of the ship-building and related industries to take part in increasing the output of badly needed new dwellings.

> Obviously here was an experiment worth trying and Walter set up a National Housing Company to try it 2,500 times. It was not to the credit of the Clydesiders – Maxton, Buchanan, Hardie etc – that they sought for every argument to discredit the steel house before it had even been tried.[36]

Coote is scathing in his indictment of the Clydesiders over their attitude on this occasion – 'the Clydeside campaign was a remarkable example of how reactionary revolutionaries can be'[37] – and he points to the ironic 'comic sequel' which was to overtake one of their number. Twenty years later, when George Buchanan 'the most fervid and sympathetic of the Clydesiders' was Minister at the Scottish Office in charge of Labour's post-war housing campaign, he

> personally sponsored a heavy programme of pre-fabricated ... 'non-traditional' houses. They were direct descendants of what he had excommunicated as monstrosities in 1925, and many were actually made by the firms Weir and Atholl ... *Autres temps, autres moeurs!*[38]

Thus during the First War and again in the period 1926–28, through the First and Second National Housing Companies, central government may be said to have experimented in Scotland both with direct intervention in house provision and with non-traditional methods of construction. The third, and major, intervention arose out of the attempt by government to drag the Scottish economy out of the crisis of the 1930s.

In 1929 the Labour Party returned to power, again as a minority government, but with the general support of a greatly reduced Liberal membership. This was a tragic period as it was the year in which a catastrophic economic crisis first struck the United States and then cast its shadow across the Atlantic. The slump which followed was of unprecedented ferocity and produced heart-breaking levels of unemployment in many parts of the country. In Scotland in 1931–33 unemployment varied between 26.1 and 27.7 per cent – the latter meaning that no less than 400,000 Scots were out of work.[39] And what made the situation so particularly horrific was that (in an age dominated by the male bread-winner) much of the distress was concentrated into a few areas, namely the heartlands of the traditional heavy industries of shipbuilding, engineering, steel and coal.[40]

In 1931, in order to relieve the drain on reserves and the damaging upward pressure on interest rates, Britain was forced to reduce the priority previously given to international exchange and to abandon the fixed link between sterling and gold. The government did not survive the crisis and when Ramsay Macdonald accepted the premiership of a National Government, the move split the Labour Party which was thereafter shattered in the subsequent general election.

One result of the economic crisis and the collapse of Labour was that the Wheatley Act was repealed in 1933. In the previous summer the government had appealed to the Scottish local authorities to suggest how public expenditure might be reduced. The committee of councillors appointed to consider the question responded that

> in view of the large reduction in building costs since the Act of 1924 was passed and having regard to the fall in the rate of interest on borrowed money, we consider that the time has now come when private enterprise unaided could supply all the houses that are required other than those necessary to house dispossessed tenants from slums and overcrowded houses and low wage earners.[41]

Broadly the government gratefully accepted this recommendation and the Housing Act of 1933, building on the Greenwood Act of 1930, concentrated public effort and attention on the business of clearing and replacing slums. In this case the subsidy was no longer attached to the house, but was instead related to the number of people displaced and rehoused. In some ways this was a reversion to late nineteenth century practice, but with the crucial difference that local authorities had to provide replacement houses for the former occupants of the slums which had been cleared.

In England the system does not appear to have worked well since doubts remained about the definition of a slum,[42] but in Scotland few councils had much difficulty in identifying slums; hence the withdrawal of the Wheatley Act produced no slackening in the pace of council house construction. In 1935, 18,814 council houses were completed in Scotland, which was the highest figure achieved thus far. In addition this period saw a sharp increase in the pace of private construction with output jumping from 5,913 houses in 1932 to 9,684 houses in 1934. This recovery in private production is interesting, but the figures just quoted do illustrate the way in which house production in Scotland in the inter-war years had become dominated by the local authorities.

The growth in private activity noted above was a pale reflection of what was happening south of the border through the 1930s. Professor Nevin estimated that 'of approximately 2,521,000 houses built during 1930–38 about 1,939,000, or 77 per cent were built by private firms'.[43] Many of these houses were purchased by 'working class borrowers' via mortgages. The relaxation in lending terms which enabled this to happen was 'a direct result of the cheap money policy'.[44] It is noteworthy, therefore, that the low interest rates which followed withdrawal from the gold standard in 1931 were able to stimulate a vast surge of activity in England even among people of modest means.

Low interest rates enabled costs of house construction to fall sharply and this had particular impact on building for the private consumer. For example, between 1928 and 1934 the average capital expense of new houses fell from £432 to £361.[45] Many builders relied heavily on bank credit facilities to carry out their projects and obviously found it easier and cheaper to raise the required loans. Similarly, on the demand side, between 1932 and 1936 interest charges on mortgages fell from 6 to 4.5 per cent and, as building society activity increased, the typical length of the repayment period also expanded while the initial required downpayment was reduced. 'Building societies were able to satisfy the demand for new mortgages since they were literally flooded with funds in the 1930s'.[46] (Incidentally, the low prices, low interest rates and huge volume of deposits in building society accounts provide the clearest indication of the rising living standards enjoyed by a large proportion of those **in work** throughout the period.)

During the 1930s then, there was a major expansion of private sector house-building and suburbia flourished around many of England's cities. On a smaller scale the same thing happened in Scotland. In the vicinity of Glasgow such activity was, not surprisingly, modest, but developments took place in such localities as Bearsden and Milngavie and these were often mainly composed of the bungalows which are so representative of the period. The small houses were a direct consequence of the subsidy limit; (Scottish private house buyers were still much more likely to be dependent on subsidy support than their English counterparts and they were often prepared to accept the restricted standards of house size involved), but to some extent there was compensation in that low land prices meant that garden space was frequently generous. The effect of this phase on Edinburgh is more obvious, because her relative prosperity meant that more of her citizens were able to take advantage of the favourable conditions confronting buyers. Frequently the houses were sold at an 'all-in' price of £760 and they were generally built to

Classic inter-war bungalows in the Craigs, Edinburgh.

high construction standards. Estates sprawled around the edge of the capital, notably, for example in the Craigs area of Corstorphine and at Duddingston. Similarly, private suburban housing spread attractively on the edge of Aberdeen.

This private sector activity occurred not just around the cities, but also made its mark on many towns and villages, particularly where there was a reasonable middle class market, such as in a resort town like Ayr. Generally, however, in Scotland there continued to be a greater degree of dependence on public sector construction. Of the total of 337,000 houses built in Scotland between the wars, no less than 67 per cent were constructed by public authorities. By contrast, 75 per cent of the 4,194,000 houses produced in England in the same period were developed by the private sector.[47] Measured per head of population there is little difference in the output rate north and south of the border, but obviously the preferred method of delivery was quite different. Presumably this was a consequence of the relative poverty of the Scots, particularly in the areas where economic conditions remained poor. However, one wonders to what extent Scottish contractors also favoured building for the public authorities, since the latter activity removed the risks involved in speculative building for sale.

The transfer of public funding to support slum clearance is not altogether surprising since in the years around 1930 there was, in fact, a considerable anti-slum campaign in which one of the key agitators was the journalist and broadcaster, Howard P. Marshall. He followed up a series of BBC radio programmes with publication of a little volume, *Slum* (1933), written jointly with Avice Trevelyan. Marshall and Trevelyan pointed out that although two million houses had by then been built since the war 'the slums have hardly been touched'.[48] In their view the problem was that

> the new houses have been swallowed up by the better paid skilled workers, artisans and clerks who consist of very many small families occupying a vast number of houses ... the poorest people have been relatively unaffected by post-war building activities.[49]

They had some very radical solutions to offer and interestingly these included the establishment of a 'Housing Corporation' which would 'build houses to let at rents within the means of the poorest people'. Such a Corporation, they argued, would provide work for thousands of unemployed people.

> It would ... carry out research into new methods of building, and without too rigid standardisation, enormous reductions could be effected in the cost of working-class houses.... a Housing Corporation, by mass production methods and a consequent reduction in overheads and waste, could in time lower ... rent(s) appreciably.

Marshall and his colleague envisaged that a Housing Corporation would be 'a central power-house, radiating energy and initiative through provincial corporations ... At present progress is hindered at every turn because there is no concentrated drive from the centre'. They strongly condemned local authorities as being unsuitable vehicles through which to provide housing because councils were frequently 'exceedingly inefficient' and often possessed a motivation which was of doubtful merit. Therefore, '… all housing questions should immediately be taken out of their hands. What is more, it is entirely wrong that housing and local politics should be mixed together …' In any case, they argued, local authorities 'could not hope to compete where cost is concerned with a National Housing Corporation'.[50]

Their views in respect of council housing would have received some reinforcement had they examined some of the activities now taking place in Scotland under the slum clearance measures of the 1930 and 1935 Housing Acts. Around the peripheries of towns and cities some ominously uniform and depressing estates were now appearing, typically in the form of grey tenements. What was to become one of the most notorious estates in Glasgow was constructed in this period at Blackhill, and another grim development took place at Possil. At Paisley the largest contemporary slum clearance estate was created at Ferguslie Park and it was to bedevil not merely generations of tenants, but the legion of public officials and politicians who have been trying to improve the situation ever since. Similary, in this period Edinburgh Corporation undertook major building at Craigmillar, Niddrie and Pilton, and Dundee and Aberdeen also produced estates of low quality. Even Stirling Corporation began to store future trouble by commencing the Raploch estate, almost unbelievably in the north western shadow of the historic castle rock.

Whether or not Walter Elliot read Marshall and Trevelyan's little volume cannot,

Inter-war slum clearance housing in Glasgow. These tenements were acquired and modernised by the SSHA in the early 1980s.

of course, now be established, but it is tempting to think that he might well have done so bearing in mind the events now to be discussed. In 1936 Sir Godfrey Collins died in office and Elliot was promoted to his place as Secretary of State for Scotland. He came to his new position at a time when his prestige was 'high from the work he had done as Minister of Agriculture in building an enduring edifice of controlled agricultural marketing and support'.[51]

In 1934 a Ministry of Labour *Investigation into the Industrial Condition in Certain Distressed Areas* had been followed by passage of the Special Areas (Development and Improvement) Act and this resulted in the appointment of Commissioners whose job it would be to promote schemes designed to aid the recovery of those parts of the country which were most severely depressed. At the time Collins had succeeded in persuading the Cabinet that although the English Commissioner would be appointed by the Minister of Labour, the Scottish Commissioner should come under his jurisdiction and this, in some ways, was the beginning of the economic development function of the Scottish Office.[52]

By 1936 the problems confronting Scotland were still enormous, but with Elliot as Secretary of State, vigorous action was not likely to be long delayed. Almost immediately he secured the agreement of his government colleagues to a practical Keynesian style economic programme. The boundaries of the 'special areas' – which already included nearly one quarter of the Scottish population – were significantly extended and the Commissioner was empowered to build industrial estates, to let factories, to subsidise new industries, and to provide assistance to an extended range of public utilities. Thereafter Elliot turned his attention back to housing.

Reviewing the situation, he was not satisfied with the progress which had been made either by the Scottish building industry or by the local authorities and concluded that the shortage of acceptable houses in the kingdom still amounted to something of the order of 250,000.[53] The survey on which he made that estimate was into overcrowding as assessed on the new standard introduced by the Housing Act of 1935.[54] If the problem was now attacked more effectively he believed this could also make a major contribution to reducing the level of unemployment. Given the background of his experience described in earlier pages, Elliot had little doubt as to how the job should be tackled. Accordingly, he set out his views to the Cabinet in a memorandum dated 18th January 1937.

He noted not only his concern at the 'deplorable' state of Scottish housing, but also what he claimed was a recent slow down in the rate of production. This presumably was his pretext for directing attention to construction processes which were most likely to do something for the unemployed, most of whom were likely to be unskilled, certainly in terms of the crafts employed in traditional house building. Considering the use of alternative methods of building, not surprisingly his first thoughts turned back to steel. The possibilities of using steel were 'being explored, but the present strain on the steel market makes it doubtful whether any substantial use of this material can be made for the time being'. (Many blast furnaces had been lost during the depth of the depression and with the cautious rearmament programme now under way, demand for steel was increasing faster than output.)

> Neither concrete nor timber is likely to be a practicable alternative of any magnitude for house building in the core of large towns. The suburbs and the less thickly populated areas generally offer the best opportunity for the use of these materials.

Even if such methods proved successful, Elliot was aware that a duty to conduct experiments in house-building by new methods and with new materials would merely add to the burden already carried by local authorities. As an alternative he proposed to turn once again to the Scottish National Housing Company.

> ... The Company's organisation could rapidly be expanded to deal with a minimum programme of say 1,500 to 2,000 houses a year, and once it gets into full swing, it would be possible for the Company to provide if desired as many as 4,000 houses annually over a period of seven years.

He insisted that the Company's activities would be 'complementary to and not in competition' with the local authorities, and that it would relieve the stresses on the labour market. Traditional skilled building workers would be released to concentrate their efforts in areas where non-traditional construction methods were less appropriate and where labour shortages existed. He argued that on

> the programme suggested a substantial direct contribution would be made to the solution of the housing problem and, indirectly, the Company's work would, I hope, be so arranged as to have a salutary effect in stimulating local authorities to press forward vigorously their organisation for ordinary construction.[55]

He then went on to plead with the Cabinet for a dispensation to provide the Company with special financial arrangements to offset the fact that it would not be able to obtain a rate-borne subsidy, and called for a campaign to upgrade some of the existing sub-standard older houses.

It is clear, therefore, that Elliot was no longer prepared to leave the resolution of Scottish housing problems to the private building industry or to the local authorities which, in some of the most economically stricken parts of the country, already had their hands more than full. Now, in his view, a major drive must come via central government. Moreover, since traditional houses could not be produced in sufficient numbers for lack of skilled labour, fresh thinking should be applied to devise new house types of timber or concrete. Such houses, he hoped, might be capable of being constructed largely by unskilled workers and the enterprise would thus be enabled to contribute in a major way to the alleviation of unemployment.

What is especially interesting about Elliot's plans is that, for the first time, a Scottish Secretary was developing and articulating a set of Scottish housing (and economic) policies which were distinctively different from those applied to the U.K. as a whole.

The basis for Elliot's views is made clear in the 1938 Annual Report of the Department of Health for Scotland. In this it is indicated that despite the 246,832 houses which had been built in Scotland since the war with the aid of Exchequer subsidy, a further quarter of a million houses were still required to satisfactorily provide for the working-class population. The Report also drew attention to the slow progress being made in the relief of overcrowding – a serious matter, given that 269,000 Scottish houses had been shown to be overcrowded in an investigation of 1935 – and it was pointed out that the slum replacement programme had also slowed down because the local authorities were switching resources to deal with overcrowding.[56] It is against this background that Elliot proposed his new central government initiative.

In view of his earlier activities it was natural for Elliot to look to the second Scottish National Housing Company as the instrument for carrying through his policy, but in the interim the management experience of the company had not been happy. Financially it had fallen into severe difficulties. Although its rents were considered to be high and tenants seem to have had difficulty in paying them, the company had enormous problems in repaying its debt. In 1934 the Treasury had had to waive arrears of interest and to suspend payment of future interest to the Public Works Loans Board, but with an increasing tax liability, with rent control and with many tenants in difficulty, there was little prospect of rapid improvement.[57] In these circumstances, and perhaps also because of problems over the nature of the company's Articles of Association, Elliot's first thoughts on the matter had quickly to be dropped. Instead, consideration now turned to the creation of a new custom-built organisation.

By 1937 the English economy was pulling steadily out of the depression but, by comparison, Scotland was still in the toils and Elliot, therefore, was desperately keen to do everything possible to stimulate the inflow of new growth industries. It was for this reason that he persuaded the Cabinet to allow the Special Areas Commissioner to establish industrial estates and it was no great leap to connect his housing plan to the Commissioner's activities. This idea was backed by Sir William Douglas, the Secretary of the Department of Health for Scotland, and so it was that the Scottish Special Areas Housing Association was established in the autumn of 1937, with the specific task of building working-class houses within the Special Areas of Scotland.

Within a few months, however, Elliot realised that it was unwise to restrict the Association exclusively to operations within the defined Special Areas; hence in the Housing (Financial Provisions) (Scotland) Act, 1938, the Association was empowered to undertake the erection of working-class houses elsewhere 'for experimental or demonstration purposes'.[58] This was an obvious attempt to encourage and stimulate the activities of local authorities wherever such help might be required. In addition, the Association was intended to embark on a substantial building programme.

The other features of the 1938 Act are also worth noting since for the first time the subsidy payable on a local authority house was related to its size, with 3-apartment dwellings attracting a central grant of £10, 4-apartments £11 15s and 5-apartments £13 – all in addition to the local authority contribution of £4 10s or £5, depending on locality. The Act was also 'remarkable' in that for the first time the subsidy was not paid on completion of dwellings, but was payable on those houses which had been commenced by an agreed date.[59] In this case the aims of the Act were to offset increasing housing costs, to stimulate local authority production and to encourage the creation of larger houses so as to attack the problems of overcrowding.

Obviously the second world war soon intervened and this makes it impossible to fully determine the effectiveness of Elliot's Act, but, in his study of inter-war housing in Glasgow, John McKee concluded that in terms of increasing the flow of four and five apartment dwellings in order to deal with the overcrowding problem 'on the Glasgow evidence … the Act was ostensibly well on the way to becoming a success …'[60]

Success or not, it is clear that a powerful and imaginative approach was now being adopted and it was thought that

> there was now the heady prospect of a Scotland without slums by 1942. A Scotland without rural slums as well, for there was now legislation to require much better standards of housing for the farm-worker and country dweller; with his agricultural background Elliot was insistent on this.[61]

The first chairman of the new housing association was Sir David Allan Hay. He had been Commissioner for the Special Areas in Scotland, a position in which he was now succeeded by Lord Nigel Douglas-Hamilton. These changes are another clear indication of the importance which Elliot attached to the activities of the association, an impression which is confirmed by the other members of the powerful first Council of Management. Included in the seven strong group were such figures as John A. Inglis KC, James Welsh, the Labour MP for Bothwell, and David Ronald, Chief Engineer at the Department of Health. Another member was Alexander McKinna, who had formerly been Secretary at the Department of Health where, in the 1920s, he had been heavily involved in setting up the Second S.N.H.C..

Exactly what the Association's initial target was is not clear, but in the minutes of the first meeting, under the heading 'Financial Estimate for the Commissioner' the following statement is made.

> The Secretary was instructed to base the estimate, for which the Commissioner had called, on 3,000 houses having been commenced in that period, including 750 completed.[62]

Presumably the period in question was the financial year 1938–39, hence these figures seem to indicate the probable objective for the first year.

Advancing from scratch to the kind of rate of construction which was being envisaged was no straightforward task. Two major problems seem to have pre-occupied the Association in these early days and neither of them was easily resolved. First, there was the problem of the acquisition of suitable building sites. Second, there was the need to identify and select an appropriate range of non-traditional houses whose forms of construction would lend themselves to the employment of workers not normally recruited by the building industry.

Theoretically sites from which the Association could choose were nominated by the local authorities and the Commissioner, but some local councils were initially dubious about, or hostile to, the Association's activities and the situation could be further complicated if a reluctant landowner was involved. As a result, the selection of land for development often seemed something of a Hobson's choice and was invariably a slow business. Moreover, the government declined repeated requests to give the Association powers of compulsory purchase and insisted that it should seek to work in harmony with the local authorities concerned.

Similarly the identification of suitable building forms proved tricky, but after considering the different methods which had been tried in various parts of England and abroad, houses of timber and poured concrete were identified as being most likely to prove successful.

Gradually the Association formulated a suitable programme and commenced operations in such places as Tannochside, Carluke, Holytown, Forth, Douglas and Coalburn in Lanarkshire, at Johnstone in Renfrewshire and at Bathgate and Armadale in West Lothian. The first completed houses were actually two red cedar Canadian timber houses, constructed on the edge of a small industrial estate at Carfin in Lanarkshire and formally visited in May 1938 by King George and Queen Elizabeth. The first tenants give an interesting view of the conditions which the Association was intended to address since Mr and Mrs Taylor and their three daughters had moved from a single apartment condemned tenement slum in New Stevenston.

If the Taylors, the Secretary of State and the Association were all delighted with the timber houses, their views were not shared by others. In addition to the S.S.H.A. houses, the Swedish Government had erected two demonstration timber houses at Carntyne in Glasgow, and this move towards non-traditional houses now sparked off one of the first shots in what was to become a fairly seminal conflict. James Maxton, MP, – perhaps the most admired of the Clydesiders – was first to challenge the Government in Parliament. He attacked the minister for encouraging the introduction of an 'inferior substitute'.

> **Mr Colville**: I understood that the honourable Member's colleague a few moments ago wanted me to investigate every method which would help the housing conditions in Glasgow.
> **Mr Maxton**: I hope that the right honourable Gentleman will not understand that he is expected to start jerry building.[63]

As it happens the Carfin houses were (and are) beautiful houses in which the first two tenants lived out their lives. The red cedar house type was used in Motherwell and elsewhere and one of the disappointments of the onset of the Second War is that it brought to a halt construction of such dwellings which, of course, depended on imported supplies of timber. In any event, four days before Maxton got to his feet, the Association had noted that so many local authorities were now interested in timber house construction that 'it could no longer be regarded as an alternative available to any great extent to the Association.' The

A Red cedar house at Fallin. The houses in this area have been modernised, but retain much of their charm. They form a strikingly pretty corner of a former mining village.

trouble was that the demand for joiners was likely to reach quickly the point where there would be insufficient numbers for normal house construction. In these circumstances the Association decided to concentrate on poured concrete since the latter method enabled the maximum use to be made of unskilled workers.[64]

If problems associated with obtaining suitable land and identifying appropriate non-traditional house types slowed the early progress of the Association, by March of 1939 its Annual Report was able to declare that significant momentum was being gained. A programme of 5,533 houses was in hand and 1,364 houses were under construction on various sites across central Scotland.[65] At that time the word 'Areas' was deleted from the Association's name and its Memorandum of Association was altered to enable it to build anywhere throughout Scotland.[66] This was in response to the appeals for help from local authorities outwith the Special Areas which had persuaded the government to agree that the organisation's remit should be broadened.

In 1938 Walter Elliot was succeeded by Sir John Colville and early in the following year the new Secretary of State met the Association's Council to explain his intentions. Henceforth the Association would not be required to work under the Special Areas Commissioner. Instead a new branch of the Housing Division at the Department of Health for Scotland would be established to work with the Association which would be given a greatly increased programme.[67] It is obvious that the government was now satisfied that the Association was sufficiently

Canadian Timber cottages built by the SSHA at Linlithgow in 1939.

prepared to enable a central initiative to be launched to address the housing problem in many parts of the country. Within a few months the immediate programme had been identified as 28,500 houses, 20,000 within the Special Areas and the remainder in other localities where there was a clear need.[68]

Thus it can be seen that on the eve of the Second War the government and what was from now known as the Scottish Special Housing Association were clearly poised to embark on the major campaign which, had it proceeded, might well have produced a very different housing pattern in Scotland from the one which subsequently developed. Reviewing the post-war housing period in the context of his history of the Scottish Office, John Gibson concluded that after the war

> too much had to be done too quickly ... the enlightened legislation of Walter Elliot's years might have saved the day. But the coming of Hitler's war was the final misfortune; for Scotland the enforced stop to house-building in the autumn of 1939 had been a national disaster.[69]

Perhaps things did have to be rushed after the war, but the need for haste was not the only problem. In fact, of course, the development of the S.S.H.A. was an initiative which roused significant political opposition and it is appropriate to consider this subject in a little detail. While, initially, contradictory opinions may not have mattered greatly, by 1945 the political climate had changed dramatically and the hostile views concerned were those of people who had gained the power and influence to change decisively the direction of policy.

Examples of no-fines concrete house types erected just before the war at Tannochside, Carluke and Holytown. The method of producing such houses involved pouring a mixture of cement and crushed whin-stone (but without sand – so no fine particles) into a mould formed from steel shutters. Even in the early days the walls of such cottages could be created in just four days by unskilled ex-miners and this became the basic technique preferred by the SSHA.

As was explained earlier, in evolving his views on housing policy in the years prior to the First World War, John Wheatley had argued passionately in favour of council housing as part of an approach dedicated to the development of a form of municipal socialism. Wheatley's views were shared by others and carried enormous influence in certain sections of Labour politics, especially within Glasgow. In particular, many members of the inter war Independent Labour Party were committed to the Wheatley position and perhaps inevitably viewed the arrival of the S.S.H.A. with great suspicion as a threat to their plans for extending municipalism.

Within four months of the establishment of the Association hostility was evident among members of the Clydeside I.L.P. group in the Commons and the latter raised angry questions suggesting that it was an ineffective organisation.[70] Similarly, as has been noted, James Maxton was quick to condemn the use of timber non-traditional house types, despite the fact that those being constructed at the time were obviously good and attractive dwellings. However, in the early months of its existence there were few other obvious grounds for conflict between the Association and Glasgow politicians since the city was not a designated Special Area.

Following the Housing (Financial Provisions) (Scotland) Act of 1938 the Association was permitted to operate all over Scotland and was subsequently authorised to build 8,500 houses outside the Special Areas. As part of this allocation the Association offered to build a first tranche of 1,750 houses within Glasgow and the episode which followed is interesting and instructive because it immediately produced conflict and helped to stimulate articulation of the various points of view. This is particularly important because of the light which the declared attitudes shed on the critical events which were to occur immediately after the war.

In 1939 housing figured largely in the columns of the Scottish Labour newspaper, *Forward*, and several of the principals used the newspaper to express their views.

In an article on December 31st, 1938, *Forward's* regular correspondent, 'Knight Watchman', who was evidently Jack Davis, a Labour councillor and member of the Glasgow Corporation Housing Committee,[71] reported on the general outlook in respect of housing.

> On all sides it is accepted that the housing question is the most important affecting the city. No other matter comes within reach of it in civic interest. The citizen has become housing conscious and the present speed of house building is seriously lagging behind the demand which has become something of a clamour.[72]

These remarks at face value contained nothing other than encouragement so far as the Association was concerned. More ominously, however, in advocating an extension of the city's own building department the same councillor wrote on April 29th 1939 –

> The direct labour experiment has been so successful that there is a danger that private profit in housebuilding will be eliminated altogether. And, frankly, that is our aim.[73]

Glasgow's Direct Labour Organisation had only recently been established, but by 1939 it was employing 2000 workmen and they completed no less than 66% of all the dwellings constructed in the city in that year. As the above example clearly illustrates, henceforward the DLO was seen by many left wingers as the means of driving private builders out of the industry.

This kind of hostility towards the private building contractor contrasts strongly with the contemporary attitude of the S.S.H.A.'s Council of Management. In some of its early concrete schemes the Association had itself used direct labour because knowledge of no-fines concrete building was not then readily available in Scotland. However, in March 1939, Council had arranged for specifications to be made to enable contractors to tender for such work in future and had declared that although –

> the Council of Management adopted direct labour for the first cellular concrete schemes they have always borne in mind that any form of construction, if it is to be of permanent value, should be capable of being used satisfactorily by contractors under the usual supervision.[74]

Clearly, then, the Association was not only willing to work with the private builder, but felt that it had a duty so to do. Within a few weeks it discharged that duty by awarding a contract for no less than 2,600 houses to be erected on six sites in the west of Scotland to Messrs William Arnott McLeod and Company.[75] Obviously, therefore, far from being inclined towards any assault on the private builder, the Association regarded itself as an employer of such contractors and, on this question, was certainly likely to provide an obstacle to the strategy favoured by Councillors such as Davis.

On May 13th, 1939, Councillor George Smith, Convener of the Glasgow Housing Committee, gave a clear and unequivocal statement of the Labour Group's official approach to housing and his words are worth quoting at length. He wrote

> 1. That what distinguishes we socialists from the others is the belief that the community should own and control the public services; in this particular instance house-building.
> 2. That we believe the community – in this case the municipality – untrammelled by profit-making, can provide this service better and quicker than private enterprise.
> 3. That those who have not as yet made up their minds on this fundamental party issue have no right to be in a party called socialist.
> 4. That if we believe, as we ought, in Labour policy, and don't work to give effect to it, we are betraying the party.
> ...
> 7. That ... the socialist way to build the greatest number of houses – not irregularly as in the past when depending solely on the private builder, but constantly and increasingly – is by the continuous enlargement of our own municipal department.[76]

In Smith's view, therefore, the official position was that housing should be provided and controlled by and through the municipality, and private builders should be progressively squeezed out through the continuous expansion of municipal direct labour. Moreover, his suggestion that any alternative viewpoint was untenable in a socialist is revealing.

We have thus a clear illustration of the attitudes prevailing within influential sections of the Glasgow Labour group in May 1939, when the S.S.H.A. made its first offer to build 1,750 houses within the city.

The first Glasgow Labour politician to comment directly on the Association was Lord Provost Dollan. On July 8th he wrote on the subject of concrete houses and said –

> Alternative methods of building are being proposed and the Special Areas Housing Association has been convened by the Government to arrange for the erection of 25,000 houses of timber, concrete and other materials not ordinarily used for building. I am all in favour of this, and any other scheme that is going to add to the output.[77]

This sympathetic response represents one ongoing strand of Labour opinion which was often to surface – namely, that since the Association would add to the supply of working class houses, it ought to be encouraged. Within a week the alternative position was expressed, this time in another article by 'Knight Watchman' (Jack Davis). Since the latter was specifically concerned with the Association's offer to build within Glasgow, this article is particularly illuminating.[78]

He began by referring to a press interview given by a 'Labour Party Organiser' welcoming the offer, but expressed the personal opinion that it was likely to be rejected. He then went on to outline the basic proposal, drawing attention to the houses of timber or concrete which might be constructed in order to avoid 'additional strain on the supply of bricklayers'. He claimed that the houses would be 'owned and managed by the Housing Association' and went on

> That is the scheme as it appears to the public. It is described as building houses for Glasgow for nothing. Because we are excused a rate contribution, which is provided by Government, it is said we are getting something for nothing. Somehow I am constitutionally sceptical about any proposal of the National Government to give Glasgow houses for nothing.

Thereafter he suggested that since the local authority would still be liable to pay for sewers and open space maintenance the saving of the rate contribution was 'imaginary'. He suggested that if the Corporation agreed to the scheme there would be very little real gain to Glasgow and that the houses when built would belong to, and be managed by, the S.S.H.A., 'so all the problems arising from dual control of housing in the city would be deliberately created by the city council'.

He argued that 'experimentation in concrete houses outwith Council control' was simply storing up trouble for the future. Where was the gain in this project, he enquired. 'Is there anything this non-elected group can do that could not be done by the public body responsible to the people?'

The S.S.H.A. proposed to build through the use of non skilled workers not normally employed in house building, but, in Knight Watchman's view, the Corporation could itself employ such workers and 'keep control and management of the houses in the hands of the Housing Department … Beware of the Greeks when they bring you gifts'.

Finally, he concluded –

> The Special Housing Association (is) a non-elected body whose activities are not controlled by the electors or their public representatives. I object to this tendency to transfer our problems from elected to non-elected bodies. ... Control by non-representative bodies ought to be fought tooth and nail.

Here we have a clear statement of the strand of Labour opinion in Glasgow which was hostile to the Association, seeing it primarily as a threat to the control over housing which its proponents wished to vest exclusively in the local authority.

Davis's blast produced an immediate counter-salvo. Under the headlines, FACTS ABOUT SCOTTISH SPECIAL HOUSING ASSOCIATION – 1700 FREE HOUSES FOR GLASGOW, *Forward* of 22nd July carried an article by Arthur W. Brady who was a member of the Association's Council of Management.

Brady pointed out that the Labour group in the Corporation had yet to discuss the offer and suggested that Davis's article had been misleading and premature. He described how he and James Welsh (MP for Bothwell) had been appointed to the Association's Board of Management with the approval of various Labour organisations including the Parliamentary Labour Party in Welsh's case, and, in his own, by the Scottish Labour Party, the Glasgow Trades Council and the Glasgow Burgh Labour Party. He claimed that neither of them would be on the Board 'were it other than a straight-forward effort to house people whose deplorable conditions are so well known'.

He then gave some further details of the nature of the organisation, pointed out that schemes were already in progress in sixteen locations and went on to describe the relationship between the Association and local authorities. The Association could not build without the consent and support of the councils to whom plans, specifications and site layout details were all submitted for approval. Once these had been agreed, however, the Association

> makes the roads, builds the houses, provides open spaces and in the case of Glasgow (will) hand over £30,000 a year of new rates. But that is not all. The local authorities select their own tenants (and) may collect the rent and rates on a payment between the parties ...

He noted that Glasgow had more sites in its possession than it could use in the next ten years. What then, he protested, was the point in a 'propaganda' campaign in *Forward* 'to reject 1,700 houses, completely free, when there are 40,000 applicants in desperation for houses? What is the reply to those on the waiting list?'

He claimed that the houses would provide work for 1,600 unskilled men at trades union rates and noted that, in addition to Glasgow's allocation, Edinburgh, Dundee and Stirlingshire – also all outwith the special areas – had been offered houses. But whereas work was already in progress on their schemes, Glasgow was being 'sticky'.

He concluded with a final swipe at 'Knight Watchman' by saying that he was writing to *Forward* because -

Misrepresentation, false calculation and bad analysis of the offer made to Glasgow required correction in the interest of those who might be employed in preference to Unemployment Relief.[79]

This then, was the alternative Labour perspective. In Brady's view the Association ought to be welcomed both because of the additional houses which it would supply for working people and because of its ability to expand the labour force of the construction industry through the employment of unskilled workers.

In essence Davis's charge boiled down to two points. First, the S.S.H.A.'s activity would introduce 'dual control' of housing because the houses would be 'owned and managed' by the Association. And second, the organisation was a 'non-elected body … not controlled by the electors or their public representatives'.

In fact, as Brady had correctly pointed out, at that time there was no intention that the Association would manage its houses. On the contrary, the local authorities were intended to have the management function – for which they would be paid commission – and rents were only to be determined on the basis of agreement between the Association and individual local authorities. Not until the rent battle of the late 1950's did the Association begin to assume responsibility for the management of the bulk of its properties.

The second charge was equally wrong. While it is true that members of the Council of Management were not directly elected, the control exercised by successive Secretaries of State and the ongoing levels of Parliamentary scrutiny would make any retrospective charge of lack of democratic control impossible to sustain for any period of the Association's history. However, at that time, not only was James Welsh, the Labour opposition member for Bothwell, a member of the Council of Management, but Florence Horsburgh, the Parliamentary Under Secretary of State at the Department of Health was one of his colleagues. The level of Parliamentary control could scarcely have been greater and it would seem, therefore, that what Davis was really objecting to was not lack of oversight by 'public representatives', but that the Association was perceived to pose a threat to Labour's control over housing at the local government level.

Davis's position seems to have been an accurate reflection of the opinion of the dominant faction on Glasgow Corporation. Towards the end of July, the Association Chairman (by then Lord Traprain), together with James Scrymgeour Wedderburn, Under Secretary of State at the Scottish Office, had a meeting in London with the Glasgow I.L.P. MPs James Maxton, John McGovern and the Rev. Campbell-Stephen to discuss 'Glasgow Corporation's unwillingness to accept the Association's offer of houses'. Apparently their reception was unsympathetic because, in a report to his Council on 28th July, Lord Traprain concluded that a favourable response from the Corporation was unlikely in the present year. The Council of Management's reaction was that such a delay was unacceptable and it resolved to demand an immediate decision failing which the houses would be reallocated to other authorities.[80]

Within weeks the war had broken out and thus ended the first brush between the Association and the Labour group within the city. However, by 1940 it was clear that the onset of war had done nothing to soften attitudes. The demands of war production led to an expansion of the Rolls Royce factory at Hillington and this created an urgent requirement for no less than 1,500 houses to accommodate incoming employees. Glasgow Corporation was initially unwilling to be involved and hence, in January 1940, the Association was invited by the government to provide the houses which were intended to be managed by Rolls Royce on behalf of the Air Ministry. (Much the sort of arrangement which was similarly and simultaneously being conducted at Rosyth for the Admiralty.) However, after 'a considerable amount of work in connection with the type and layout plans' had been undertaken, the Corporation abruptly changed its mind and insisted on taking over the project.[81] It seems, therefore, that even the emergency requirements of wartime were quite unable to soften or deflect the views of members of the Corporation housing committee in their single-minded commitment to council housing.

It is clear from the situation recorded above that direct central government intervention in the provision of housing via the S.S.H.A. was deeply unwelcome to powerful sections of the Labour movement within the west of Scotland. While this was a minor irritation in the period 1937–1940, after the war the conflict between the two positions was to produce a distortion to Scottish housing policy which can only be described as disastrous.

CHAPTER THREE

The Watershed Years

*T*HE housing problems in Scotland which confronted the government at the end of the Second World War were particularly acute. It is true that of the U.K. total of 475,000 houses destroyed or permanently rendered uninhabitable by enemy action, only about 7,000 were in Scotland, and these were mainly concentrated in Glasgow, Greenock and Clydebank.[1] However, many other houses in these areas were damaged, and once the residue of the pre-war housing programme was completed by 1940, the flow of new houses was reduced to a trickle, with only 15,633 houses being erected from 1940 to 1945 – mainly for essential war workers who were required to move into particular localities. Furthermore, the condition of many of the older existing houses deteriorated significantly during the war, both from the scarcity of tradesmen for maintenance purposes and in consequence of the shortage of materials.

If the quality and condition of the housing stock was inadequate, it was also hopelessly short in quantity. The war years saw a recovery in both rates of population growth and family formation. No census was conducted in 1941, but in 1945 the Scottish population was estimated at 5,150,000.[2] In 1931 it had been recorded at 4,800,000.[3] Similarly the number of marriages per year increased, while the average age at which people married fell. Thus the demand for accommodation was growing sharply at precisely the moment when the supply of new houses dried up.

Throughout the U.K. the housing shortage was severe.[4] And if this was particularly true in London and the heavily bombed cities of the Midlands, it was also true in Scotland, and the problem was not confined to the industrial heartlands. All over the country thousands of people had to make shift as best they could. In 1946, about 40,000 squatters[5] including 6,800 in Scotland,[6] were believed to have taken possession of disused service properties of one kind or another. Moreover, throughout the war years it was almost a patriotic duty to share any available spare accommodation space (compulsory powers could be used to enforce sharing if necessary). With the return of peace this practice naturally came to be regarded as increasingly burdensome and unsatisfactory.

The earliest attempts to increase the stock of dwellings as rapidly as possible involved the repair and adaption of war damaged houses, the modification of various wartime buildings such as government hostels and service properties, the adaption and erection of huts which had originally been intended for war purposes, and the production of temporary houses – often the celebrated 'prefabs'.

Nationally by the end of 1946 a little over 300,000 units of this kind had been provided : '80,000 in 'prefabs', 45,000 in conversions and adaptions, 107,000 in repaired unoccupied war-damaged houses, 12,000 in temporary huts and service camps, 25,000 in requisitioned houses, and 52,000 in new permanent houses. About 1.25 million occupied dwellings which had suffered war damage and had been repaired'.[7] In Scotland 32,000 'prefabs' were erected around this time.[8]

Looking to the longer term, however, it is interesting that in housing, as in so many other areas, the war seems to have stimulated rethinking on the grand scale, and throughout the years 1939–1945 an astonishing number of committees and commissions were at work preparing to contribute to the reshaping of post-war society.

The first committee to report, the Barlow Commission, had actually been set up before the war and in 1940 it produced its recommendations on the *Distribution of the Industrial Population*, urging the further redevelopment of congested areas, the dispersal of population and industry and the establishment of a national planning authority. It was followed in 1942 by the Uthwatt Report on *Compensation and Betterment* and the Scott Report on the *Utilisation of Land in Rural Areas*. The former encouraged the State to assume the right to take up undeveloped land for development purposes, while the latter looked at development and conservation in the countryside and made recommendations on the improvement of rural housing. In 1943, while the Ministry of Town and Country Planning was set up in England and Wales, its duties in respect of Scotland were devolved to the Scottish Office, and the Town and Country Planning (Interim Development) (Scotland) Act brought all land under planning control. (Planning procedures were consolidated in the post-war era by the Act of 1947.) This enabled the Scottish Office to accelerate its own preparations for the return to peace.

In his Cabinet reconstruction of early 1941 Prime Minister Winston Churchill appointed the respected Labour MP Tom Johnston to be Secretary of State for Scotland.[9] On agreeing to take the post Johnston asked for the right to form a committee – a sort of Council of State – composed of all the living Secretaries for Scotland and which would plan for the kingdom's future. Churchill responded 'sympathetically', indicating his willingness to look favourably 'upon anything about which Scotland is unanimous'.[10] Thus was born Johnston's 'Council on Post-War Problems', which, in addition to himself, included in its membership Ernest Brown, Sir John Colville, Sir Walter Elliot, Sir Archibald Sinclair and Lord Alness. John Gibson describes the 'Council' in the following terms.

> Here was a mechanism which neatly brought together Labour, Conservative, Liberal and National Liberal, which turned to advantage the important posts at the Health and Air Ministries respectively held by Brown and Sinclair, and secured the maximum co-operation between the parties on proposals brought before it.[11]

In Gibson's view the, what came to be called, 'Council of State', was intended by Johnston to be a lever – endorsed by the Prime Minister – which could 'prise out of Whitehall' powers required by the Scottish Office.

From September 1941 to February 1945 this committee met frequently to co-ordinate plans and dealt with a multitude of matters including hydro-electricity, the future of the herring industry, hill farming, the regionalisation of water supply, the unification of hospital services, industrial redevelopment, education reform and housing. As a result of these activities the grip of various Whitehall departments on Scottish affairs was loosened and more and more came under the direct authority of the Scottish Office. In this way the momentum towards a separate housing policy for Scotland, which had been implicit in Elliot's pre-war programme – including the setting up of the S.S.H.A. – was maintained.

When the Council turned its attention to housing in March 1942 the Under-Secretary of State at the Scottish Office, H.J.Scrymgeour-Wedderburn, was appointed to the Council of Management of the S.S.H.A. and the Association was asked to produce a briefing paper for Tom Johnston.[12] This task was rapidly accomplished and was followed up by a meeting on 29 June, at which the Secretary of State and his senior colleagues discussed the way forward with Members of the Council of Management.[13] During this meeting – the minutes of which are worth examining in some detail – Johnston indicated his intention to expand the Scottish Housing Advisory Committee and to instruct it to engage in full-scale consideration of the housing problems likely to confront Scotland after the war.

The Secretary of State also referred to his discussions with other Ministers about problems south of the border during which he had advised them of the nature and functions of the S.S.H.A., which he 'regarded as the government's building agent for Scotland' and which, among other things, he considered to be capable

Wartime concrete houses built by the SSHA at Motherwell. The flat roofs and spartan design was partly the result of the scarcity of timber.

of preventing 'price ramps in the building of houses after the war'. In view of these conversations 'he thought it was probable that similar organisations would be established for England and Wales'. A 'National Housing Corporation' was likely to be formed, but its writ would not extend to Scotland since 'the Scottish Special Housing Association (was) already in being'. Following this interesting opening, the meeting went on to consider the Association's paper and explored the general terrain which the Advisory Committee should be asked to examine.

Generally there was broad agreement on the main problems which needed to be addressed. Johnston drew attention to the 'appalling disparity between England and Scotland' in respect of the production by private enterprise companies of houses for the working-class and

> stated that this matter would be fully examined with a view to private enterprise being encouraged to contribute its share of building in Scotland. The Association's suggestions with regard to the encouragement of working-class people to own the houses in which they lived would be carefully considered.

The length of the designated post-war housing programme was discussed and eventually it was agreed that a ten year time scale should be adopted. The Minister made clear the government view that 'the maximum number of houses should be built as rapidly as possible' and indicated that measures would be implemented to increase supplies of labour and materials. The Secretary of State also commented on the Association's proposals in respect of its powers and functions, but declined to make a decision until 'it was seen what type of association the Minister of Works and Planning and the Minister of Health proposed to set up in England and Wales'.

One interesting suggestion which was also discussed was that if the Association was given a 'large post-war building programme' it might be

> desirable to establish branch offices or subsidiary associations in various parts of the country so that the work might be supervised in detail on a regional basis. The Secretary of State anticipated objections from local authorities to the proposal and stressed the desirability of avoiding antagonism on the part of local authorities.

In addition, Johnston wished to look carefully at the notion that the Association be funded directly from the Treasury rather than, as hitherto, via the local authorities. This was a proposed change which was pushed strongly by the Association representatives in view of the delays which had previously 'frequently occurred in reaching agreement with local authorities'.

As this meeting illustrates, many of the key issues were being addressed from an early date in the war. Each of the matters discussed may be said to be of interest, but in retrospect, two points seem particularly important. First, it is clear that the Secretary of State – and presumably everyone else present – was convinced that an English and Welsh equivalent of the S.S.H.A. was likely to be established. Obviously Johnston did not want it to be a 'National Housing Corporation' in the sense that its writ might extend to Scotland and so threaten the developing authority of his own office. But his real doubt seems not to have been whether such an organisation would be set up south of the border, but rather 'what type of association' it would be. Second, it is apparent that everyone at the meeting was aware of the potential hostility of local authorities towards an extended role for the Association and that the Secretary of State, in particular, was keen to minimize the grounds for antagonism. (In passing, it is also interesting to note that in speculating about the Association's post-war structure, talk of 'subsidiary associations in various parts of the country' seems almost to presage the format of the Housing Corporation – and attendant associations – which, of course, was not brought into existence until the 1960s.)

As the minute of this meeting makes explicit, the S.S.H.A. was well aware of the need to make an early start by obtaining sites, preparing layouts and making experiments to surmount the problems which were bound to arise immediately after the war from shortages of materials and skilled labour. Indeed, at the meeting, the suggestion was made that additional plant and shuttering should be purchased at an early date so that a capacity to build large numbers of no-fines concrete houses would be available as soon as peace returned. The response was 'that it would be difficult, if not impossible' to obtain authority for such a purchase while the war was in progress, but that it should be given priority 'immediately after the war'. However, it is clear that the Association wanted to make as many early preparations as possible. For example, in September 1942 it asked the government for permission to proceed to develop one or more sites where new techniques, materials, house designs and building methods could all be examined while the war was going on. In this way the findings would be available for general use as soon as conditions permitted a major building programme to be initiated.[14] But it was not until 1944 that permission was given to proceed with this project, at Sighthill in Edinburgh, with the result that most of the houses there were actually built between 1946 and 1952, by which time they were too late to be as useful as was originally intended.

In August 1942 the Scottish Housing Advisory Committee was reconstituted with Joseph Westwood, Under Secretary of State for Scotland, as chairman and Scrymgeour-Wedderburn as his deputy, and these appointments provide the clearest evidence of the high priority which the Secretary of State gave to the Committee's examination of Scotland's likely post-war housing problems. The eventual report, *Planning Our New Homes*, was of great importance and deserves careful examination. However, at the outset it should be noted that the full committee, which included twenty-eight members, was supported by three sub-committees – one on House Design, chaired by Robert Adam, another on Furniture, chaired by James Welsh (the Labour Lord Provost of Glasgow, 1943–45), and the third on the Distribution of Houses, led by Mr Laidlaw. Most of the Committee members were represented on one or another of these sub-committees (or on them all) and a further fourteen individuals were co-opted directly onto the sub-committees. Hence it is clear that the net was cast widely in order to bring the best available advice to bear, a conclusion reinforced by the extent of the Committee's investigations. Not only was evidence taken from housing authorities, institutions, companies and housing professionals of one kind or another, but members of the public also had their say with detailed questionnaires being returned by no less than 15,634 individuals. The latter were grouped into categories headed 'H.M.Forces' and workers in 'Industry'. Thus in many respects the Committee has left us with a clear account both of professional and public opinion at that time.

The table below[15] shows the responses of the public when asked to indicate the most favoured types of dwelling. The massive support for the cottage type house is impressive although it is interesting that, for a town dwelling, servicemen and women preferred the two storey house while industrial workers were relatively more in favour of a bungalow. Whether this kind of variation was partly a reflection of an age difference (presumably the average service respondent was younger than his civilian counterpart) or whether the people in the forces were illustrating a taste broadened by recent travel, it is impossible to say. What is clear is that the cottage fitted the aspirations of the great majority even in an urban context.

		In a Town		*In the Country*	
		Forces	*Workers in industry*	*Forces*	*Workers in industry*
		%	%	%	%
a) Bungalow	– detached	21	29	41	42
	– semi-det	11	7	8	8
	– terraced	3	2	3	2
b) 2-storey house	– detached	30	13	19	11
	– semi-det	12	7	7	3
	– terraced	2	2	1	1
c) Flatted house,flats in 2-storey, mostly in blocks of 4 houses – '2 up & 2 down'		4	6	1	4
d) Block of modern flats		14	15	1	2
Not answered		3	19	19	27
Total		100	100	100	100

In the light of these figures it is not surprising that the committee concluded that although evidence had been submitted in favour of various types of dwelling – 'the overwhelming balance of preference is in favour of the cottage'. The main reasons given for this choice were the desire for privacy, accessibility of playing space, and the advantages to a family of a private garden.[16] The latter factor is borne out by the responses noted at question 1(a) of section G where 95% indicated that they wanted a private garden while only 5%-6% thought a jointly maintained communal garden would be acceptable. When, at question (d), attitudes to allotments were examined, only about a quarter of respondents indicated an interest.[17] Clearly, therefore, in 1944 the Scots were overwhelmingly in support of the building of houses which stood in their own gardens.

Much other interesting information may be gathered from the survey. For example, when asked whether they would prefer to rent or own a house the civilians were almost exactly evenly divided (49% in favour of renting and 48% wishing to buy, with 3% undecided). The (younger) service personnel were somewhat keener on renting, but even so, 40% of this group wanted to buy their future homes. About 50% of those in favour of house purchase expected to do so via a mortgage or other loan, but 43% of civilians and 39% of service people in this category evidently expected to have sufficient savings to purchase outright by means of a one off payment. Again, on this evidence it is safe to conclude that towards the end of the second war, roughly half of the Scots wanted to own their own homes and most expressing such a desire had no doubt that, other things being equal, they possessed the financial means to do so.

Moreover, so far as those wishing to rent are concerned, the overwhelming majority (around 70%) of those questioned considered that rents should be of the order of from 10% to 20% of an income range of from £4 to £10 per week. In other words, effectively most respondents who wanted to rent accommodation thought that typical reasonable rents at that time should be in the range 8s to 16s for low income workers and so on up to between £1 and £2 per week for those who were better paid.[18]

When the surveyors pressed on the question of flats the public indicated (80%) that buildings without lifts should be of only two or three storeys. With lifts, six storeys was the most popular height.[19] In addition, there was widespread agreement that good housing estates required more than just dwellings and day nurseries, community centres, health clinics and libraries were the community facilities which were thought to be most important.[20]

The Advisory Committee, therefore, had a good view of public opinion on many of the key questions. Indeed, it is worth keeping firmly in mind the attitudes indicated above when reflecting on the conclusions reached by the Committee and on the way in which housing policy was actually to unfold in the years immediately after the war.

Although unpopular with the public, the flatted house seems to have been favoured by many local authorities. The Committee felt this was because the type was regarded as a compromise between the cottage and the tenement; but it took a poor view of excessive reliance on such dwellings.

> Since 1919, however, 137,380 houses or 57% of all houses built by local authorities in Scotland have been of the flatted type. In this period this type of development has been consistently cheaper than the cottage type, but we cannot help deploring the disproportionately large concentrations of flatted houses which are familiar in almost all local authority housing schemes.[21]

These estates, which were normally made up of blocks containing four flats, were said to have stimulated much unfavourable comment because of their 'depressing uniformity of design'. Poor sound-proofing, a general lack of privacy and a propensity to produce tension between neighbours were the main other sources of complaint in respect of such houses.

As far as tenements were concerned the Committee's position was somewhat shifty. The Report argued that tenements should be described as flats, since the 'old-fashioned' 'traditional' tenement was 'completely out-of-date by modern standards'. It was recognised that only a minority of potential tenants were in favour of flats, but the majority of the Committee insisted – 'in some districts … flats will, without doubt, continue to be required, *particularly in the redevelopment of the central areas of our cities and larger burghs*'[22] (my italics) – a view which, in so far as it referred to 3 or 4 storey tenements, was more or less in keeping with the line advocated by the S.S.H.A. in its submission to the investigators. Where opinion diverged was on the question of larger buildings.

The thoughts of the majority of the Committee's members on the subject of flats ('tenements' and larger blocks) were subsequently noted on four key points. First, effective sound proofing was an essential requirement. Second, without lifts, blocks of flats should not be constructed to a height above three storeys. Third, if lifts are provided '… we do not altogether exclude the possibility that in some districts, particularly in the large cities, blocks of flats of from 6 to 10 storeys may be appropriate, provided that the over-all density of development is not excessive and ample provision is made for open space, recreational facilities etc.' And finally, if flats were contemplated, then the site layout assumed priority and the Committee strongly opposed the erection of 'blocks of multi-storey flats on the frontages of arterial and sub-arterial roads as has been the habit in this type of development in Scotland in the past'.[23] (Here the curious proposition is almost that the buildings were fine, so long as they were kept away from main roads – and middle-class eyes!)

Despite their general approval of flats, the majority fully realised that excessive reliance on such house types could give rise to major problems.

> In conclusion, we should like to stress the fact that great care must be taken to avoid planning schemes of flats on such a scale that they become 'garrisons' or 'colonies' with no proper social focus.

After having visited and inspected many schemes of flats the Committee held that 'each scheme should comprise not more than 400–500 flats if it is to be planned on a compact community basis'. A single site could include a greater number, but flats and attendant facilities should be grouped in 'residential units' which had no more than the numbers suggested'.[24] (Clearly members were trying to have it both ways.)

In view of the post-war widespread use of both tenement type and high-rise blocks of flats in some parts of Scotland, and especially in the greater Glasgow area, one of the most interesting features of *Planning Our New Homes* is the debate which it contains on this type of housing. Two Committee members, Mrs Jean Mann and Mr F.A.B. Preston, went to the length of including 'notes of reservation' on this matter – two under their joint names, one by Mr Preston alone and a 'Dissentient Memorandum' by Mrs Mann.

Jean Mann had already been deeply involved in this question. In the 1920s almost 70% of the council houses built in Glasgow had been cottages, but by the early 1930s the increased emphasis on slum replacement in the city had produced a transformation, with almost 80% of the new council dwellings constructed in such (then) peripheral estates as Possil and the wretched Blackhill being in the form of inferior tenement flats. From 1933–1935, however, Jean Mann had been Labour's Convener of Housing and she had insisted in switching the emphasis back to cottages and gardens so that by the outbreak of the war 47% of the city's output of new council houses met her preference. It is not surprising, therefore, that she was willing to take up the cudgels on this subject.

Essentially the concern of Mann and her colleague Preston was that the urgency of the housing problem had pressurised the Committee into advocating housing types which were unsatisfactory and which would give rise to unnecessarily high densities. Perhaps the most impressive comments are contained in their lengthy *Note of Reservation on Paragraph 22.*[25]

Agreeing that a cottage has 'pre-eminent advantages as a home', Mann and Preston conceded that 'under certain circumstances and conditions houses of other types should not be disregarded'. However, they dissented from the recommendation in respect of flats and pointed out that the Barlow Commission on the *Distribution of the Industrial Population* had argued that flats 'should not be encouraged'. In particular, they protested against the idea of flats above six storeys.

> We are of the opinion, that only in exceptional circumstances, should flats be built above *three* storeys, and in no case above six storeys. Where in these circumstances it is found essential to build six storeys, the upper three storeys, at least, should be reserved for single people and households without children.

They referred again to the Barlow Report in which it had been concluded that 'for young children, residence in the higher floors is undesirable'.

They then went on to point to the lack of support for flats among the general public as assessed by the Committee's own survey. Ninety per cent of respondents in the forces and eighty -five per cent of civilians had agreed that flats should be for single people and childless households. Only fourteen per cent of respondents in the services and fifteen per cent of industrial workers had expressed any desire for flats.

In summary their objections to 'modern' flats were noted as a) overcrowding, with adverse effects on public health and mortality rates; b) the unsuitability of the Scottish climate with its lack of strong sunshine; and c) the 'strain and noise due to the nearness of neighbours in such houses'.

> We note that references have been frequently made to New York and Continental multiple-storeyed housing. The inference appears to be that this practice should be copied in Scotland. We feel that those who have advocated this move have not given

sufficient consideration to the differences of climate, sunshine and the nature of the soil in many of our Scottish towns.

On the question of health they drew attention to the evidence submitted to the Committee by the Royal College of Physicians of Edinburgh where tenements had been stigmatised as an expedient which could only be accepted 'under duress of circumstances, such as limitation of building sites, proximity to work, and the easement of travelling to and from work, etc.' Where tenements had to be used the physicians had urged a height limit of three storeys and 'no shops ... in the block'. They also condemned the type as unsuitable for young children and urged that ground floor flats be reserved for the elderly or disabled. On the other hand, they agreed that young unmarried persons could be accommodated in upper storey flats.

The Housing and Town Planning Committee of the Scottish Branch of the Institution of Municipal and County Engineers was also quoted by Mann and Preston as arguing that – 'the tenement with the common entry either by close or balcony, should only be used where circumstances warrant it and it should be limited to three storeys in height'. The Sanitary Inspectors Association of Scotland had similarly stated – 'Tenements are not recommended, but where circumstances necessitate their erection these should, as a general rule, be restricted to three storeys'.

Mann and Preston then referred to some of the developments in England which the Committee had inspected. The blocks of flats examined had not impressed in architectural terms and had not appeared as a reasonable 'solution to the housing problem'. They noted that five storeys had appeared to be the general upper limit. Again, the Barlow Committee was cited as objecting to the noise and nerve strain associated with life in such dwellings.

With remarkable perception Mann and Peters then got right to the heart of the matter.

> The recommendations of the Committee appear to have been arrived at by consideration of what is practicable at the moment and without full regard to the need for decentralisation, as would result from a balanced planning policy for the whole of Scotland, which we regard as essential if highly overcrowded areas are to be properly dealt with by other means than a simple re-shuffle of their population into multi-storeyed flats.

They particularly emphasised the problems which would result from a failure to restrict upper flats to adults.

The battle lines for a crucial argument, which was to rage for several years, were thus clearly delineated in the report of 1944. Interestingly the S.S.H.A. was drawn into the dispute in March 1945 when Edinburgh Corporation's Housing Committee asked the Association to construct, at its Sighthill experimental site, a block of flats of from six to eight storeys in height. The proposal was discussed fully with the Department of Health and Tom Johnston was consulted on the matter.

While the Secretary of State fully realised that there might be a place for the building of multi-storey flats in the more populous centres of Scotland, he could not reasonably advise the Association to direct any part of their resources towards the building of a block of demonstration multi-storey flats at this stage, especially having regard to the experimental work which had already been done in the field elsewhere – notably in Leeds.

Johnston felt that, at this time, the Association had more pressing demands on its attention both from its duty to demonstrate forms of construction of more general interest, and in pushing ahead with the 'large building programme which had been entrusted to the Association'. If Edinburgh or any other large authority wished to develop an interest in multi-storey flats the Secretary of State would consider the proposals and perhaps make available the assistance of his department.

On receipt of the guidance the 'Council unanimously concurred with the views of the Secretary of State and instructed the General Manager to reply accordingly to the Town Clerk'.[26]

The question of the use of flats – both medium and high-rise – is obviously one to which we shall return. However, it is clear that, although no doubt well-intentioned, and despite the significant qualifications which they set out, the majority on the Scottish Housing Advisory Committee did open the door to the subsequent widespread adoption of flats by urban local authorities. With the benefit of hindsight, those, such as the S.S.H.A., and the College of Physicians and so on, who advised against the general use of flats and in favour of cottages, were not only far more in tune with public opinion as expressed through the Committee's own survey, but were on much firmer ground in reality. Indeed, given the problems which were later to be associated with such post-war flatted estates as Drumchapel, Easterhouse, Castlemilk, Hutchesontown, West Granton, Wester Hailes, or Whitfield, it is painfully obvious that the protests of Preston and Mann, in particular, were fully justified and that their position has been entirely vindi-cated by the passage of time. Moreover, the use of tenement flats, not in the redevelopment of inner city areas, but on massive green field peripheral estates was clearly a tragic rejection of the explicit advice which had been provided during the war years by the S.S.H.A. and other well informed organisations and individu-als. The costs, human and economic of ignoring or over-ruling their guidance, can only be described as appalling. Just to give one specific example, as has been illustrated, on health grounds, Mann and Preston repeatedly warned against the general and careless use of flats, and the price of neglecting this argument can clearly be seen in west central Scotland where bad environmental living conditions are still (in the 1990s) being held to be principally responsible for the relatively poor state of health of citizens of the greater Glasgow area.

In addition to discussing various dwelling types, the Committee was concerned with many of the problems which would have to be confronted in the early years after the return to peace. In particular the members understood that at a time of chronic housing shortage, authorities and builders could be expected to face grave scarcities of both skilled labour and materials.

It is feared that the shortage of building craftsmen and of some traditional building materials will be acute in the immediate post-war years at the very time when the demand for housing accommodation will be at its height … It will be absolutely essential to adopt alternative methods of house construction of proved reliability and efficiency.[27]

The Advisory Committee, of course, was aware that a Committee chaired by Sir George Burt had been established specifically to investigate this matter, but it did not hesitate to make its own views clear.

During the inter-war years a great deal of enterprising work in alternative methods of house construction has been carried out in Scotland and the special powers given to the Scottish Special Housing Association in 1937 to employ alternative methods of building have been most valuable in this respect.

As a result of this work Scottish public opinion was fairly receptive to new ideas in house construction and the Advisory Committee hoped that a 'high degree of enterprise and initiative will continue to be displayed in this field in Scotland'. The government was urged to make early preparations on this subject so that appropriate innovations were available for use immediately on the return to peace.

The Report referred enthusiastically to 'the speed and volume of output which can be secured by the poured cellular concrete method of house construction which has been successfully adopted by the Scottish Special Housing Association'. The method was promising, but it was recognised that further work also needed to be done on internal and external methods of finishing. This system enabled 'foundations and walls of ten two-storey houses to be constructed in one week, but comparatively little research has been done on the possibility of accelerating further work on the house when this stage has been reached'. The subsequent delays involving the conventional 'finishing trades' had typically been sufficient 'to nullify the most valuable acceleration secured in the initial process of building.'

The Committee also foresaw other alternative methods as being important and these included building in timber and steel. In many areas of Scotland, particularly in rural areas, timber houses could make a 'valuable contribution'. In addition, 'in the inter-war years about 2,500 steel-clad houses of various types were erected in Scotland and these houses have been most favourably received in recent technical reports which have been made available to us'. (Presumably by the second S.N.H.C..)

In view of the capacity of the steel industry in Scotland and the extent to which methods of building involving the use of steel lend themselves to prefabrication, we think that further experiments should be carried out into the possibilities of developing the potentialities of steel in house building, not only as cladding material, but also for the structural framework of the house.[28]

(Interestingly, on the question of steel houses, Jean Mann again dissented from the general view on the grounds that the 1920s houses had not been very popular with tenants and that the take up of any vacant steel dwellings had often been slow.[29] In this case, she may have been on less secure ground in that the pre-war problem with the S.N.H.C. houses from the point of view of tenants was almost certainly mainly connected to their relatively high rents and had little to do with their utility as living space. Indeed, a tenant who has lived in one of the houses in question from her childhood in the 1930s until the present time, described it to the author as, 'very comfortable, but a bit like living in a ship.')

Planning Our New Homes and the various submissions to the Advisory Committee, provide a clear insight into the ways in which the various issues were being addressed during the later war years. Most regrettably, in the hectic building after the war and for various reasons to be examined shortly, many of the more enlightened recommendations were either forgotten or abandoned by building authorities and this was very much to the detriment of thousands of post-war Scottish tenants.

Again, with the benefit of hindsight, it is not possible to argue that everything which was suggested in 1943/4 was entirely sound. As has already been pointed out, for example, the majority on the Advisory Committee were clearly too sanguine in their expectations of the quality of life likely to be available in large scale 'modern' flatted developments. That major criticism apart, however, the flaws in the Report are rarely obvious. Most of the recommendations (including those set out in the S.S.H.A.'s submissions to the enquiry) have easily withstood the test of time and one wonders what the framers of these documents must have felt when, in the early post-war years, their careful considerations and wise counsel were either ignored or swept aside. Douglas Niven, writing in 1979 of the products of the post-war era, described them as being 'undersized and of poor quality'. In his view they contained many 'built-in' defects, the rectification of which was subsequently to prove a major drain on housing budgets. 'Many of these houses were planned for peripheral city or town sites with indecent haste and without proper thought for layout or for community services'.[30]

And again –

> Long term investment potential, quality, maintenance and the provision of attendant social and commercial services were either ignored or given low priority in many housing programmes. It was somehow imagined that these services could be added at a later date. It was also believed that little harm would be caused by the lack of these facilities in new housing areas. The consequences of this misguided policy are now obvious to all concerned with housing problems in Scotland.[31]

As far as they go, these criticisms are entirely valid and will be amplified later when an attempt will be made to examine the wider results. Importantly, however, it is also clear that those who came to control the building policies after 1945 must accept by themselves by far the greater part of the burden of responsibility for the creation of such sadly inadequate dwellings and estates. Beyond argument many of the schemes constructed after the war were built in defiance of the explicit advice which had been provided by the post-war planners during the war years.

At about the same time as the S.S.H.A. submitted its evidence to the Scottish Housing Advisory Committee, it was also consulted by the Burt Committee on the question of alternative methods of construction which might be used to speed up post war rates of house building. In January 1943 Mr J.W. Laing, a member of the latter committee, inspected some of the poured cellular concrete (no-fines) houses which the Association had built and examined the shuttering which had been used.[32] Mr Laing was obviously impressed because the method was strongly recommended in the Burt Report of 1944 and the publicity given at that time resulted in many requests for information and advice in respect of the technique.[33]

Indeed, it is clear that the Association fully gained the confidence of the Burt Committee since its chairman, Sir George Burt, agreed that the Department of Health for Scotland and the Association should be given a free hand to experiment with demonstration house types which might be appropriate within the Scottish context. As noted previously, as early as 1942 the Association was pressing on the government the need to conduct experiments while the war was still in progress, and the Advisory Committee had forcefully argued the same case. The Ministry of Works in fact established a national demonstration site at Northolt near London and in April 1944 permission was granted for the Association to establish a Scottish experimental development at Sighthill. Initial plans were immediately drawn up to erect pairs of houses of no-fines concrete (8 inch walls); foamed slag (poured *in situ* and for which the Association's own shuttering might prove suitable); 'Gyproc' – similar to those erected in heavily bomb damaged Coventry; steel-framed (Hill's Patent Glazing); Weir steel; and houses identified as 'Duplex'. These represented first thoughts, but other houses which were considered at that time were of foamed slag – prefabricated blocks, prefabricated brick houses and steel framed resin bonded plywood houses. It was also planned to order and erect a pair of timber houses to be imported from either the USA or Canada.[34]

In succeeding months many other house types were considered for the Sighthill scheme. The objectives behind the project were fundamentally to devise methods of house construction which would circumvent the chronic shortage of certain types of material such as timber, and which would also enable large numbers of demobilised servicemen who had little training for the building industry to find employment in the forthcoming assault on the housing problem. In addition, however, the disastrous consequences of the recoil of industry from the dislocation caused by the First World War were well remembered. There was determination to ensure that history did not repeat itself. For example, throughout the Second World War the steel industry (and, therefore, the coal industry) had been fully stretched by the requirement for ships, tanks, military vehicles of all description and aircraft. With the return to peace it was imperative to find some alternative outlet which would keep the furnaces and factories busy. In the same way during the war the demand for concrete had expanded, while other industries – such as brickmaking – had contracted. In all of these circumstances, houses of steel or concrete were going to be essential if recession was to be avoided, but inevitably this involved the risk of a major and self-defeating reduction in the quality of houses. A key purpose of Sighthill – as with Northolt and the Burt Committee's activities generally – was to ensure that sufficiently high standards of design were maintained.

As has been noted, there were subsequent delays to the project; nevertheless houses demonstrating twelve different systems of non-traditional construction were built by the S.S.H.A. between 1944 and 1952, and later a number of other houses were erected on the site to demonstrate a variety of economic techniques, including space-saving design, economic use of softwood, and alternative methods of whole house heating. The last pair of houses were built as late as 1964 and these were two timber dwellings built on behalf of the Canadian government.

The sixty-nine houses on the Sighthill estate (two Weir 'Paragon' steel houses were demolished in 1966) eventually included thirty different house types, some of which are quite unique in Scotland since they were never used elsewhere. Others were widely adopted both by the Association and by local authorities. Once these houses had been built, it was obviously important to monitor their performance. When the Association was expanding rapidly in the late 1940s and 50s Edinburgh, like other towns and cities, suffered from an acute housing shortage; hence to provide for staff and to ensure that the houses were constantly checked, these dwellings were originally allocated to employees. At the time of writing 52 of the houses have been sold to tenants and the 21 oldest were modernised in the late 1980s. (Interestingly, while fifteen houses remain in stock, ten of their current tenants are on housing benefit and are presumably financially unable to purchase. That such a high proportion of the houses has been sold clearly indicates not only that they are in fundamentally sound condition, but that they have been well maintained and modernised. Given that many of the residents are knowledgeable – typically retired housing professionals, the high level of sales can only be regarded as an overwhelming endorsement of the quality of many of their houses as well as of the attractive layout of the estate.)

The second major report published by the Scottish Housing Advisory Committee in 1944 was the one produced by its sub-committee on the *The Distribution of New Houses in Scotland in the Immediate Post War Years*. This was a much less 'glossy' production and it seems never to have been given the wide public circulation accorded to *Planning Our New Homes*. Presumably the sub-committee's report was intended to inform and augment the main paper. However, this study on population distribution is a very important document in its own right since it provides critical insights into the way in which ideas were evolving both in government and within the wider Scottish housing community.

The authors of the report estimated that Scotland required 500,000 new houses in the immediate post war period,[35] and concluded that 'the need for houses in Scotland is so great that the responsibility for building them should be shared by housing (local) authorities, private enterprise, and housing associations'.[36] On housing associations in general it was argued that 'in view of their potential contribution … to the national distribution of housing in Scotland the question of their encouragement should be the subject of a further enquiry'.[37] (Interestingly, in an internal Department of Health for Scotland memorandum in the autumn of 1944, it was indicated that the Secretary of State wanted to extend the use of housing associations by granting them 'the same priority for labour and materials as would be accorded to the local authority ... He recommends local authorities to encourage the establishment of housing associations under the Housing Acts by private persons or by industry ... (He indicated) that housing associations may receive Exchequer subsidy through a local authority'.[38])

On the Scottish Special Housing Association specifically the Committee commented that its functions deserved 'special mention since they have an important bearing on the distribution of houses in Scotland'.[39] The committee explained that

> In providing houses, the Association enters into arrangements under Section 26 of the Housing (Scotland) Act, 1935, with the local authority of the area in which the houses are to be built.
>
> ... In short the Scottish Special Housing Association gets the same grant subsidy (£10 10s for each 3-apartment house, £11 15s for each 4-apartment house, and £13 for each 5-apartment house for forty years) as the local authority ...[40]

The committee was particularly concerned about what was perceived to be the previously inadequate standards of planning in respect of the relationship between housing and industrial development. Members argued that decentralisation and dispersal of industry and of the industrial population was 'likely to be inevitable'[41]; that 'broad industrial trends can be studied more effectively on the regional and national levels than on the local level'[42]; and that immediately after the war the housing of families moving from one area to another as a consequence of industrial changes of national importance should be the subject of 'a special programme initiated by the Central Department and carried out by housing authorities or by the S.S.H.A. without encroaching upon the commitments of housing authorities to their own people'.[43] In summary -

> a) The endeavour should be made to make a *general* allocation to all housing authorities of *some* houses, with *special* allocations to those areas in most urgent need.
> b) In the event of a housing authority being unwilling to build houses for transferee families, or unable to build timeously, the Central Department should arrange for them to be erected by the Scottish Special Housing Association.[44]

The committee concluded that 'the broad aim of the national distribution of housing ... is to devise some means of ensuring that the needs of both 'static' and 'transferee' families are given due weight'.[45] As far as the S.S.H.A. was concerned, the Committee believed that it had particular advantages when it came to meeting the needs of families having to move in response to industrial change. As with private enterprise or other housing associations, but unlike local authorities, the Association was not tied or restricted to a particular locality or area. 'It does not operate .. without an agreement with the housing authority' and it had the great advantage of direct financial backing from the Exchequer – an asset which could be augmented if local authorities wished also to assist it from their own resources.

The Association is therefore in a position to meet the needs of 'transferee' families wherever they arise and, subject to the availability of labour and materials, as soon as they arise. ... We look to the Scottish Special Housing Association to be the main alternative building agency to the housing authorities for the housing of 'transferee' families during (the initial post war) period.

It was further argued that the Association could provide a useful restraint on the building costs of other agencies and, through the use of alternative forms of non-traditional construction, it could tap supplies of labour which would otherwise be unavailable for house building.[46]

The idea of the S.S.H.A. being 'the main alternative' to the local authorities for housing families moving in response to industrial developments was quite acceptable to Departmental officials. An internal D.H.S. memorandum commented, 'the purpose of this recommendation will be largely accomplished by the arrangement now agreed with the Treasury and embodied in the Housing (Scotland) Bill whereby the Association will build in the areas of greatest need', and it was suggested that no amendment to the Bill was required.[47]

The Committee also had another task for the Association. In rural areas where suitable construction workers were scarce, 'the Scottish Special Housing Association should, as soon as possible, experiment in building houses with the aid of flying squads of building operatives equipped with the necessary plant, materials and temporary accommodation.'[48] In the Departmental memorandum referred to above it was noted that this proposal was largely as a result of an initiative led by Major Stirling, Convener of the County of Ross and Cromarty. The suggested response was that 'the proposal is not inconsistent with the formula agreed with the Treasury for the operations of the Association except in so far as it implies that the Association might build in very small groups'. The report, however, recommended only an experiment and on that basis it was argued that 'the recommendation should be accepted'.[49]

While mentioning the Departmental memorandum on the *Distribution of New Houses* report one other response is worth noting. The Committee had accepted the need for a 'Transitional Period' up to 1st October, 1947 and argued that local authorities should be given a 'subsidy for general needs' for ten years after the war. In the light of what was to happen in the Housing (Financial Provisions) (Scotland) Act of 1946, it is interesting to note that in May 1944 the official attitude was that the government could *not* accept that a general needs subsidy was necessary for ten years. *'Continuance of the subsidy after October, 1947 will be considered in the light of the circumstances prevailing' at that time*[50] (my italics).

One of the fascinating points about the official records connected with the *Distribution of New Houses* is that they give us a very clear picture of how and when policy was formed and of which personalities were particularly responsible. The papers of the Scottish Housing Advisory Committee Sub-Committee on Distribution include early drafts of the Report. The draft which was circulated to committee members late in December 1943 includes only one brief reference to the S.S.H.A., and that is the short sentence quoted previously indicating that the functions of the Association deserved 'special mention since they have an important bearing on the distribution of houses in Scotland'. It may be likely that further comment would have been included in the appendices, but it is clear that at New Year 1944 the Committee did not intend to recommend any particular role for the Association. Indeed the strong, near exclusive, commitment of members to local authority housing is perhaps best indicated by the invariable use not of the term 'local authorities', but of the definitive, 'the housing authorities'.

However, on 28th January, 1944 the secretary of the sub-committee on the Distribution of Houses, Dr A.B. Taylor of the Department of Health, wrote to his chairman, Mr Laidlaw, in the following fascinating terms.

He explained that Mr Westwood (who was, of course, at the time not only one of Johnston's junior ministers, but was also chairman of the main Scottish Housing Advisory Committee) -

> would like to have a chat with you … He is likely to suggest that the most important step that could be taken would be a big expansion of the operations of the Scottish Special Housing Association under the general direction of the Central Department. I am not certain how far this recommendation would be welcomed by the local authority members of the Sub-Committee, some of whom, particularly in the Glasgow area, are not enthusiastic about the Scottish Special Housing Association. It may be, however, that a recommendation of this kind would be a way out of giving an undue prominence to a recommendation for the encouragement of private enterprise.
>
> … The Secretary of State has been looking at one of the copies of the report which we sent to Mr Westwood, and has made one or two suggestions, which I can discuss with you when you are here next week. His main point is that we do not make enough of the Scottish Special Housing Association.[51]

Since the subsequent draft of the report includes the various references to the Association which have been quoted, it is clear that changes were included following this letter and presumably the meeting between Westwood and Laidlaw. The relationship between the S.S.H.A. and local authorities – especially some of the Glasgow Councillors – clearly remained a difficulty. In addition, the grim attitude towards private enterprise displayed here is a clear reflection of a position being adopted in many official circles at the time. However, probably the key point to note from this letter is that Tom Johnston's mark on the emerging strategy for post-war housing, particularly as it related to the use of the S.S.H.A., has been established beyond doubt. Clearly, he accepted the need for national and regional housing plans in the immediate post-war era, accepted the likelihood of industrial reconstruction and a consequent significant redistribution of the population, and intended the Association to take a leading part in future housebuilding. In addition, it is also evident that in 1944, Westwood, who was to succeed Johnston in the following year, supported Johnston's policy.

Johnston's attitude to the Association as indicated in Dr Taylor's letter is actually a reflection of comments which the Secretary of State had made earlier in Parliament. In November 1943 he assured the House of Commons that comprehensive measures were in hand to meet Scotland's grave housing problem, that he was considering such matters as the expansion of the building industry, the acquisition of sites, alternative methods of construction and the provision of emergency housing accommodation.

He added –

> We already have a national house-building agency in Scotland, the Scottish Special Housing Association. This Association can provide housing in any part of Scotland and I am at present planning for a large scale programme of building by the Association after the war.[52]

In answer to a question, he confirmed that he would willingly extend the Association's statutory powers if necessary, a similar response to one which he had previously given to the former I.L.P. stalwart, David Kirkwood.[53]

Another significant report of 1944 was the *Interim Report on Housing* of the Clyde Valley Planning Advisory Committee. In keeping with his views on the need for national and regional planning, Johnston invited three such committees to produce plans for the regions of Scotland and the Clyde Valley Committee felt that housing was of such pre-eminent importance that it rushed to produce an interim report on the subject within six months of its formation. The conclusion offered was that the total requirement 'to replace unfit houses, relieve overcrowding, and for 'general needs' is approximately 202,000. Taking four persons as representing an average family, this means the rehousing of 808,000 persons, or 35 per cent of the population of the region'.[54]

The Clyde Valley Committee estimated that between 1919 and 1939 172,000 houses had been built within the region and that 74 per cent of these had been erected by local authorities. However, members were not greatly impressed with the quality of either the planning or the housing.

> All the faults of unplanned and haphazard building present themselves throughout the Region in a marked degree. As in most areas the great bulk of residential building has been carried out by local authorities, it is not easy to put the blame for this unco-ordinated development upon private enterprise, or the 'spec' builder.

In general terms the Committee felt that the great drive to improve national housing conditions between the wars had failed entirely 'to realign our towns and villages in accordance with the best principles of modern planning' and had merely produced a proliferation of 'piecemeal creations'.[55]

Nor were the Clyde Valley Committee members enthusiastic for the early efforts of the S.S.H.A..

> In this connection we regret that the Scottish Special Housing Association has not taken the opportunity to set an example of good planning in the selection of housing sites for experimental building.

They accepted that the Association had had many difficulties in the location of sites, but with few exceptions Association estates exhibited 'the same planning faults as are found in local authority schemes'.

It is to be hoped that, in post-war years, when we understand that the activities of this Association may be considerably extended, a lead may be given, not only in building technique, but more importantly from the planning point of view, in the techniques of community planning and sight layout.[56]

Here then was the clearest statement of recognition of some of the lamentable failings in public sector house provision in the inter-war years, and a clamant plea for central government, via the S.S.H.A., to give a stronger lead in the direction of higher standards of planning in the design of viable and well located communities. If the belief in planning is somewhat touching, the position of the committee can only be regarded as fundamentally sound, particularly when proper note is taken of the achievement of the garden city pioneers in the years around the First World War. Then the possibilities of well planned, balanced towns and estates had been demonstrated for all to see and the high quality living standards which they offered to residents had been amply illustrated. The committee was clearly correct in pointing to the deterioration which had then followed as councils were launched into the main inter-war housing programmes. By the Second World War, as the committee indicated, the dubious and potentially disastrous trend was obvious. Mere involvement of the local authorities (and other public agencies such as the S.S.H.A.) was demonstrably far from being a guarantee that good standards would be achieved. Indeed, as the Clyde Valley committee hinted, councils, by mass, repetitive building had demonstrated a potential capacity to proliferate poor quality housing on a scale far beyond the scope of even the most rabid private developer.

In *Planning Our New Homes* the Scottish Housing Advisory Committee provided the Secretary of State and the public at large with its assessment of the magnitude of Scotland's national housing problem in 1944. It was indeed 'grave'. The Committee indicated the housing need as follows –

Replacement of unfit houses

i) Houses found in 1938 to be so unfit as to require replacement	66,538
ii) Houses estimated to be required to replace those which will have become unfit between December 1938 and December 1943	55,000

Relief of Overcrowding

Houses estimated to be required in 1938 to end overcrowding (after taking appropriate account of the use of houses to be vacated by overcrowded families)	200,000

General Needs

i) Houses required to meet general needs and to replace those destroyed by enemy action.	64,000
ii) Houses required as a result of marriages between December 1938 and December 1943	133,750
Total	*519,288*

From this total approximately 50,000 could be deducted as being the number of houses completed between December 1938 and December 1943. In consequence, the estimated requirement in the three categories was for 470,000 houses.[57]

It was then pointed out that there were many houses in Scotland which were technically not capable of being classified as unfit, but which nevertheless lacked such basic amenities as an independent water closet or reasonable sanitary convenience. Such houses were not yet included in calculations, but could scarcely be regarded as adequate. In these circumstances the overall requirement in Scotland was for at least 500,000 houses.

Moreover, this took

> no account of additional demands for housing accommodation arising after December 1943 as a result of further marriages and further wastage of existing properties, nor does it take account of progressive improvements in housing standards which might make public opinion require the termination of the effective life of existing dwellings rather earlier than would otherwise be expected.[58]

By May 1944, armed with this assessment, and following completion of the Report on the *Distribution of Houses*, Johnston was ready to flesh out his plans into a realistic programme and the S.S.H.A.'s Council was summoned to the Department to be given an outline of his intentions. These involved a massive increase in the Association's activities and, as a first step, he proposed significantly to enhance the political and technical authority of the Council of Management. Lord Traprain had played little part throughout the war and was in any case fully occupied as Controller of Coal for Scotland; James Welsh,MP, had resigned on account of poor health. All the other members of the wartime Council were retained, but now, Sir Garnet Wilson,JP, the Liberal Lord Provost of Dundee, was appointed as chairman. In addition, three experienced Labour councillors, John C. Forman, JP, John J. Robertson, JP and Thomas Paterson, JP – the first two of whom were Labour parliamentary candidates who were successfully returned at the 1945 General Election – were added to the Council, where they were joined by John Stirling, the Chief Architect from the Department of Health for Scotland.[59]

On 31st July, the new Council assembled at the Association's offices, then at 11 Drumsheugh Gardens in Edinburgh, where they were joined by the Secretary of State and Mr G.H.Henderson, the Secretary of the Department of Health for Scotland. Mr Johnston complimented the Association for the work which it had carried out during the war in the provision of emergency accommodation for evacuees and others. The Secretary of State then turned to the Housing (Scotland) Bill which was then before Parliament and which contained provisions affecting the Association.

> He stated that, subject to the Bill becoming law, it was intended that the Association should build 100,000 houses within a period of 10 to 12 years after the conclusion of

the European War: that the Association would build in the areas where the housing needs were greatest: and that so far as could be foreseen at present, it seemed that those areas would cover about one half of Scotland .... Subsidies would be payable to the Association direct by the government, instead of through the local authorities, as formerly, and loans would be available to the Association through the Secretary of State.[60]

The Secretary of State then instructed the Association to recruit a competent staff adequate to meet the heavy demands which would be placed on them and, before leaving, paid tribute to several individuals, notably Alexander McKinna the acting chairman, for their sterling work throughout the war.

The interesting thing to note about Johnston's plan is not simply the sheer magnitude of the programme which was being allocated to the Association, but also its target area. *The areas where the housing needs were greatest* were undoubtedly in the Clyde valley, in and around Glasgow and Lanarkshire and, to a lesser extent, in Dundee. Clearly, therefore, his intention was not to leave the old industrial heartlands of Scotland to their local authorities, but to use the Association as an agent of major change in these localities.

The Housing (Scotland) Act of 1944 duly passed into law on 26th October. Among other provisions, this Act defined the so-called transitional (from war to peace) period as extending to the first day of October 1947 and during which time the normal arrangements for holding local inquiries in respect of compulsory purchase orders would be suspended. This was obviously an attempt to reduce planning delays to an absolute minimum during the first two post-war years. It was also under this Act that many of the emergency measures outlined earlier were initiated. (In fact, the S.S.H.A. was invited to construct the Scottish prefabs built in the transitional period, but, anxious to push ahead with its large permanent housing target, it declined and urged the use of private contractors for the building of the temporary dwellings.)

A few weeks earlier the Department of Health had suggested to the Association the rough outlines of an initial 10,000 permanent house programme and this had been discussed on 13th September. It was then noted that to minimise costs the Treasury was pressing for the Association to build estates of not less than 100 houses in urban areas and not less than 50 houses in more rural locations.[61]

On the passage of the Act the Association's first programme was declared. The distribution, which was guided by the Secretary of State, gives an explicit illustration of where the emphasis was to be placed. Glasgow was offered 2,000 houses (20 per cent of the programme), Dundee 700, and Aberdeen 600 houses. For the 'Large Burghs' the allocations were – Arbroath 200, Ayr 300, Clydebank 600, Coatbridge 300, Dumbarton 300, Greenock 600, Hamilton 200, Inverness 500, Kilmarnock 300, Motherwell 500, and Stirling 200. The 'Small Burghs' of Bathgate, Brechin, Galston, Hawick, Irvine, Johnstone, Kilwinning, Leven, Saltcoats, Tranent and Whitburn were each to have 100 houses, the exception in this group being Buckhaven and Methil which was offered 300 houses. Of the counties, Midlothian and West Lothian were each allocated 400 houses while Lanark was to have 500 as its first instalment. In other words, only 1,300 houses were awarded to three counties and 1,400 to eleven small burghs. By contrast 7,300 houses were to be built in the cities and large towns and almost 60 per cent of this first programme was intended for the Clyde Valley area. Beyond doubt, Johnston was directing the Association towards the heart of the problem.[62]

On 1st November, 1944, Department of Health for Scotland Circular No 158/1944 was sent to the local authorities to clarify the purposes of the new housing Act as well as to encourage councils to co-operate in full with the Association and to allay any possible fears or suspicion. It is interesting in respect of the latter point, for example, that the relevant section of the circular is headed 'Supplementary Housing By Scottish Special Housing Association', the clear implication being that the Association's activities were not to replace, but to supplement local authority housing programmes.

It was pointed out that Sections 3 to 7 of the Act enabled the 'Secretary of State to assist the Scottish Special Housing Association to build working-class houses in areas of the greatest housing need'. The Association would no longer be restricted to the Special Areas, but would be authorised by the Secretary of State to build 'in the areas where the need for houses was greatest ...' The activities of the Association were to be financed directly from the Exchequer and, in accordance with the Act, loans and grants would be advanced by the Department without the need for local rate borne support and without a requirement for formal arrangements between a local authority and the Association. It would be 'essential' for the Association to work in full 'consultation and co-operation' with local authorities.

> In particular the Association will consult local authorities with regard to the selection of sites, the types of houses to be built, the rents to be fixed and the selection of tenants, and their proposals generally will have to comply with the requirements of the Planning Acts.

It was then explained that the Association's building activities were being deliberately restricted to the areas where housing needs were greatest in order to assist hard pressed local authorities.

> The Secretary of State therefore appeals to these authorities, in their turn, to co-operate with the Association to the fullest extent by giving them every possible assistance in making their arrangements. The Association's most urgent task will be to secure housing sites and it is in this respect that local authorities could particularly render valuable help...

Johnston then urged co-operation on all sides in order to solve the housing problem in the affected areas as rapidly as possible.[63]

On the next day (2nd November, 1944) the Association followed up the circular with a letter to each of the various authorities directly affected by the initial programme outlining its intentions in respect of their locality and setting out the conditions involved. It was also explained that the Association was being financed directly from the Treasury and that the houses would be provided without contribution from local rates.

> The local authority would, however, be expected to carry out, free of cost to the Association, any necessary extensions of water and drainage services and the public utility undertakings would similarly be expected to provide any necessary extensions of gas or electricity services ...

The identification and acquisition of a suitable site or sites was requested as a matter of urgency. It was explained that the Association was proposing to build at least one hundred houses per site except in rural areas where the minimum was reduced to fifty. It was also pointed out that, in view of the earlier D.H.S. Circular (149/44), the houses would be of 4 or 5-apartments and the local authorities were asked to indicate their choice of ratio between the two sizes.[64]

Over the next few months the Association pressed ahead, recruiting staff and pushing on with drafting site and layout plans. In some cases – as with Dundee, bomb damaged Clydebank, Motherwell, Coatbridge, Inverness, Kilmarnock and most of the small burghs and counties, the local authorities seem to have been co-operative and for these areas the activity advanced. Elsewhere there was notice-able reluctance to identify sites.[65]

A matter which created difficulty at this time was the selection of suitable house types which could be employed as soon as peace returned and this problem was compounded by the delay in approving work at the Sighthill experimental development. The first house erected there was a Weir 'Paragon' steel house. Remark-ably its foundations were commenced on 3rd July 1944 and by the 18th of the same

The Weir 'Paragon' steel bungalow. The example of this house erected at Sighthill, Edinburgh, in 1944 was demolished in 1966. This design was quickly superseded by the later Weir 'Quality' type.

month it was completed and furnished.[66] Two days later the press were invited to inspect the building and it was open to the public from 31st July until 2nd September. Towards the end of August it was reported that no less than 4,340 visitors had looked over the house and a month later, even although the building was now closed to the public, various delegations were still being received from local authorities.[67]

The demonstration house, then known as prototype '3', was not without its faults, but modifications were agreed which would be incorporated in prototype '4'. In August 1944 the Secretary of State and members of his Departmental staff met with Lord Weir and representatives of the S.S.H.A.. It was decided that the Association would erect 100 of the Weir houses on various sites throughout Scotland.[68] The reasons for this initiative are not specified in the relevant minute, but presumably the idea was to familiarise both the public and local authorities with housing of the type. At the meeting it was agreed that three-quarters of the houses would be built in mining areas and the remainder in semi-rural districts. Messrs Weir hoped to have the first five houses ready for delivery by the end of November and thereafter to deliver and put up five houses per week through to May 1945, a target which, in the event, the company was unable to meet. The price of the houses was estimated to be £950 per house, 'delivered and erected on sites within a radius of twenty miles of Glasgow' and with a supplementary charge for destinations further afield.[69] Eventually the programme identified fifteen locations ranging from Newton Stewart to Inverness and even included some for construction in Stornoway and Kirkwall.

At the same time as this demonstration programme of 'Paragon' houses was agreed the Department of Health also proposed to Weir that the S.S.H.A. should agree to erect 1,000 of the company's steel houses per annum on condition that the price did not exceed that of comparable brick or concrete houses. These houses were to be fully modified to take account of criticisms of the prototypes and eighty per cent were to be of two storeys. They were what came to be called the Weir 'Quality' houses and many were indeed ultimately constructed in developing mining communities in various parts of central Scotland.

The other steel house building company which was quick to declare an interest was Atholl Steel Houses Limited. By March 1945 this company was offering to supply 40 four-in-a-block 4-apartment houses which could be erected for demonstration purposes in different parts of the country. These were claimed to be priced at £1000 per house, plus a delivery charge outside Glasgow as well as the cost of land and sewerage.[70] Closer inspection revealed that in a scheme of 20 Atholl houses the total cost would be £24,790 including costs of land, services, foundations, fees etc, and that this gave a price of approximately £1,240 per house. The S.S.H.A. agreed to acquire the 40 houses and decided to construct 20 in Clydebank and 20 in Dundee, provided suitable sites could be obtained.[71]

The Association was, of course, equally interested in other types of house and pushed to have various specimens erected at Sighthill. At the end of May 1945, however, it was noted with regret that the Department of Health had suggested that the only houses which should be located at Sighthill were those already adopted by the Ministry of Works for mass production after completion of experimental schemes of not less than 50 houses. Clearly the estate had now become a location for the demonstration of non-traditional sponsored house types rather than for the genuine experimentation originally envisaged.

Timber houses also attracted early interest. In June 1945 the Association was informed by the Government that it had succeeded in purchasing 5,000 Swedish timber houses, and that one half of these were to be built in Scotland. The Department offered the Association 1,000 of the houses with the remainder being shared among appropriate local authorities.[72] Within a few days more than six hundred of the Swedish timber houses had been included in the S.S.H.A.'s plans for Dundee, Inverness, Motherwell (Watling Street and Muirhouse), Polbeth, Bathgate, Lochore, and Fallin and Plean in Stirlingshire.[73]

In August the *New Statesman* told readers that 'prefabrication of either temporary or permanent dwellings will work only if it is organised upon a really large scale, in factories as thoroughly equipped for it as the war factories were for the mass-production of planes'.[74] This was very much the mood of the moment and there is little doubt that most planners looked to mass prefabrication of dwellings as the main way of tackling the immediate crisis. It is equally clear, however, that the traditional building industry was less convinced. The Royal Incorporation of Architects in Scotland, for example, submitted a brochure of designs suitable for public sector housing, all of which relied on traditional methods of construction.[75] Similarly the Standing Committee of the House Building Industry invited all regular house builders to submit plans for houses to be built by traditional means in order to 'show the contribution which private enterprise builders were able to make in the provision of post-war housing'. This was a viewpoint with which the S.S.H.A. Council sympathised and it decided to urge the Department of Health to allow space to be made available at Sighthill to demonstrate suitably designed houses built by traditional builders.[76]

The Association had a very good reason to favour the use of ordinary bricks and mortar in the right circumstances. On 21st September 1945 the Council studied a detailed breakdown of the final costs of 372 houses which had been built for the Admiralty at Rosyth in the year 1941–42 at a total expense of £249,000.[77] 209 of the houses were of cellular concrete and 163 of standard brick construction. While the average cost of a concrete house had worked out at £683 the equivalent brick house had been eleven per cent cheaper at just £608.

The Rosyth houses had undoubtedly been built to extremely spartan war-time specifications and no doubt prices had risen somewhat between 1942 and 1945. However, when compared with the £950 to £1,240 quoted for the Weir and Atholl steel houses, the above figures certainly suggest that the case for prefabricated housing did not rest on any cost advantage and that traditional building methods were still the cheapest. The point seems to have been well understood within the

Department of Health for in June the interim Conservative administration had given permission for the Association to proceed on a rather larger scale than had been envisaged for Sighthill. Now instructions were given to build an experimental scheme of fifty houses of a traditional type 'with such modernising as might be made necessary, or desirable, by the supply position, or cheaper methods of construction'. The Association's intended development at Holytown, Lanarkshire, was considered to be suitable for this scheme.[78] By the autumn of the year, however, the political climate had changed and there was far less sympathy for the cheaper solutions proposed by the traditional building industry.

As the war in Europe came to an end, and brought in its wake notice of the demise of the National government, the general lines of a coherent housing policy were clearly in place. Within the S.S.H.A. in particular there seemed no reason to fear the outcome of a general election. The Association had been set up by a Tory government and could expect to have its planned programme broadly maintained if the Conservatives were successful. Equally, throughout most of the war it had been guided and directed by a Labour Secretary of State and the plan to which it was working was his. Johnston was retiring, but with a Council dominated by Labour politicians, there seemed no obvious reason for the Association to fear the return of Labour to power. Indeed, on 27th July 1945 the Council happily intimated its congratulations to members Forman and Robertson on their election to Parliament.[79] However, those in touch with Scottish local political currents may have felt some unease when the composition of the new government was announced and it was realised that the Parliamentary Joint Under-Secretary of State with responsibility for housing was to be the former I.L.P. (now Labour) Member for the Gorbals constituency of Glasgow, George Buchanan, MP. But even those with the profoundest suspicions can scarcely have anticipated that, within a matter of months, Tom Johnston's carefully prepared plans would have been reduced to a shambles and that the S.S.H.A., in particular, would be in deep crisis.

Following the general election it did not take long for matters to come to a head. On 21st September the S.S.H.A.'s council met with Mr Buchanan and were apparently rebuked for lack of progress, although members considered the Minister's criticisms to be 'vague and unspecified' and demanded in writing that he should set out his complaint.

> The Council of Management, comprised as it is of persons experienced in public affairs, consider that they are competent to judge the quality and extent of the work being done by the Association and that you must have made the statement referred to without having had the opportunity of making yourself completely familiar with the work of the Association and the difficulties which have confronted them.

The Council then indicated its willingness to remedy any deficiencies speedily and pleaded once more for the Minister to say precisely wherein lay their fault.[80]

At the Minister's request the following statement of progress was drawn up on 10th November and submitted.[81]

Association's Programme for Transitional Period – 11,300 Houses
The progress of this programme is shown as follows:–

		Sites	*Houses*
1)	Nomination of Sites by Local Authorities	83	9,400
2)	Sites approved	87	7,498
3)	Road lay-out plans approved	41	2,936
4)	Roads contracts placed	33	1,947
5)	Of which roads completed	22	578
6)	Approval of type and final lay-out plans	39	1,815
7)	House Contracts placed (including 464 Swedish timber houses)	32	922
8)	House Contracts received and being checked for an additional (?)	8	613
9)	Houses completed (demonstration houses – Sighthill)		7

In the accompanying notes it was explained that all local authorities had now suggested suitable sites, with the sole exception of Glasgow. In the case of the latter city, it had still only agreed to take 100 Swedish timber houses. However, the Association expressed the hope that the Corporation would within the next few weeks identify locations for its remaining allocation of 1,900 houses. In some cases planning approval had been granted by the Department, but not yet by local authorities, and in other cases the reverse situation obtained. Similarly, some local authorities had reservations about accepting steel houses and securing agreement from several authorities on this question was slowing progress in places. The notes also indicated that work was under way on 21 sites and 255 houses, that contractors were being recruited for other areas and that Messrs Weir had overcome some initial delays and now expected to complete 19 houses before the 17th of the month.[82]

On the basis of this report, are there any grounds to support Mr Buchanan's claim that the Association was making slow progress?

Certainly, seven completed houses, and work in progress on a mere 255 houses, cannot be described as a rapid rate of advance in a programme which had been announced roughly a year earlier. However, bearing in mind that the war in Europe had only come to an end six months previously; that the country's economy was only beginning the process of readjustment; that scarcities of men and materials remained severe; that much of the national effort was going into transitional temporary housing, converting war premises and making good war-damaged buildings; and that the commitment to factory produced houses meant that the Association was to some extent dependent on the efforts of others for the supply of houses as well as for planning approval and land acquisition; the progress made does not seem unduly slow. Under the prevailing conditions, it was bound to take a little time for the permanent housing programme to gain momentum and there is nothing at all in the evidence to suggest that the Association was being laggardly in any realistic sense.

This judgement is fully endorsed when the contemporary national position is considered. Indeed, on 17th November, a week after the S.S.H.A.'s report was completed, the *New Statesman* had commented on the subject of housing. After explaining that the Government had decided against nationalising the building industry, which would thus remain composed of a few large and a host of small contractors, and that the industry would receive contracts from the 'local authorities' on whom the the Government was placing 'exclusive reliance' for the formulation and implementation of housing programmes, the article went on –

> The result at present is that, apart from a limited number of temporary structures, practically no houses are being erected at all. Lord Listowel announced in the House of Lords' debate on Tuesday that tenders had so far been approved for 12,000 permanent houses ... but he did not claim that one brick had yet been laid upon another.[83]

If Lord Listowel's statement was an accurate account of the contemporary national position, the S.S.H.A. would seem to have had very little with which to reproach itself. Indeed, in comparative terms, its record, such as it was, was quite respectable and may have contributed to the following intriguing comment by 'a leading civil servant' (E.M. Nicholson) in a Cabinet Memorandum dated 6th November 1945.

> ... it certainly looks as if the Ministry of Health ought to try and increase the number of houses started and reduce the time lag between authority to go to tender and the beginning of construction. *Scotland is making much better progress than England and it would be interesting to know the reason for this.*[84] (my italics)

On the broad general point the economist Douglas Jay advised the Prime Minister on 2nd November that 'the picture is gloomy and the building of permanent houses is likely to remain the weak point in the government's record for many months'.[85]

As may be seen, therefore, Buchanan's accusation of lack of progress could not fairly be levied specifically at the Association in the autumn of 1945 and, interestingly, it was not a charge which was raised in any of the subsequent recorded exchanges. However, the crisis for the Association was now at hand. On 10th December the Council was summoned to St Andrew's House – though noticeably neither Mr Forman nor Mr Robertson (the new MP's) were present – to meet Mr Westwood, the Secretary of State, and Mr Buchanan and to learn the Government's verdict.[86]

The bland minute of the meeting does nothing to conceal the blunt message. The Association's activities were being directed 'beyond the areas of greatest need to which they are at present limited' and it was to be encouraged to concentrate on rural areas. Among other changes the Secretary of State wished to 'develop a strong direct labour force as an essential feature of the Association's organisation' and to 'strengthen the higher whole time staff and the Council of Management' by several appointments including that of a full-time chairman. To facilitate these changes the majority of the members of Council were invited to submit their resignations by the following Friday.

Despite the careful wording and Mr Westwood's talk of the object being 'to extend the Association's activities' and enabling it to 'undertake an extended programme', the reality, from the point of view of the Association, must have been bitterly disappointing.

Two points are clear. First, the focus of the Association's operations was being shifted from the 'areas of greatest need' (the cities, and greater Glasgow in particular) to 'the rural areas where labour supply was difficult'. Without alarming the public at this time of extreme sensitivity on the subject of housing, or completely undermining the morale of the Association's staff, the Ministers could not, of course, explain the major shift in policy in blunt terms. (Indeed, as far as the Treasury was concerned the legal position remained that the Association was funded to work in the 'areas of greatest need'.) But the fact remained that the Association's intended key role in the rehousing of the population of the old industrial heartlands was clearly and emphatically being downgraded by the new administration at the Scottish Office. Second, the ministerial team were no longer prepared to permit the Association to be led by political heavyweights of the order of Sir Garnet Wilson and Messrs Forman and Robertson. Now the key members of the S.S.H.A.'s Council were to be employees capable of being subjected to an employer's discipline.

Lest there should be any doubts on these conclusions, it is perhaps worth stressing that there was nothing at all in the previous policy or in the Association's regulations which would have prevented it from being active in the rural areas. Indeed, it had already built houses in some fairly remote places including the Orkney Islands and, as we have seen, several small burghs and three counties received allocations in the first post-war programme. So long as a genuine need could be identified, there was nothing to prevent the Department from approving allocations to county communities or any locality. It was, of course, precisely this ability to build anywhere throughout Scotland which had made the organisation so attractive to Tom Johnston. In other words, Mr Westwood was not in any sense extending the Association's sphere of activity to embrace new areas. On the contrary, he was redirecting it away from the territories of key local authorities.

Similarly, the objective of developing 'a strong direct labour force' has, to say the least, a somewhat strange ring. In June of 1945, following detailed study by a sub-committee, the Association had decided to expand its direct labour force. Council had estimated that with the present no-fines concrete plant there was a capacity to construct 600 poured concrete houses per year in schemes of from 150–200 houses. Consequently it was decided to use direct labour for walling and jointing, while letting the other tasks out to contract. Moreover, members agreed to obtain more equipment as soon as circumstances justified the acquisition, and thereafter to expand direct labour and to appoint a manager to run the department. It was expected that manufacturers of sponsored prefabricated houses would carry out erection work and Council decided that it was not appropriate to use the Association's direct labour for road works, pipe laying and so on. However, it was agreed to give further consideration to having an in house squad of skilled workers capable of building up to 100 houses per annum using traditional methods.

Clearly, therefore, well before the new Government was in office the Association had decided to have a substantial direct labour organisation to supplement the efforts of traditional contractors. Provided the intention was that the Association should work with the private sector, while using its own labour force where required or where that gave some advantage – such as when no-fines construction was being used or in remoter rural districts where labour was in short supply – there is no reason to believe that there was any opposition to such a policy within the existing Council. It would seem, therefore, that either this was another 'red-herring' on the part of the Secretary of State, or the intention was actually much more radical.

Within five months of taking office, then, the new Government had effectively overturned a key part of Johnston's policy, namely his intended role for the S.S.H.A.. To explain why this happened and the significance of the development, it is appropriate here to examine both the Scottish and national contexts and, in the case of the former, to recall the division of opinion which had developed within the Labour Party about the Association.

As was explained previously, sections of Labour opinion, particularly within Glasgow and the west of Scotland and among members of the old I.L.P., had been distinctly hostile to the S.S.H.A. virtually from its formation. Essentially it was perceived to be a threat to the plans of those Labour followers of the Wheatley tradition who believed strongly in an extreme form of municipal socialism. To those who shared this point of view housing policy was not simply a matter of securing good dwellings, but was rather a method of propagating socialism at the local authority level as well as of undermining and replacing the private building industry. Thus when, in 1939, the Association first offered to build houses within Glasgow its overtures were rejected. The outbreak of war had prevented this issue from coming to a head in 1939, but clearly the slow response of Glasgow Corporation to the Association's first post-war request for city sites for 2,000 houses is indicative of continuing hostility.

As this chapter has made clear, between 1942 and 1944 Tom Johnston led the development of a housing strategy to suit post-war Scotland. This process drew on major reports prepared by the Scottish Housing Advisory Committee under two of his junior ministers, while his Council on Post-War Problems (Council of State) provided the guiding hand in the background. Interestingly, Christopher Harvie, who studied the minutes of this wartime Council, has hinted that Walter Elliot's was the dominant voice, and the former Secretary of State may indeed have persuaded Johnston of the wisdom of giving the Association an extended role. However, that Johnston personally came to favour such a policy is clearly indicated in Dr Taylor's letter to Mr Laidlaw quoted previously.[87]

As has been explained, the Housing (Scotland) Act of 1944 provided for the central funding of the Association and thereafter Johnston gave it a target of 100,000 houses to be built in 'the areas where the housing needs are greatest', and which 'would cover about one half of Scotland', the houses to be built within 'ten to twelve years' of the end of the war in Europe.[88] Earlier, the Scottish Housing Advisory Committee had estimated Scotland's housing requirement in 1944 as approximately 470,000 houses[89] and had assumed that something like nineteen years would be required to achieve that target. Obviously, therefore, an objective of 100,000 houses to be completed in the first ten years or so in the areas of greatest need, must mean that Johnston intended the Association to provide roughly half of the required houses in the problem areas. (Interestingly, these estimates were fairly accurate for the actual outcome in the first ten years was 223,173 houses, while 491,843 houses were built over the nineteen year period.[90]) In 1946 the Clyde Valley Regional Planning Advisory Committee (also set up by and working for Johnston) suggested that over 500,000 people in Glasgow required to be rehoused and a further 40,000 in Greenock.[91] There is no doubt, therefore, that Clydeside in general and Glasgow, in particular, was the main 'area of greatest need' and that Johnston expected the Association to be fully involved in the reconstruction of the city and the region.

Moreover, as has also been shown, the war-time administration did not believe that general needs housing subsidies would be required by local authorities for a period extending beyond the ten years immediately following the end of the war. Clearly, therefore, it was intended that private sector production would become a main source of housing supply by the end of the first post-war decade.

A key problem which had been examined by the Scottish Housing Advisory Committee on the Distribution of Houses was the difficulty posed for local authorities by movements of the population as a result of industrial change. The pre-war emphasis on linking housing subsidy to slum clearance and to the relief of over-crowding had prevented 'housing (local) authorities (from) building subsidised housing for work people transferred from other areas'.[92] As the committee pointed out, this was not a problem to the S.S.H.A. which was intended to build where needs were greatest. Indeed, in the spring of 1945 the Association had been given a supplementary programme of 1,000 houses for 'transferred miners' and these were located in 37 small estates scattered throughout Ayrshire, Dumfriesshire, Fife, Lanarkshire, Midlothian, Stirlingshire and West Lothian.[93] (In passing, this programme clearly makes patent nonsense of Westwood's claim that he was extending the scope of the Association in permitting it to operate in rural areas.) Nothing could more vividly illustrate the Association's ability to react to the requirements of movements in population caused by industrial change, and Johnston's plans for the S.S.H.A. explain why no long-term measure was introduced in the 1944 Act to enable the local authorities to respond to the problem. This is particularly significant when one bears in mind the war time planners' conviction that dispersal of both population and industry on a large scale would be inevitable in the post-war era. In framing the 1944 Act Johnston was, therefore, prescribing for movements in the population which, in terms of the 1940 Barlow Report, The Distribution of Houses

The meeting point of two cultures; Millar Street, Stirling. On the right, a terrace of Edwardian houses built c1914; and on the left, some of the first council houses completed c1920.

Early council houses in Knightswood, Glasgow.

The first SSHA houses (Canadian red cedar) built at Carfin in 1938.

SSHA red cedar timber houses in Linlithgow.

The inter-war bungalow, still the *beau ideal* as far as many urban Scots are concerned. Built and sold originally for about £750, these houses today sell for prices in the range £100,000 to £175,000 (depending on such factors as location, condition and size). The economy of this type of house is quite remarkable, especially when contrasted with, for example, the life-cycle costs of much of the public sector housing built from the 1950s to the 1970s which is now having to be either radically reconstructed or demolished and rebuilt at huge public expense. This is perhaps the classic example of the inherent superiority of consumer choice over bureaucratic decision making in determining the nature of a product.

A fine 1950s house at Hillpark, Edinburgh. This was one of the first private houses built c1956 after the licences restricting the private sector had finally been removed. Note the interesting corner windows.

Transformation at Whitfield, Dundee. This photograph of houses belonging to Ormiston Housing Co-operative was taken in 1993.

'Partnership' modernisation at Ferguslie Park, Paisley (1992).

Similar reconstruction at Castlemilk.

394 Gallowgate. An 18th Century tenement restored by the SSHA in 1983 during the G.E.A.R. project. A few years earlier much finer buildings than this were being knocked down without a second thought.

Housing by Link Housing Association at Auchmithie Place, Glenrothes in 1992.

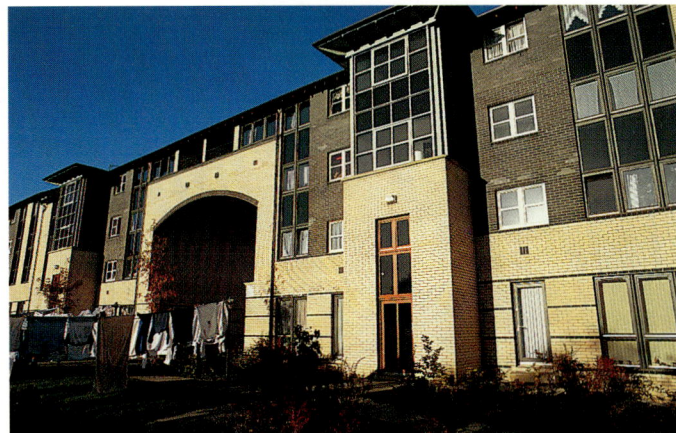

Restoration and renewal in Glasgow. Weavers Building 1993. This property was developed by Hillhead Housing Association (now Glasgow West Housing Association).

Tenemental restoration, Westend Park Street, Glasgow, c1990, by Charing Cross Housing Association.

Housing for low cost home ownership at Southloch Gardens, 1991.

Tenemental modernisation under way at Fielden Drive. Contrast this picture with the photograph of the same location at the beginning of the century. (Bill Spalding)

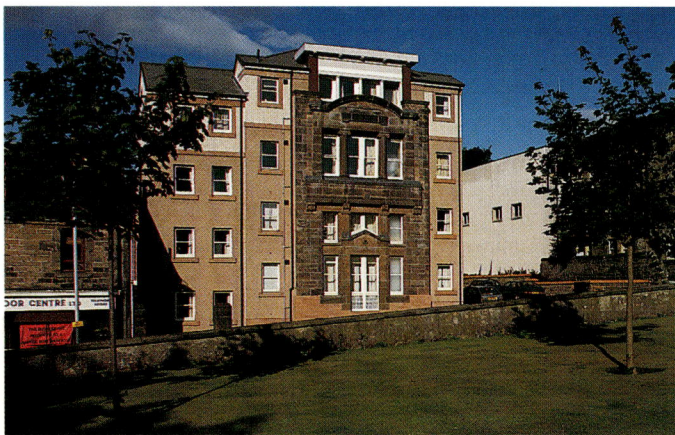

Lauder Technical College, Dunfermline (1994). This project by Kingdom Housing Association provided barrier free accommodation for rent.

New build tenement housing mainly for rent, but also for shared ownership, by Wester Hailes Community Housing Association in the Wester Hailes Partnership area, September 1995.

Modern luxury housing off Craigcrook Road, Edinburgh 1995.

Two views of Gribloch in Stirlingshire. Not as large as it appears in the photographs, this must be a contender for the most elegant 'family' house constructed in Scotland in the 20th Century. It was built for the steel manufacturer, John Colville, in 1938 and is included here as an example of the best work of the architect, Basil Spence.

Morrison Circus and Morrison Crescent, Edinburgh. When the circus was opened in September 1995 it marked the 300,000th houses built in Scotland since 1979. A remarkable mixed urban development involving Canmore Housing Association (including some accommodation for disabled tenants), Malcolm Housing Association, providing housing for market rents (and including some student accommodation leased to Napier University), and Woolwich Homes providing flats for sale at prices of about £78,000. Evidently this is the first circus to be built in the city in the 20th century and it vindicates the concept of modern tenements in an appropriate setting. It is interesting that tenants consulted in the contemporary reconstruction of the Gorbals in Glasgow, also pleaded for a return to this form of inner city housing.

Sir James Mellon, Chairman of Scottish Homes, in conversation with the Princess Royal during the rural housing conference at Aviemore in 1990.

Queen Elizabeth Court, the Gorbals, Glasgow; also designed by Basil Spence. (Julie Muir, *The Herald & Evening Times*, Glasgow.)

Symbol of the end of an era? The demolition of Queen Elizabeth Court in September 1993. (Jeff Mitchell, *The Herald & Evening Times*, Glasgow.)

Report and the subsequent Distribution of Industry Act of 1945, were regarded as desirable and necessary.

Johnston's intention's for the S.S.H.A. should, therefore, not be seen in isolation for, in his view, *regional* planning was required if there was to be a genuine long-term solution to Scotland's deep-seated social and economic ills. 'Heaven knows', he wrote later, 'there was a great need for co-operation among local authorities for planning on a regional basis'.[94] The main Clyde Valley Regional Plan, although not published until 1946, was very much in tune with his philosophy. Under the leadership of Sir Patrick Abercrombie and Sir Robert Matthew the study team, composed largely of officials from the Department of Health for Scotland, investigated the physical, social, recreational and economic development possibilities of the entire Clyde region. In addition to calling for the creation of New Towns it pointed to the need to reduce drastically the density of Glasgow's population – three-quarters of a million people were crammed into three square miles around the city centre – to the imminent and inevitable decline of both the Lanarkshire coalfield and the shipbuilding industry, to the need to relocate the steel industry towards the coast, and to the essential requirement for a Clydeside Regional Planning Authority to co-ordinate the immense tasks involved in social and economic reconstruction.[95]

It should also be noted, of course, that the Clyde Valley planners saw themselves in a wider than regional context and called for 'a national plan for the repopulation of Scotland as a whole'.[96] They pointed out that the regional provision of new towns and further planned development of towns in the Clyde Valley other than Glasgow, would still only produce a partial solution. They strongly urged 'that this vital problem of the over congested central part of the Clyde Valley should not be considered in its local or even its regional aspects only', and pointed out that in relative terms greater Glasgow was considerably more over-burdened in relation to Scotland than was London relative to the English population. Moreover, topographically the Clyde Valley was far less able to absorb urban sprawl than the Home Counties of south east England. Attending only to the Clyde Valley, therefore, their proposals would not be able to provide measures to 'decrease *regional* as distinct from local congestion'.

> We recommend as a necessary corollary to our required proposals for decentralisation, the immediate setting up of machinery for linking together all the regions of Scotland for the purpose of working out the basis of a National Plan for the location of industry and population.[97]

The vision of the planners clearly required not only national planning co-ordinated by a central department, but some mechanism which extended well beyond the frontiers of local government and this brought them '*to the crux of the problem. The outward movement of population and industry cannot be stopped against municipal boundaries*'.[98] (My italics) They had thus found it necessary to consider the current local government arrangements 'in respect that, if the proposals of the Plan with regard particularly to housing, industrial development and provision of open spaces and a green belt are given effect to, they will at once 'cut across' the system of Local Government as that obtains at present'.[99] The Report, therefore, concluded -

> The Regional Enquiry that has taken place has shown unmistakably that the present system of Local Government with its water-tight compartments of Local Government areas is altogether inadequate and unsuited to the problems that face the development of the Area in its best sense.

> Accordingly, they urged that a Regional Authority should be set up.

> In the sphere of Industry, the great potential changes that have been envisaged for the Area in the fields of coalmining, iron and steel and shipbuilding and docks ... can only be successfully dealt with and equitably balanced by a common policy suitable and applicable to the Area.

Without regional co-ordination of policy the planners feared for 'the future of the conurbation' and feared that good government and planning would be 'delayed indefinitely, if not altogether sacrificed'.[100]

It is within the context of this regional (and national) approach that Johnston's intention for the S.S.H.A. should be considered. Having utilised the war years to explore and investigate the extent of the problem, and the way in which it could be expected to unfold in the post-war era, he and his advisers were in no doubt that the range and scale of operations extended well beyond the resources, means and frontiers of the local authorities of his day. The whole thrust of Johnston's war-time approach was, therefore, that direct central government involvement through the S.S.H.A. was required to facilitate the coming migration of industry and of the population (and, to the same end, he was also in favour of major contributions from both the private sector and voluntary housing associations).

But there were also critical immediate reasons for central government intervention. The war-time planners were acutely conscious that on the return of peace housing authorities would be faced by four key problems. First, the shortage of available accommodation would be desperate virtually all over the country. Second, for several years to come, building operations were bound to be severely restricted by a chronic shortage of skilled craftsmen. Indeed, the retraining of demobilised servicemen would take years and was bound to conflict with traditional craft practices. Third, certain materials such as cement, bricks, plaster, glass and, above all, timber, would be extremely scarce. And fourth, the resources with which to purchase large quantities of material from abroad simply would not exist.[101]

Under these circumstances, central control of a large part of house building must have seemed as essential as the rationing of, for example, tea, sugar, meat, or petrol. Indeed, for a time it appeared as though house-building might have come under the overall control of the Ministry of Works and it may have been the existence of the S.S.H.A. which enabled Johnston to retain responsibility within the Scottish Office during the war. (It is interesting that Westwood should have raised this possibility at the meeting of 10th December, 1945 and one cannot help wondering if his comment was actually aimed at Mr Buchanan, since it provided a rationale for retaining rather than abolishing the Association.) As early as 1942 Johnston, in fact, had advocated the establishment for England and Wales of an organisation similar to the S.S.H.A.[102] Indeed, in 1944, the Labour Party Annual Congress actually adopted the creation of a National Building Organisation as official party policy, and it is clear that in the autumn of 1945 many powerful voices were still in favour of such a move.

On 17th November the *New Statesman* set out the case. It explained that while building labour would be underemployed in some districts in others, perhaps 'where the need for houses is most acute', work would be impeded for lack of workers.

> We have argued before, and we return to our contention, that the housing problem will not be solved unless the work of the local authorities in canalising private enterprise is supplemented by a National Building Corporation run directly by the Ministry of Health and charged with the task of mobilising ... all available building resources in man-power and machinery not absorbed by local authorities' needs.

In addition to making good deficiencies of finance or progress by local authorities, such a Corporation 'would be of immense psychological advantage' under current circumstances.[103]

Earlier, in August, the same publication had been even more in harmony with Johnston's case, urging the Government to 'create a mobile National Building Corporation ... to go to the help of areas in which conditions are particularly bad'.[104]

On 2nd November, in the memorandum to Mr Attlee mentioned previously, Douglas Jay condemned the Ministry of Health's over reliance on the local authorities. His 'solution was for a new Housing Corporation to act in default of inefficient local authorities, and for more direct building by the Ministry of Works', and evidently his views were advanced in Cabinet by Lord Addison.[105]

(Interestingly, in one part of the country Johnston's ideas seem to have been adopted. It seems that the establishment of the Northern Ireland Housing Trust in 1944 was 'inspired ... by the Scottish Special Housing Association'. Moreover, Unionist local politicians opposed the initiative on the grounds that it was an attack on 'the competence and integrity of the local authorities'.[106])

It is clear, therefore, that the notion of direct central government participation in house provision was not simply a Scottish suggestion, but was rather an approach which commended itself to politicians at the U.K. level as an obvious response to the critical complex of post-war housing problems.

The question then arises, why was a National Housing Corporation for England and Wales not brought into existence in 1945? Perhaps the course of events in Scotland to be outlined shortly may shed light on the matter, but the explanation seems fairly straightforward. So much of the Labour Party's strength was based on local government, and public sector housing to most Labour politicians meant 'council housing'. Professor Smout commented in the Scottish context that Labour's appeal was to the working-class voter, frightened by the immense scale of unemployment and industrial collapse (in the inter-war years) ... but nevertheless impressed by the practical energy of Wheatley in getting the Housing Act through in 1924 ... Labour in Scotland became synonymous with the defence of council housing ....[107]

What was true in Scotland was only less true by degree in other parts of the country. Hence, with Labour enjoying majority power at Westminster for the first time, (and with many new MP's who had cut their political teeth in town halls up and down the country), while its nationalising programme might mean developing and extending central control of the rail, steel or coal industries, or the creation of a National Health Service, control of house building had fundamentally to be through local authorities. The Tories in Parliament mocked the continued division of responsibility for housing south of the border between the Department of Health and the Ministry of Works, and criticised the failure to create a unified authority.[108] But the last thing many Labour activists across the country wanted to see was a strong centralising Ministry of Housing, still less a National Building Corporation. Douglas Jay condemned Aneurin Bevan as 'very doctrinal' in his support for local authorities, but no-one more clearly understood the popular psyche of the Labour Party of his day than the Minister of Health.

The strength of the local government lobby in the Labour Party, and the securing of the key Government offices by its supporters, was what killed the notion of a central house-building agency south of the border. However, it was the existence of the S.S.H.A which encouraged Johnston in his attempt to develop the idea into a practical, major proposition in Scotland.

Following the passage of the 1944 Housing (Scotland) Act, when Johnston's plans became known they inevitably sparked off a lively debate. The redoubtable Jean Mann was among the first to take up the cudgels in *Forward*. In January 1945 she asked, 'what is the Scottish Special Housing Association?' She accused members of the Association of being 'too remote' and asked, 'Who appoints them? When can they be chucked out? Is it a matter for local or national elections?' She went on –

The S.S.H.A. do not appear to be responsible to anyone but themselves ....

If the S.S.H.A. has to be responsible for the erection of most of Scotland's post-war housing, it is necessary that we should understand this Association, who it is, what it is, and that its constitution should be sound from the start.

Having raised these questions, remarkably she then concluded -

The S.S.H.A. is controlled by the Secretary of State for Scotland, who ... changes rapidly and has no fixed tenure here ...[109]

which suggests that her apparent confusion as to the constitution of the Association was somewhat synthetic.

S.S.H.A. Council members Thomas Paterson and Arthur Brady both responded and, over the next few issues, the argument continued, degenerating eventually into the kind of bickering which left Thomas Paterson concluding ironically – 'It may be, perhaps, that the wrong socialists have been appointed to the Council of Management of the S.S.H.A.'[110]

(As a matter of interest, as far as can be determined, there were no known Conservatives on the Association's 1944–45 Council. Messrs Stirling, Rose and Ronald were civil servants and Alexander McKinna was a retired civil servant whose original appointment was presumably because of his expertise in public sector housing administration. Sir Garnet Wilson, the chairman, was a Liberal. And Messrs Forman, Robertson, Paterson and Brady were all Labour politicians. Coutts Morrison – a local government education officer – and Mrs Menteith were involved purely because of the operation of the Association's war-time evacuation camps for children – and the vice-chairman, W.C. Davidson was a full-time Association employee. The political allegiances – if any – of the three last named are not known, but in no sense could this be described as a Council which was hostile to the incoming Labour Government.)

Mrs Mann's reaction to Johnston's intended role for the Association may have been shared by many of those involved in local politics in Scotland. For example, in the summer of 1945, David H. Halley (who was to serve with distinction for many years as the Association's secretary), was given an insight into the feelings of Robert Adam, the Town Clerk of the Burgh of Perth. Adam had chaired the Scottish Housing Advisory Committee's sub-committee on design and was, therefore, deeply interested and involved in housing. When Halley, then depute town clerk in Perth, told Adam that he was going to apply for the post of assistant secretary in the Association, the response was 'words to the effect that the S.S.H.A. would never get in the door of Perth'.[111]

Through the early months of 1945 it is certain that Johnston came under increasing pressure from the local government lobby – both as represented by Labour activists such as Mrs Mann (she was then a Glasgow councillor, and was to be Labour MP for Coatbridge, 1945–50), and local government professionals such as Robert Adam. 'Adam believed that housing was a local government function and the Scottish Office should keep its nose out'.[112] Whether or not it was in response to such pressure, or whether it was a natural reaction to the ending of hostilities in Europe, one of Johnston's last acts before relinquishing office was to allow the local authorities to make a start on permanent housing. A Scottish Office circular was distributed relaxing the embargo on new permanent house building by local authorities and encouraging them to prepare schedules of quantities and tenders both for new buildings and the reconstruction of war damaged houses.[113]

One of the most intriguing questions of this period concerns Tom Johnston's decision to withdraw from Government. Why he chose to retire in 1945 in spite of Clement Attlee's expressed desire to retain his services has never been adequately explained. Why did he resign? He was still at the height of his powers; Labour was preparing to take office for the first time with a House of Commons majority – something which he had spent a life-time working for; he was one of a small handful of Labour leaders with significant experience of ministerial office and could expect to have possessed a very powerful voice in Cabinet; and, all other things being equal, he should in 1945 have been looking forward to the ultimate satisfaction of having the chance to implement plans which he had prepared throughout the long years of war and which could only be regarded as seminally important to the future of Scotland.

On the face of things Johnston's decision to leave politics in 1945 makes no sense. But were 'all other things equal'? By the spring of the year he must have had few doubts about the storm which was gathering in Party circles in respect of his housing plans. Had he lost the will to fight his corner? Had he come to the conclusion that he was bound to lose? Could he simply not bear to be part of a government which was about to dismantle the programme which he had spent so much time and effort constructing? Or did he have some deeper insight into the devastating consequences of the alternative approach to housing which his successors were about to deploy? These are questions which require answers. But whatever the truth, it is clear that the events in the development of Scottish housing policy in the period 1942 to 1946 do provide a more than plausible rationale which might explain the voluntary departure of a much admired Scottish Secretary in the hour of his Party's major political triumph. In the author's opinion, Johnston decided to quit in 1945, disgusted and disillusioned by the vehemence with which his housing plans were being assaulted from within his own Party, and that thereafter he chose to remain silent on the matter out of loyalty.

This then was the background to the arrival of the new administration at St Andrew's House. The appointment of George Buchanan is in itself extremely interesting. In forming his Government Mr Attlee evidently offered Buchanan the post of Minister for National Insurance which, given the intended legislative programme, would seem to have been a key and senior appointment. Buchanan, however, declined and chose the relatively junior position of Joint Under Secretary at the Scottish Office with responsibility for housing. Nothing could more vividly illustrate his passionate interest in housing and the importance which he attached to reforming Johnston's policies in this area.[114] Indeed, in a debate in the Commons on 29th July 1944 he had made his strong feelings obvious by urging that housing should get absolute priority.

> I almost express hatred of the conditions prevailing in my native country, and I ask the Secretary of State for Scotland to make it a first duty … to ask the War Cabinet that something should be done to get on with housing now, and try to make Scotland a better country than many of us have known in the past.[115]

The strength of Buchanan's commitment to transforming the housing conditions of the mass of working people in Scotland generally, and in the Glasgow area in particular, cannot be doubted. As he was Member of Parliament for the notorious Gorbals he had perhaps more reason than any politician to be interested in a crusade on housing. An acquaintance categorised him as 'a rude, strong man of passions, full of emotion which may be regarded as either love or hate, an emotion centred on a limited object … bestowed only on the working class'.[116] David Halley who, as the newly appointed assistant secretary, attended the meeting of 10th December remembers the minister as 'a sincere rough diamond who desperately wanted to stage a major attack on the housing problem'.[117] However, for most of his parliamentary career, Buchanan had been a member of the I.L.P., joining the Labour Party only in 1939.[118] His views were very much in tune with those represented by the old I.L.P. and, in terms of the Labour Party, can only be regarded as traditional Wheatleyite left of centre. His belief in local authority provision of housing was unquestioning and his loyalty to his colleagues, many of whom, like himself, had been on Glasgow Corporation, was undoubted. But as Middlemas commented, 'the Clydesiders were ... sometimes surprisingly conservative and rooted in local politics ...'[119] Moreover there are good grounds for believing that there was latterly no great affinity between the Clydesiders and Tom Johnston, who had at times been a sharp critic of the I.L.P..[120] It seems clear, therefore, that Buchanan's mind was closed to any other approach to the housing problem than by means of the local authorities, and this was particularly true in so far as Glasgow was concerned. The extreme political prejudices on the housing question which the new junior minister embodied simply ran far too deep to be in the least deflected by the careful planning and thoughtful, reasoned arguments of Johnston and his advisers.

As shown in the report of 10th November, 1945, Glasgow had been easily the least co-operative of the local authorities in relation to the S.S.H.A.'s first 10,000 house programme. Although offered 2,000 houses as a first tranche, the city Corporation had still only suggested sites for 100 Swedish timber houses. (These were eventually erected at Balornock.) Given the background hostility illustrated earlier it is perhaps not surprising that many Glasgow Labour councillors were still far from willing to co-operate with the Association. Shortly after the offer was announced a dispute erupted over the rents to be charged and the method of allocating tenants to Association houses. This dispute seemed to take up time at every meeting of the Association's Council throughout 1945.

Certainly the issues were significant and boiled down to determining the extent to which the Association's houses would be under the Corporation's control. But these were matters of interest to all the local authorities with which the Association had dealings. It is interesting that only in the case of Glasgow was the argument pushed to the extent of freezing identification of sites for houses. One is thus left with the thought that,up to a point, this may have been a stalling operation on the Corporation's part – stalling to give time for a change of government and to give time for the new minister to curb the Association. However, be that as it may, the most striking and obvious feature is the three cornered nature which the various exchanges assumed.[121] These were not straightforward negotiations between the Association and Glasgow Corporation. On all points of contention the minister had become involved and it is quite clear that he invariably gave complete support to the Corporation. Thus was established a pattern which continued over the next two years. It is also interesting to note, however, that throughout this debate, and even under ministerial pressure, the Council of Management was still attempting to assert its responsibility for the Association's operations and it was obviously reluctant to be bullied into the premature acceptance of conditions which might not be workable.

In the main the purge of the Association's Council was a reflection of the minister's intention to downgrade the Association's role. But it seems that the sacking of the new MP's Forman and Robertson was particularly significant. As has been pointed out, James Welsh MP, had been a member of the Council from its inception until ill-health had forced his retiral during the war; Florence Horsburgh,MP, had served for a few months in 1939 when she was a junior minister; and James Scrymgeour Wedderburn,MP, also a junior minister, had been a member of Council in 1942 when the Association first became involved in post-war planning. The direct involvement of junior government ministers and MP's was, therefore, a notion which was apparently acceptable to a reasonably broad spectrum of political opinion and is itself an indication of the way in which the successive Secretaries of State – Walter Elliot, Sir John Colville and Tom Johnston – wished to use the Association to enable central government to play a leading part in the housing drive. From its establishment up until 1945 when Mr Buchanan intervened, therefore, MP's had always been on the Council and at one level this idea can scarcely be considered remarkable. It is perfectly normal, and always has been, for MP's to hold directorships in major companies and institutions. At another level, however, the presence of two MP's was bound to enhance the prestige and authority of the Council, as well as being an obvious manifestation of public representatives being in control of the Association. Buchanan's friends on Glasgow Corporation, however, bitterly opposed the whole concept of MP's being directly involved and this goes some way to explain the rapid removal of Forman and Robertson in particular.[122] Ironically, ever after the Association was typically attacked by Labour activists on the grounds that Council members were not subject to democratic election.

It would seem that events in relation to the S.S.H.A. in Scotland in the winter of 1945/46 were a reflection of the same forces which prevented the emergence of a National Housing Corporation south of the border. In Aneurin Bevan, as Minister of Health, and George Buchanan, Under Secretary of State with responsibility for housing at the Scottish Office, the left wing Labour local government activists had their supporters in the key positions so far as housing was concerned. Hence we are not simply considering a Scottish phenomenon. But while it is important to keep the wider context in mind, the reality is that in few parts of the country was the position of the left more rigorously advanced. Douglas Niven claims that the local authority housing policies in the immediate post-war period were 'disastrous' in effect. Some of the Labour councillors believed that it was possible to municipalise all private rented housing and 'some even believed that all houses in a burgh or city should be owned by the local authority'.[123]

In Niven's view, the results of this 'ridiculous notion', together with the continuation of rent controls, produced high local rate borne taxation and an absolute concentration of attention on new council building in what virtually amounted to a sustained assault on the private rented sector. In turn this meant continued decay and deterioration in many older but reasonable properties so that the high density new building in the three decades after the war proceeded cheek by jowl with the neglect and destruction of far too much of Glasgow and of other towns and cities, particularly in the Clyde Valley. Niven's damning indictment is no exaggeration. Indeed, it will be argued later that some of the consequences of the policies pursued from 1945/46 were considerably more devastating than he suggested.

In short, then, in the mid 1940s many local Labour politicians regarded council housing fundamentally as the means by which the loyalty and support of working people would be secured in the long term. Because the S.S.H.A. was seen as a threat to that end – as a threat to the sovereignty and autonomy of local politicians – it had to be excluded or confined. However, it should also be noted that in this attitude the left received encouragement from many local government bureaucrats keen to expand their empires. (In David Halley's words, 'They – the councillors – often just said what the officers told them to say'.[124])

Thus it was that Buchanan rushed to deflect and curb the Association's activities. In 1953 Tom Johnston reflected somewhat ruefully, but politely on what had happened and it must be accepted that his regrets were not focused against his nominal political opponents of a lifetime. He commented that with the ending of the National Government the 'experiment in political co-operation for Scottish national ends' had been terminated. Into that experiment he had put many of his aspirations.

> For a certainty there are considerable achievements in housing, in health, and the right to work, which could be rapidly secured for this generation if they were taken outside the realm of party strife.[125]

What he was perhaps too polite (or too loyal) to say was that the political fanaticism which had replaced his housing policies had set the country on a course which would result in immense and enduring damage in precisely these areas.

The immediate resignation of the senior members of the S.S.H.A.'s Council had been demanded on 10th December, but they eventually took their leave with rather more dignity two Council meetings later, on 31st January, 1946. At the intervening meeting at the end of December Sir Garnet Wilson recalled that the Secretary of State had said he had 'nothing but praise for the work of the Association', and this may have been a reflection of the latter's innermost opinions. But Joseph Westwood had little chance of standing up to Buchanan on an issue of this kind, particularly since behind the latter stood the formidable Minister of Health, Aneurin Bevan. (It has been pointed out that Westwood was ill and absent from office for many of the early months of the life of the Government, and that he was never subsequently able to make up the ground which he lost in terms of the formulation of Cabinet Policy. If there is truth in this analysis, it would seem probable that his absence during the critical autumn of 1945 may have made it so much easier for Buchanan and his friends to prepare their attack on the housing policy which the Government had inherited. In any event, Westwood's continued poor health throughout his period of office must have compounded his problems.[126])

Clearly Wilson and his colleagues had to go since Buchanan was not prepared to tolerate an S.S.H.A. led by people who were capable of challenging policy. Interestingly, he did nothing to democratise the process by which members were appointed to Council. Obviously the reality is that he wanted an organisation which would be quite unable to exert any kind of strong public influence on policy matters, which is why he insisted that the chairman should be the chief executive and a full-time salaried officer. From a purely management point of view, however, this was an extremely doubtful proposition. On the day to day running of affairs, it placed far too much authority, responsibility – and temptation – on the shoulders of one individual.

Against the background of the chronic post-war housing shortage, Mr Buchanan could not, of course, dispense entirely with the Association, although that presumably would more closely have matched his views. But in some ways he wanted to throw every available public resource at the problem of working-class housing, and it clearly would have been demonstrable nonsense to have abolished the Association under current conditions. He told the House of Commons that

> the Secretary of State considered it essential, in view of the proposed expansion of the scope of the Association's work and the development of a direct labour organisation, to re-organise the Association under a full-time chairman with experience in building industry techniques and large scale production.[127]

At the time some Association staff felt that the minister wanted the new chairman to be a 'supremo' who would be able to 'cut all sorts of corners and get on with the job',[128] and that may well have been his hope – provided the Association did not impinge too much on the territory of local authorities, and as a purely temporary expedient.

The decisive shift away from Tom Johnston's policy came in the Housing (Financial Provisions) (Scotland) Act of 1946. This Act provided the legislative basis for placing the primary responsibility for the provision of post-war housing firmly into the hands of the local authorities. The Act virtually doubled the subsidies to councils (from £13 to £25 for a five apartment house) and permitted them to follow an open 'general needs' building policy.[129]

The initial consequence of the 1946 Act was a hopeless competition for scarce or unobtainable resources and a general identification of building plans which had no chance of early fulfilment. Within two years huge programmes of construction had been earmarked all over the country which could not possibly be completed in the short term. The market for materials and labour became grossly overloaded and the pressure to resort to ill-considered methods of construction became almost irresistible. In other words, a situation which was inherently very difficult was turned into something approaching an uncontrollable nightmare.

Almost the last thing which the outgoing S.S.H.A. Council did was to consider a report on the various forms of non-traditional housing which were being offered by industrial concerns.[130] It was noted that the full output of Weir steel houses in 1946 would be taken up by the Association and Glasgow Corporation and therefore nothing more could be expected from that source in the short term. Similarly, although the Association had ordered 500 Atholl steel houses that company's houses were now already also fully committed for 1946 as well as for much of 1947. 200 Braithwaite Unit houses and similar numbers of Hill's Presweld Frame and Fairhurst Frame houses were recommended for erecting at Clydebank provided in each case specification details and prices proved satisfactory. It was noted that Scotland might get an allowance of about 1,000 British Iron and Steel Federation (B.I.S.F.) houses and it was recommended that the Association should accept any that might be available.

> *Precast Concrete – Orlit House.* The Orlit company have offered to supply and erect 1,500 houses during 1946 and, while some doubt was expressed as to the company's ability to provide this number in view of their other commitments, it was recommended that a contract for a suitable number should be entered into, provided plans and prices are satisfactory.

Messrs Holland, Hannen and Cubitts had offered about 500 houses for Clydebank by the summer of 1947, and discussions were being held in Leeds about the possibility of securing some 'Airey' houses.

The most striking feature of this report is perhaps the way in which it points up the change which had already occurred in the Association's position. In June 1945,

Swedish timber houses at Motherwell. These were part of the batch purchased by the government immediately after the end of the war in Europe.

when the first batch of Swedish timber houses was ordered by the Government the Association's share had been 1,000 out of 2,500 houses allocated to Scotland. Now, six months later, it was having to scratch around for whatever houses might be had. Nothing could more clearly illustrate the way in which it had been downgraded as the government's building agent.

The Association, of course, had always been concerned with non-traditional methods of construction and, with the Sighthill demonstration site it struggled to sort out the wheat from the chaff, but under the developing conditions the risks of inferior products being adopted were obviously high. (Four of the house types mentioned above were actually constructed at Sighthill.)

In March 1946 the Association houses on which building was in progress were classified as follows:-

Traditional	776
Weir 'Paragon'	46
Orlit	2
Swedish timber	968
Association's no-fines	68
Total	*1,860*

At the same time agreement in principle had been reached to order 1,000 Weir 'Quality' houses and 500 Atholl houses.[131]

The Association was never very enthusiastic about steel houses, fought endless battles with their manufacturers, and, in fact, did not itself erect very many. Where

Weir 'Quality' houses at Kirkcaldy. Houses of this kind have now all been either demolished or radically reconstructed with outer (usually brick) walls and pitched roof.

98

non-traditional houses were concerned the preference was always for the no-fines technique which the Association had pioneered and which it was subsequently to use with success down to the late 1970s. Regrettably, however, right through the 1940s it was unable to utilise its knowledge and experience in this type of construction. With the wholesale expansion of local authority building the Association found itself compelled to use its direct labour force not so much for building no-fines houses – as had been intended by the war-time Council – but instead for site servicing (ie laying the drains, etc and preparing foundations) so that others might build less satisfactory houses.

The pressure exerted by the government at this time in favour of various prefabricated non-traditional techniques which might be used by the local authorities was intense and, at the request of the Ministry of Works, two additional small experimental sites were planned for Danderhall and Holytown. These estates, involving three different house types were to be built to English standards to see if they were capable of standing up to Scottish weather conditions. In addition, the Department of the Chief Scientific Adviser co-ordinated a variety of experiments into tenants' 'ways of living' by incorporating within the designs variations in the interior layout and in facilities for cooking and heating.[132] Similarly, throughout 1946 sites were required to be provided in various parts of the country for manufacturers of prefabricated houses to erect such house types as Orlit, B.I.S.F., Hills Presweld, Whitsun Fairhurst, Brydon and Wimpey.

The new Government favoured the production of such houses fundamentally in order to maintain levels of employment in the factories as the firms concerned

British Iron and Steel Federation houses at Campbeltown.

adjusted to post war conditions. Traditional and, in particular, 'no-fines'-techniques would almost certainly have produced better and cheaper dwellings more quickly, but clearly the matter was at least as much a question of industrial, economic and labour strategies as of housing policy. The post-war Labour Government was absolutely committed to the maintenance of jobs in the traditional workplaces of heavy industry and adapted its housing strategy accordingly.

In June 1946 Mr Buchanan met the S.S.H.A.'s new chairman, Mr Dalziel and, ironically, berated him for lack of progress.[133] In fact, of course, Dalziel's task was now almost impossible despite a recruitment drive and an attempt to restructure the organisation. In August the Department gave its general approval of his reconstruction plans on the understanding that the work of the Association 'would be subject to a comprehensive review in July, 1948'.[134] Now, it may well be that what the Department had in mind was nothing more than the normal monitoring of the Association's performance. But this early intimation of an intention to hold a 'comprehensive review' in July, 1948 does suggest that Mr Buchanan may well have hoped that from that date the entire responsibility for housing could be passed on to the local authorities. Perhaps that is reading more into the comment than is entirely safe, but there is no evidence of any such major review having taken place in 1948 and it seems probable that the intention died with Mr Buchanan's departure from office.

As things turned out Mr Dalziel's tenure with the S.S.H.A. was very short and his resignation was forced by his Council colleagues in October 1946. It is impossible to establish the precise cause of Dalziel's dismissal – the relevant documents are discreetly worded and memories of the incident are hazy, although it has been suggested that 'money and alcohol were both involved'.[135] However, with his departure a proposed deal with the Orlit company was terminated. Under this plan the Association would have been pledged to accept the entire output of an Orlit factory in Scotland, but since the houses were to be erected by direct labour it is impossible to see what advantage the scheme might have had over building by the Association's own no-fines technique. As it happened, the S.S.H.A. erected only a

Orlit Framed houses, photographed at Ayr shortly before they were demolished in 1986.

few Orlits in Ayr, Hamilton, Kilmarnock and Aberdeen, and this was to prove to be a fortunate escape for, although they served well enough for many years, by the 1980s a fatal flaw had been discovered in the structure of these buildings. Deterioration in the concrete framework exposed the steel reinforcement in places to corrosion, and this necessitated complete demolition and replacement. But if Dalziel's plan had gone through, the Association could have faced a disaster of major proportion rather than a relatively minor problem.

What the Scottish Office thought of Council's decision to remove its chairman is unclear. (The minutes only refer to a meeting with the Secretary of State and Mr Buchanan at which there was 'an exchange of views'.[136]) But the outcome was accepted and Council member A.G. McBain succeeded to the chairmanship, which now reverted to a part-time appointment. McBain, a close personal friend of Mr Buchanan, was a fine accountant and a man of considerable character and he was largely responsible for rescuing the Association from a desperate predicament and for enabling it to develop usefully throughout the late 1940s.

As far as permanent housing was concerned, the period from the summer of 1945 to the autumn of 1947 can only be described as chaotic. The truth is that with so many local authorities competing for scarce resources of men and materials the process of house building was being strangled. On sites up and down the country the situation degenerated into a shambles with work in one place being held up for lack of bricks, cement or joiners, while on other locations these resources were plentiful, but could not be used because there was no timber or because bricklayers were unavailable.

The situation confronting the S.S.H.A. reflected the general situation and was illustrated in its annual report of March 1947.

Progress on Schemes as at 31–3-47

Sites nominated	21,038
Entry to site granted	15,608
Contracts placed	8,993
Completed	615 [137]

At a meeting in that month the Association's new general manager, Mr S.A.-Finlay, explained to Mr Buchanan that the organisation's proposed target of 6,879 houses for the year ahead was hopelessly unrealistic since it would require a labour force of 11,000 men as compared to the 2,816 then employed.[138] Consequently the target for the year would have to be reduced to a more reasonable level. Under the prevailing circumstances there was no possibility of the additional building workers being recruited. Indeed, the Association was having a very hard time hanging onto existing labour in the face of the fierce competition for experienced men.[139] Similarly the position in respect of some materials – notably timber and steel – was also extremely difficult.

1947 was, in general terms, a difficult year for the country and a traumatic one for the government and its policies. It was, in the words of Kenneth Morgan, 'a truly bleak, bad year', and the 'main causes' of difficulty 'were rooted in the economy'.[140] It began with a particularly severe winter with bitter weather and heavy snow falls extending from late January until well into March. This precipitated a disastrous fuel crisis which Mr Buchanan blamed for some of the problems concerning building materials.

Mr Buchanan claimed that there should 'be no deficiency of labour', but stated that 'timber and steel were the two materials which were causing the Government most concern at the moment.'[141]

He anticipated improvement in the supply of timber by the latter part of the year. As far as steel was concerned, the Minister admitted that the fuel crisis was affecting the steel industry, but he did not believe that production of Weir, Atholl or B.I.S.F. steel houses would be interrupted although there might be delays in respect of other types. He urged the Association to 'consider alternative methods of construction in concrete rather than steel'.

But the solution was not so simple. Four months later the monthly report for July showed that the situation remained grim and conditions in respect of concrete were as bad as for any other material.

Labour and Materials
The phased labour required for the completion of the (adjusted) 1947 programme as at the end of June was 5,013. The actual head of labour employed was 2,873, a difference of 2,140. The actual shortage intimated to the Ministry of Labour was 180. The difference between the figures of 2,140 and 180 is mainly due to the shortage of materials.[142]

Timber and cement were the main materials in short supply and consequently disrupting progress. But shortages were also noted in 'fireclay drainage goods, cast iron soil goods, electric conduit and electrical fittings, and hardwall plaster'.

In order to speed up a priority programme of 1,002 houses for coal miners, the report indicated that resources were being diverted from some locations to concentrate work on a limited number of sites. A special investigation had also been conducted into the position of cement.

It is understood that 15,000 tons of cement per week are available to Scottish cement merchants and that these merchants have agreed to supply 25 per cent of their quantity (3,750 tons) for housing work. (The Association's estimated weekly requirements are 750 tons.) It was also agreed that the needs of the miners' schemes should be met in full before allocating cement to the general housing programme.

As may be seen then, the S.S.H.A. had every reason to believe that the whole building industry in Scotland was over-loaded. (In passing it is interesting to note that the Association was finding it impossible to obtain one fifth of Scotland's output of cement for house building. This vividly illustrates the extent to which it had been pushed away from Johnston's target of roughly half the houses to be built in the first ten years of peace.)

By the end of September the problems of hanging on to labour were once again under consideration.

From replies to a recent questionnaire addressed to Clerks of Works it appears that there is a small drift of labour from housing schemes to work in factories, steel works, shipyards and mining, where better terms of employment seem to be obtainable than in the building industry.[143]

Almost certainly the problem was lack of continuity of work and overtime as a result of inadequate supplies of materials. Under these circumstances the earnings of employees were almost bound to be depressed in relative terms.

By the end of March 1948 the Association's performance still seemed very poor and the Annual Report explained the situation thus. The slow progress was principally the consequence of 'erratic supply and prolonged shortages' of such materials as 'cement, timber, electric conduit, steel cast iron materials, plasterboard, hard wall plaster and glass'. Throughout the year, by a variety of expedients, the Association had attempted to overcome shortages by transferring materials between sites, and this had provided 'some slight success'.

It, however, was clear that the number of houses under contract in Scotland was far in excess of the number which could be completed in a reasonable time, having regard to the supply of labour and materials. It was thought by the government early in 1947 that … it was not unreasonable to expect the completion in Scotland in that year of 24,000 houses, of which the Association's share was 4,234 … but it soon became evident that this output could not be attained.[144]

The annual report for 1948 also records the various house types for which the Association had placed contracts in the post war programme and including those houses completed at that date.[145]

Houses

Traditional	4,021
Weir Steel (Paragon and Quality)	2,511
Atholl Steel	1,342
B.I.S.F. steel-framed	1,000
Hilcon steel-framed	138
Orlit concrete framed	358
Whitsun Fairhurst concrete framed	654
Swedish timber	968
No-fines poured concrete (including Brydon and Wimpey types)	402
Keyhouse unibuilt	2
Foamed slag poured	2
Tarran-Clyde pre-cast units	162
Hostel conversions	57
Total	*11,617*

As this list indicates, the Association had been quite unable to concentrate its resources on the no-fines technique which it favoured for a semi-skilled labour force. The reasons are quite clear. First, the necessary supplies of cement were inadequate and what was available was required for the sponsored houses. But

These SSHA 'no-fines' semi-detached houses were built at the Sighthill demonstration development in 1946 and for this particular model the consultant was the well known architect, Sam Bunton. This was the form of construction which was neglected during the 1940s. Note that the house on the right has been purchased and modified.

second, the Association's direct labour force had been diverted into site servicing for local authorities and could not be deployed to undertake much building work.

Even in England and Wales the performance in respect of housing in the immediate post war period was poor. 'During his first eighteen months or so at the Ministry of Health, so little progress was made in relieving the housing shortage that it began to look as though Bevan's head would have to roll'.[146]

If the situation for the government had started badly in 1947 with the fuel crisis, it seemed to get worse as the year progressed. 'The climacteric of Labour's troubles was reached with the grave financial crisis over the convertibility of sterling in August ...' according to Kenneth Morgan. It 'left Britain facing bankruptcy, the Cabinet was brought to its knees ...'[147]

The financial crisis quickly became trading and, for the government, budgetary crises, and Attlee responded to mounting criticism by making major changes in the composition of the government. The *New Statesman* concluded that 'the old type of working class leader gives way to the disinterested expert who had studied Keynes'. To Morgan this comment referred particularly to the replacement (at the Ministry of Fuel and Power) of Shinwell, of impeccable Glasgow proletarian background, by the Wykehamist Gaitskill', but he agrees that 'the balance of authority within the government was much altered. In the first place, the leftish element in the Cabinet was somewhat undermined ...'[148]

So far as Scotland was concerned, Westwood was replaced as Secretary of State by Arthur Woodburn, and George Buchanan was transferred to become, for a few months, Minister of Pensions. Why had the latter changes occurred? Christopher Harvie's assessment is blunt. Westwood had 'proved a failure and was sacked'.[149]

If his tenure in charge of the Scottish Office is evaluated in terms of the housing programme, poor, sick Mr Westwood was indeed a failure, although the criticism might be more accurately levied at his junior colleague. But if the short-term consequences of the policies followed in this period were unfortunate and frustrating, the legacy of the era for housing and for economic development in many parts of Scotland has to be regarded as infinitely more damaging.

CHAPTER FOUR

The Scottish Urban Predicament

*F*ROM the perspective of the 1990s the long term consequences of post-war policies are obviously both more interesting and more significant than short term matters. However, it is important not to lose sight of the immediate pressures to which ministers were subject. Again, in this context, the archives of the SSHA are revealing since it was natural for the Scottish Office to turn to the Association both for intelligence and as a means of direct intervention.

George Buchanan's replacement as Joint Parliamentary Under-Secretary of State with responsibility for housing was J.J. Robertson,MP, the former member of the S.S.H.A.'s Council who, of course, had been one of those dismissed in December 1945. Now he lost no time in coming to the Association's offices for wide-ranging exploratory discussions.[1] One can at once detect an easing in the relationship between the Association and Government[2], but it was not within the Minister's power to restore complete order in the short term, nor could he reverse the fundamental policy shift engendered by Buchanan in 1945–46. However, important instructions were rapidly forthcoming.

The situation which confronted Robertson and his Secretary of State on assuming office is illustrated vividly by the Association's progress report dated 9th October, 1947.

In the light of these figures (just 1544 houses completed out of a 29728 house programme), it is not surprising that later that month and in November Government circulars to the local authorities and to the Association instructed that only houses on which work had been started by 24th October were to be continued if they were being built by traditional methods. Work on other houses for which approval had earlier been given was not to proceed until further notice, although special arrangements might be made in respect of non-traditional houses to prevent disruption to factory production.[4] In effect this meant that the future programme was being suspended while an attempt was made to apportion resources more strictly between the various authorities. The report to the Council of Management at the end of March 1948 explained that in the previous October, the Government had announced that work should not continue on contracted houses unless their erection had already been commenced. The only exceptions were in the cases of houses for agricultural workers or miners and non-traditional

Statement summarising the progress of the 1st, 2nd and Supplementary Site Acquisition Stages of the Association's Housing Programme as shown in Statements 1 to 6 of the Monthly Report dated 9th October 1947.[3]

	1st Stage (Houses)	2nd Stage (Houses)	Supplementary Site Acquisition Programme (Houses)	Total (Houses)
Programme	11680	14848	3200	29728
Sites nominated by Local Auths......	11486	8754	2164	22404
Sites approved by all interests....	11440	7694	1964	21098
Sites to which entry is available..	11266	6332	840	18438
House Contracts placed..............	8829	1926	116	10871
House Construction started.............	6963	1106	–	8069
Houses Roofed........	3318	112	–	3430
Houses Completed.....	1522	22	–	1544

houses where work in the factories had been started. In addition, the policy was confirmed of limiting new contracts to the production of houses required in support of farming and coal-mining.

> The object was to reduce by the latter half of 1949 the total number of houses under construction at any one time to the number which it was estimated might be completed in 12 months. Incidentally, it is hoped that this realistic policy of avoiding the overloading of the market will result in reduced prices.[5]

A year later, on 25th October, 1948, the Minister and George Crow of the Department of Health for Scotland discussed an improving situation with the Council of Management. After congratulating Council for the Association's 're-markable activity' in the past year Mr Robertson explained that the policy was to attempt to bring house building into balance so that the number of starts was realistic when compared to the number of houses capable of being completed. To obtain a properly balanced programme it would be necessary to continue the policy for a further year. The only exceptions were still houses for miners or farm workers or where a local authority with 'extensive housing needs together with labour available to undertake new work' already had its construction programme in balance.

The minister then noted with approval the 'record' progress which had been made in 1948 despite the difficult economic conditions.

Robertson's words of encouragement must have been welcome to Council members and tend to confirm a sympathetic attitude towards the Association. In addition, his willingness to help local authorities which had 'extensive housing needs' suggests something akin to Johnston's emphasis on the 'areas of greatest need'. However, it is clear from these minutes that the Minister was aware of a sharp increase in the pace of construction in 1948, and this was also confirmed by the subsequent annual report. In the year to the end of March 1949, the Association completed 3,305 houses – an increase of about 1,100 on its performance in the previous year.[6] The calendar year output figures for Scotland as a whole show an increase in total public sector output from 10,795 completed houses in 1947 to 19,670 in 1948 and 24,745 houses in 1949. No doubt as the national economy became increasingly reconciled to peace-time conditions some acceleration in house production was bound to have occurred, but the figures certainly suggest that the action taken by the new Scottish Office team in the autumn of 1947 was reasonably effective.

Nevertheless, the Association's report for the year to March 1949 made it clear that all was still far from well, and there was frustration in the belief that far more could be done. Shortages of plasterers, joiners, and painters were noted although the supply of most materials was slowly improving. In particular, however, the Association was disgruntled about the use to which its direct labour force was being put. 'The main activity of the organisation during the year has been site-servicing and constructing foundations for steel houses...' It had commenced actual building operations on two small schemes and similar projects were being prepared. However, 'practically all the Association's site servicing work is being done by direct labour, and includes in many cases the provision of sewers for local authorities'.[7]

The calendar year figures for the output of houses in Scotland in the initial post-war period are set out below.

	Local Authority	New Town	SSHA	Housing Assocs.	Other Govt Depts	Total Public Sector	Private Sector	Total All
1945	1351	–	77	–	–	1428	141	1569
1946	3321	–	490	–	–	3811	499	4310
1947	8919	–	1854	20	2	10795	1354	12149
1948	16615	–	2932	14	109	19670	1541	21211
1949	20004	60	4116	72	493	24745	1102	25847
1950	20989	158	3167	91	624	25029	782	25811
1951	17971	120	2906	139	647	21783	1145	22928

These figures show clearly the improvement in overall output which was achieved following the changes in personnel and policy which were introduced from the autumn of 1947. More strikingly, however, they also illustrate the early consequences of the policies flowing from the Housing (Financial Provisions) (Scotland) Act of 1946. The near doubling of the general needs subsidies to local authorities taken together with the building licences and controls restricting the sites and materials available to the private sector and the diversion of the S.S.H.A. had allowed the local councils to establish overwhelming domination of house production in Scotland.

Despite all the initial difficulties described above, the momentum built up by the local authorities in Scotland (and elsewhere in the U.K.) was obviously of critical importance in dealing with the post-war housing shortage. At the time, there is no doubt that the public looked to Government for answers to their urgent housing needs and, through the war years, had become accustomed to State directed economic and social activities. Clearly, no political Party could have avoided extensive intervention during these years, but under the first post-war Labour Administration councils secured a quite remarkable degree of ascendancy over house provision.

On the credit side, the efforts of the local councils in the 1940s and early 50s did gradually ease the overall shortage in a manner which was then generally acceptable to the public. Moreover, it is also true that most of the sponsored houses constructed by councils in the period at least had the merit of being of a large family size cottage style and thereby conformed to the basic house concept favoured by the public as indicated in the 1944 survey. In many parts of the country some very reasonable estates were built and gradually these matured into thriving communities. This was especially the case in some of the smaller towns and villages where the typical development was of fifty or so houses, but some good urban estates were also built on green field sites. Where problems did occur in the latter areas they were typically a consequence of the size of the schemes and the uniformity of design.

By the 1970s and 80s many of the dwellings erected in the 1940s had to be radically reconstructed and a few, designated as defective (such as Orlit concrete framed), had to be demolished. On the whole, however, considered in context, most of the houses in question have to be regarded as relatively successful and they are likely to be still in use for many decades to come. Fundamentally, they succeeded because, despite design flaws and some of the inherent problems associated with industrial methods of production, they almost always conformed to the pre-eminent consumer preference for a family size cottage and garden. Anyone who doubts that conclusion might reflect on the similar story in respect of the 'pre-fabs' of the transitional post-war period. These tiny dwellings were generally intended to have a life-span of little more than fifteen to twenty years, yet in the event, they must have far exceeded the initial expectations of designers, builders and the first generation of tenants. Most have now gone, but some, in areas such as rural Stirling, were extensively modernised in recent years with a brick outer wall, and these undoubtedly have long term futures. Others, for example, those at Prospecthill adjacent to Hampden Park stadium in Glasgow, survived in their original condition until as late as 1993, and the Glasgow houses were only relinquished by tenants after a prolonged campaign for their retention. A few of the last of the pre-fabs were actually developed as 'permanent' houses and some of the latter, located at Moredun in Edinburgh, are still in use. Indeed, as a curious footnote, when, in September 1995, the author went to photograph the Moredun houses he was promptly stopped by Mrs Snedden of the Moredun and Craigour Pre-fab Action Group and advised of the strenuous efforts being

Prefabs at Moredun and Craigour, Edinburgh photographed in September 1995 and showing clearly how proudly gardens have been maintained.

made to dissuade Edinburgh District Council from demolishing the houses. The tenants want their pre-fabs to be modernised. When Mrs Snedden was asked to explain why they should be retained, she replied that not only did the long-standing community not wish to be broken up, but that the pre-fabs were excellent houses in which to live. It is to be hoped that these little buildings, so evocative of the post-war years, are not lost to Edinburgh, but clearly, the secret of their success as dwellings is essentially that they meet the basic criteria preferred by many consumers.

The initial post-war council housing programmes, therefore, have, even in retrospect, a significant credit side. However, there is another aspect to the account and it is now appropriate to begin to consider some of the longer term consequences of the policies pursued from 1945.

The plans of the Scottish Office as developed under Tom Johnston during the war assumed a regional approach to housing and planning. As has been shown, this was very much in accord with ideas being developed elsewhere in the U.K., and the Barlow Report of 1940 in particular had considered the dispersal of the population and industry as crucial elements in the twin tasks of addressing the problems of urban congestion and the predicted decline of many of the traditional heavy industries. Two key elements in the intended approach were the use of designated green belt areas (within which development would be prevented) around the old cities; and new towns beyond the green belts to which a proportion of the population would be decanted.

To further these proposals a New Towns Committee was established in 1945 under the chairmanship of Lord Reith and its task was to consider how new towns might be developed, organised and administered. Meanwhile, from 1944 a division of the Scottish Department of Health, led by J.H.McGuinness, was dedicated to planning implementation of the system within the context of west central Scotland, and some of his staff were seconded to assist in the development of the Clyde Valley Plan.

Inevitably the Clyde Valley Plan recommended precisely such a strategy. Sir Patrick Abercrombie had advocated something similar in respect of Greater London, but the situation of both industry and housing in and around Glasgow made the case for such an approach particularly strong. The post-war future for the shipbuilding and heavy industries of Clydeside was uncertain to say the least and the need to attract new light industries and other businesses into the district was a vitally important consideration. As early as 1936 in a report on the distressed areas it had been indicated that the region needed to attract an additional 60,000 jobs. By 1945 it was also realised that a significant decline in the Lanarkshire coalfield was inevitable. Moreover, the proposed relocation of the steel industry to the coast to give it a long term future was bound to require a restructuring of other elements of the economy and to increase the importance of bringing in more modern industries. New towns were considered to be the most promising magnets for precisely such a purpose.[8]

As far as housing was concerned, the primary need in the area was to tackle the slums of the central parts of Glasgow and some of the other towns of the region, in particular, Greenock, Hamilton, Motherwell, Coatbridge and Airdrie. As we have seen, in the case of Glasgow, some of the housing conditions were absolutely atrocious with typical inner city densities of the order of 865 persons per hectare. Indeed, in that respect, one of the worst locations comprised of a set of tenements in a six hectare space in which resided an almost unbelievable 12,500 persons.[9]

As early as 1936 the splendid Councillor Jean Mann had argued the case for tackling the problem by dispersing some of the city's population to new towns and she also saw how this could be combined with bringing new factories to such communities.[10] The same logic was favoured by both the Clyde Valley Planners and the McGuinness team at the Scottish Office and, as has been shown, it provided much of the intellectual thrust of Johnston's post war planning.

In 1946, therefore, the Clyde Valley Planners recommended the imposition of a broad green belt around Glasgow to prevent its further sprawl and the reconstruction of the city, the latter to be facilitated at least in part by the construction of four new towns, at East Kilbride to the south, Cumbernauld to the north east and Bishopton and Houston to the west. There would also be some dispersal of the population to other growing towns of the region and, as the Lanarkshire coalfield declined, so miners and their families would move from there to the east, especially to new developments in Fife and the Lothians. This was the broad plan within which Johnston had intended the S.S.H.A. to operate when he gave it its 100,000 house target in 1944.

Westwood was, of course, part of the war-time planning group and it is not surprising that he was very enthusiastic for the new town concept. Indeed, he believed so strongly in the possibilities of new towns that initially he wanted no less than twelve to be developed in Scotland in the post war era. When the New Towns Act was drafted in 1946, in his eagerness to move on the matter, he waived the convention that Scotland should have separate legislation, hence the Act applied to both England and Scotland. He was able to do this because McGuinness and his colleagues were prepared and ready to produce the necessary Scottish clauses. Two months before the Act became law and a few weeks after publication of the Clyde Valley Plan, Westwood called together the relevant local authorities to discuss the development of East Kilbride New Town. By October 1946 he had already designated the land on which the town would be built.

Subsequent commentators have remarked at the speed with which Westwood moved to have Scotland included in the terms of the New Towns Act and to initiate

'Traditional' cottages built in the early 1950s at Prestonpans for 'incoming miners'.

the development of the first such town.[11] Perhaps, however, his haste is not at all surprising. Given that the regional planning/ green belt/ new town strategy was obviously in conflict with the local authority based approach to housing which was being so urgently advanced by George Buchanan and his friends, (and now empowered by the 1946 Housing (Financial Provisions) (Scotland) Act), it seems certain that Westwood came under enormous pressure to abandon the whole approach which he and his colleagues had spent so many of the war years developing. Presumably, therefore, he moved swiftly because he had to do so in order to rescue something from the wreckage. The New Towns Act and the swift designation of the land for East Kilbride can be regarded as something of a salvage gesture by Westwood. It was almost all that he could save, for, with the sole exception of Glenrothes in Fife, he was shortly persuaded or compelled to drop his plans for the ten other intended new towns.

Apart from Jean Mann (by now an MP) and Hugh MacCalman (Chairman of the Clyde Valley Regional Advisory Committee) the Councillors on Glasgow Corporation were almost entirely opposed to a planned programme of overspill. Not surprisingly, the city lodged a vigorous objection to the designation of East Kilbride and the case was heard at an Inquiry in January 1947. MacCalman commented that 'if Glasgow does not think of her industrial future in terms of the region, she is destining her future citizens to become the undistinguished burghers of a decadent town'; but many of his colleagues on the Corporation were committed inflexibly to resolving the city's housing problems via the Council's own housing programme.[12]

From 1942 Glasgow's Master of Works and City Engineer, Robert Bruce, had been working on municipal plans intended to enable the Corporation virtually to reconstruct the city, but by 1944 it was already clear that his scheme would be in conflict with the probable proposals of the regional Planning Committee. If a green belt was imposed, there would be little council controlled land around the edge of the city on which to build new council estates. Nevertheless the Corporation decided to reject the regional approach, resolved to build all the required houses within the city boundaries and Bruce accordingly completed proposals to refashion the city into nineteen neat community areas each accommodating 50,000 people in five neighbourhoods of 10,000 persons.[13]

At the East Kilbride Inquiry, Bruce led most of the case for Glasgow and one of his objections was that construction of the new town would make it more difficult to hang on to the 6,000 construction workers then employed in building council houses for the city. To build the numbers of houses in mind he required a labour force of 12–14,000 men. His main objection, however, was to the green belt which would be bound to limit the amount of available land and, therefore, severely restrict his ambitious plans for the city.[14]

Westwood had already sanctioned the building of the huge estate at Castlemilk on intended green belt land, but he refused to go further. The green belt was imposed – indeed, second thoughts persuaded Westwood to reduce the land approved for Castlemilk – and East Kilbride was formally designated with effect from March 1947.

Left wing opposition to the planned overspill of a part of Glasgow's population and industry had its roots not just in a passionate commitment to council housing, but also in the desire to protect the city's traditional heavy industrial base. The view was that Glasgow had to remain big if it were to have the continued capacity to support ship-building and heavy engineering and left wingers were not willing to contemplate the kind of industrial renewal proposed by the regional planners. One suspects that the politicians were supported in these opinions both by their municipal officials as well as sections of the business community committed to the old industrial structure. Those commercial and other groups which objected to the costs and drastic upheaval implicit in an attempt to reconstruct the city seem to have been more or less ignored. According to the Bruce scheme, many of the workers would have to be relocated to new estates around the edge of the city, but the City Engineer hoped to meet this problem by constructing a new municipal rapid transport system. (Not only in housing does his plan have many of the hallmarks of the post-war cities of eastern Europe.)

Glasgow Corporation, therefore, continued with the attempt to devise its own solution and in the later 1940s modified plans were produced to redevelop the city on a 'community area' basis. However, the situation which emerged was almost the worst possible of muddles. On the one hand Buchanan and his friends had succeeded in a) killing off key elements in the regional planned approach – planned overspill via the full quota of new towns and extensive use of the S.S.H.A. – and b) obtaining for the local authorities (in this case, Glasgow Corporation), the powers and subsidy system needed to carry forward large scale 'general needs' council house building. But on the other hand, Glasgow (and the other cities) now had to deal with those aspects of the regional system which Westwood had salvaged, a green belt which restricted the development land available to the city and the designation and growth of East Kilbride. (Glenrothes in Fife, approved in 1948, was not originally intended as an overspill town, but was rather planned to support the opening of the Rothes colliery. Only from 1962 after heavy underground flooding had aborted the latter project did Scotland's second new town assume a role in overspill.)

Recently the first post-war Labour government has been the subject of heavy criticism, particularly in Correlli Barnett's massively authoritative study, *The Lost Victory : British Dreams, British Realities 1945–1950* (1995).[15] Specifically, Barnett castigates the Attlee government for its failure to give priority to the essential reconstruction and modernisation of the country's obsolete and out-dated industrial base. In the immediate aftermath of shattering military defeat both Germany and Japan funnelled all their energies and resources into new factories, new technologies and into modernising their economic structure and work practices, and Germany, for instance, despite the battering which her cities had sustained during the war, succeeded in restoring no less than 90% of her industrial capacity by as early as 1948. In consequence of this effort and sense of priority these two 'defeated' countries rapidly turned themselves into two of the three major economic powers of the post-war world. By contrast Britain's Labour government gave priority to the immediate effort to improve living standards by means of the creation of the welfare state, the nationalising of the health service and the massive council housing programmes. Moreover, the policy of nationalisation of the coal, steel and railway industries in order to 'protect' employment, merely had the effect of committing the state to the techniques, practices and structures of the decaying economic order of the past and of inhibiting the development of a modern infrastructure. For example, while the Attlee government moved quickly to nationalise the railway and other transport companies, not one mile of motorway was built – blissfully ignoring the obvious examples and significance for the future of the modern roadways constructed by Italy, Germany and the USA in the 1930s. Germany, for instance, had, by 1940, a high speed road system extending to 1,300 miles of autobahnen; but not until eighteen years later was Britain's first short stretch of motorway opened in the form of the Preston by-pass. Not surprisingly, the need for new investment in British car manufacturing was also largely ignored in the immediate post war period, thus handing over to the country's international competitors leadership of what was to prove a key industry of the subsequent fifty years.

In other words, Barnett argues, the first post-war government concentrated on the redistribution and consumption of wealth rather than on giving first attention to the means by which such wealth was to be generated. The 'priorities were monumentally wrong' and a complete contradiction of the warning of the war-time Chancellor of the Exchequer, Sir Kingsley Wood, that 'the time for declaring a dividend on the profits of the Golden Age is the time when those profits have been realised in fact, not merely in imagination'. However, the tragedy is that, once set, the wrong orders of precedence proved appallingly difficult to correct and soon left the British with an inferior economy and living standards well below those enjoyed by their former enemies.

As far as Scotland's economy and her urban communities are concerned, the legacy of this period is well in accord with Barnett's thesis and the consequences of false priorities and misdirected resources proved to be little short of tragic.

The story of the muddle which now distorted the post-war redevelopment of west central Scotland has been well told elsewhere and there is no need to repeat it here in detail.[16] However, the key points are as follows.

Glasgow Corporation pushed ahead as best it could with its own designs, significantly modified in the approved plan of 1951. In this it was aided by the system of controls and licences imposed by George Buchanan which had prevented private developers from taking up some of the available land, thus securing a virtual monopoly position for the council. Inevitably, however, land scarcity dominated municipal thinking with the consequences that the new estates to be built on the periphery of the city were designed to increasingly high densities. The low density 'garden city' approach implicit in regional and new town dispersal was consequently abandoned by the city authorities. Bruce and his colleagues always had assumed widespread use of flats, but they had also initially envisaged a considerable quantity of cottage style housing. Now, however, to accommodate the numbers to be rehoused on a restricted amount of land, cottages almost disappeared from estate plans and ever increasing reliance was placed on rank upon rank of tenements. Almost before the post-war builders were into their stride, therefore, all the war-time guidance and reservations in respect of flatted developments on greenfield sites had been cast aside. Indeed, had they been able at first to build such things there is no doubt that high rise blocks would also have been used to meet the necessary population densities. In 1947 a team from the Corporation visited Marseilles to inspect multi-storey housing in the Le Corbusier mould, but such structures were initially delayed both by inexperience in respect of the required constructional methods and by the cost implications.[17]

During the years around 1950 vigorous efforts were made to produce satisfactory and economic designs for higher density flats, but, as we have seen, such was the scramble for building resources that there was frequent scarcity of materials and labour and, therefore, almost continuous upward pressure on prices. In desperation the Corporation even attempted to obtain S.S.H.A. assistance to lead a move in the direction of high rise flats by pleading with it to produce such buildings at Toryglen, but the Association's leadership of the day was firmly committed to cottage housing. In February 1950 its Council of Management had argued that

> multi-storey flats had certain inherent disadvantages which rendered them less desirable as a family dwelling than the normal two-storey house, and they came to the conclusion that such flats should not be erected, unless it was impossible otherwise to achieve the density fixed by Glasgow Corporation.[18]

Cannily the Association then pointed out to the Corporation that in the face of existing costs, if it did agree to construct high flats, high rent levels would be inevitable. Since the Labour councillors on the Corporation were absolutely committed to a low rent policy supported by a substantial local subsidy and the city's rates were already significantly higher than in comparable cities elsewhere in the U.K., that effectively postponed the construction of the Toryglen high flats for several years.

Some of the earliest post war building was to the east of the city at Barlanark where more than 1900 of the 2300 planned houses were in four-storey tenements. Other similar contemporary developments were at Cranhill, Ruchazie and Garthamlock and at Pollock (where more than 9000 dwellings were completed) initial cottage building rapidly gave way to grey lines of three and four storey tenements. Such estates seemed to mushroom around the city, but with the council now rapidly running up against the green belt some kind of compromise had to be struck between the city and central government.

Bruce resigned in 1951 and the initiative within the city was now taken up under the leadership of the city architect, A G Jury.[19] His subsequent report and 1954 plan, while listing 23 areas for new council housing, also showed an acknowledgement of a requirement for 100,000 overspill houses to be built outwith the city boundaries. As a result the Corporation agreed to repeal its 1946 resolution, which had committed it to rebuilding entirely within the city, and this ultimately permitted designation in 1955 of another overspill new town at Cumbernauld.

However, the Scottish Office had been first to blink as far as the green belt was concerned. Westwood's successor, Arthur Woodburn had sanctioned the expanded development of Castlemilk to the south of Glasgow on additional green belt territory and similar clearance followed to permit other huge estates to go ahead on the protected land at Drumchapel and Easterhouse. Indeed, much of the contemporary developments at Pollock, Priesthill, Nitshill and Darnley were on land which the Clyde Valley Planners had originally also wanted to include in the green belt. These concessions were crucial to some of the most disastrous of the post-war activities of the Corporation for, in the 1950s, and 60s, grim mono-tenure council schemes were constructed in each of these locations and with truly evil consequences.

If, by giving councils virtual domination of house production through the 'general needs' subsidy system, the 1945–51 Labour administration has the main responsibility for much that is most wretched about the housing developments of the post war era, the Conservative ministers of the 1950s are also blameworthy, particularly for their failure to stand up to Glasgow Corporation and to protect the green belt. Had they done so, much damage and distress might have been avoided.

For example, the 1954 Jury plan reduced the requirement for new houses to be built in the city from 73,000 to a mere 30,000, yet by 1959 no less than 45,000 houses had already been built in the peripheral estates and work was continuing at a furious pace. Much of this could have been contained had the Conservative governments of 1951 to 1964 been prepared to adopt a more sceptical line and to challenge the system which they had inherited.

The estates in question were massive and the numbers of dwellings ultimately constructed in the main ones are indicated below.[20]

Castlemilk   9,700
Drumchapel 10,345
Easterhouse 14,959
Pollock   11,566

Overwhelmingly the accommodation was in the form of three and four apartment tenement flats and in an era when average household size in Scotland was 3.5 persons, this means that these entirely single tenure estates were intended to house communities of from approximately 34,000 people, in the case of Castlemilk, to 52,000 people in Easterhouse.

The significance of this activity will be discussed further later, but at the moment it should be noted that in the rush to build houses (and in dramatic and devastating contrast with the new town development process) consideration of the wider needs of these new communities was given scant attention. At first, for example, schools were not adequately provided in Castlemilk and for several years children had to be bussed back to the old schools in the central areas. Similary cinemas, public halls, and other community facilities did not appear, being at first deferred and then

Typical 1950s peripheral estate tenements.

subsequently virtually forgotten. Even decent pubs were not built, as much as anything falling foul of archaic corporation licensing laws. Shopping facilities were typically utterly inadequate, being confined to a few purpose-built outlets where the high rents inevitably led to high prices. Major retailers showed no willingness to move out to the new estates hence, from the beginning, the tenants, whose incomes were usually low in the first place, were confronted with either buying expensive products from a very limited range or paying the additional cost of travelling to the inner city shops. Finally, also often neglected were the churches which, contrary to popular belief, had frequently flourished in the old inner city parishes.[21] Transplantation of churches to the peripheral estates proved almost impossible to effect and the ground lost by almost all denominations at this time has never been recovered. Key traditional institutions around which a multitude of organisations, clubs and societies had hinged, therefore, almost disappeared from the lives of thousands of tenants and their families. Time after time this pattern of neglect and social and economic disruption was repeated in the peripheral estates of Glasgow and in other large contemporary developments.

The forms of development adopted by Glasgow were repeated elsewhere so that similar estates rapidly appeared around towns such as Airdrie, Coatbridge, Motherwell, Port Glasgow, Clydebank and Dundee. Of course they were not of the sheer size of Drumchapel etc, but relative to their own towns they were often big and they were invariably single tenure in form. Edinburgh was, at this stage, rather more restrained and most of the work in the 1940s and 50s to extend inter-war council schemes at locations such as Sighthill, Bingham and Moredun tended still to rely on cottages or four-in-a-block flats, but some of the work being conducted at Craigmillar and Niddrie became more ominous as the 1950s advanced and some fairly dire building was done to the north of the city at West Pilton. Ironically, in this period the philosophy of the garden village estate of houses and gardens was most vividly being given expression a mere seven miles from Castlemilk in the new town of East Kilbride where by 1959, the ratio of houses to flats was of the order of 70% to 30%.

The official Scottish house building returns for the 1950s are as follows.

	Local Auth's	New Town	SSHA	Other Housing Assoc's	Govt. Depts.	Total Public Sector	Private Sector	Total
1950	20,989	158	3,167	91	624	25,029	782	25,811
1951	17,971	120	2,906	139	647	21,783	1,145	22,928
1952	22,393	485	4,745	285	797	28,705	2,242	30,947
1953	29,719	1,316	4,957	217	946	37,155	2,393	39,548
1954	29,748	1,466	4,117	115	799	36,245	2,608	38,853
1955	24,210	1,323	3,745	131	1,137	30,546	3,523	34,069
1956	22,084	1,073	3,133	148	887	27,325	4,576	31,901
1957	24,239	951	3,136	105	493	28,924	3,513	32,437
1958	22,622	1,474	3,277	93	643	28,109	4,061	32,170
1959	18,665	1,551	2,493	4	348	23,061	4,232	27,293
1960	17,913	1,519	2,071	127	433	22,063	6,529	28,592

These figures illustrate many aspects of the effects of policies throughout the period. The most obvious feature is the way in which building by the public authorities remained dominant while private construction was a relatively minor source of new houses in Scotland over the decade. Right at the beginning of the period production of dwellings for the private buyer had fallen from 1,541 in 1948 to a mere 782 in 1950 and this was a direct result of Government measures following the devaluation crisis of 1949. Confronted with the need to reduce public spending and to restrain imports of construction materials, the Government was forced to cut back on housing expenditure. Aneurin Bevan, however, was 'anxious that the £35 millions of cuts proposed should fall on houses built privately for owner occupation, and that there should be no reduction in houses built by the local authorities'.[22] Accordingly, the controls on the private developer were further tightened.

Public building did not entirely escape this episode however and a drop in output in this sector in 1951 can also be seen. More significant were the simultaneous measures to reduce building costs. Interestingly, A.E.Holmans has pointed out that in the U.K.

> between 1938 and 1947 building costs increased in real terms by about 35%, and unlike the increase in building costs between 1913 and 1920, was never fully reversed. By the early 1960s building costs had fallen back by about 10% in real terms compared with 1947–48, but that still left them some 20% higher than before the war.'[23]

Holmans then goes on to remark that a 'wholly convincing explanation' is lacking as to why the fall in productivity of the war years was not subsequently made good.

In fact, however, it seems probable that public sector production involving the extensive use of high priced factory made sponsored housing was at the root of the problem. In the post war years the Government relied heavily on such houses. Why they should have been more expensive than traditional houses can only be explained either by the relative cost of raw materials or by costs linked to factory production. Since both steel and concrete houses were affected, raw material prices do not seem likely to have been the major problem. Indeed this view is supported by the fact that the SSHA's own no-fines concrete houses were sometimes cheaper even than traditional houses. It seems obvious, therefore, that the relatively expensive labour cost patterns in the industrial factories which were transferred to house manufacture at the end of the war had the effect of dragging up the scale of costs throughout the traditional building industry. Whatever the explanation, it is clear that the Labour Government was at first quite prepared to tolerate uneconomic production of a significant proportion of houses in order to maintain employment in the factories in question. (This is a good example of the profligate misuse of resources condemned by Barnett.)

By 1949 the 30% devaluation in the currency forced a closer examination of the cost of the housing programme and the SSHA was among those to whom Prime Minister Attlee appealed for help. Writing on his behalf to the Association in

Ministry of Housing and Local Government/Ministry of Works Timber Economy Construction. These houses, built in 1952–53, are of traditional brick, but demonstrated various means by which softwood timber could be replaced by other materials either home produced or imported from within the Sterling area.

October 1949 the Secretary of State explained that while no reduction was intended in the public sector programme, it would be necessary to reduce costs by building more 3 apartment houses, by otherwise reducing the size of dwellings and by making such other economies in designs as could be devised.[24]

The Association responded to this appeal in two ways. First, at the Sighthill experimental development it co-operated with staff of the Department of Health for Scotland, the Ministry of Housing and Local Government and the Ministry of Fuel and Power in designing and erecting a number of specimen houses with reduced space standards, more economic use of softwood and more efficient forms of space heating.[25] Secondly, it turned back increasingly to developing improved techniques of deploying the no-fines method of *in situ* construction which it had devised before the war, but had been prevented from using in the 1940s.[26] Each of these initiatives were being deployed from 1950–51.

In October 1951 the Conservatives returned to power when responsibility for housing in England and Wales was assumed by the new Minister of Housing, Harold Macmillan with a national production target of 300,000 houses per annum.[27] As can be seen from the figures noted above, production in Scotland jumped to record totals of 30,947 in 1952, 39,548 in 1953 and 38,853 in 1954. Noticeably there was a significant improvement in private production, but it is clear that to make good their promise the Conservatives remained overwhelmingly dependent on the public sector and stimulated a fresh surge of building wherein

Department of Health for Scotland 'space saving low cost cottages' built at Sighthill in 1952.

numerical targets took precedence over considerations of quality or social and economic development.

The new minister with responsibility for housing in Scotland was Commander Galbraith (later Lord Strathclyde) and to speed the flow he made full use of the economic methods developed by the SSHA and others in the preceding years. The Association's general manager explained his desire to concentrate more fully on no-fines building by explaining 'that a squad of 25 men – 50% unskilled – could pour 10 houses per week' and that further improvements and efficiencies in production were in course of development.[28] Costs of no-fines cottages were thereafter carefully monitored and in 1952 it was indicated that the average cost of building a no-fines cottage in a 100 house scheme at Prestonpans 'was £1,395, which was equivalent to a rate of 29/3d per square foot'.[29] This compared very favourably with other techniques, but full economy could only be achieved in substantial schemes where the capital costs of the steel shutters required in the construction process were spread over a reasonable number of houses and where men could move swiftly from one task to another. Depending on the size of development, no-fines seems to have been much cheaper than sponsored houses, but, where small numbers of buildings were involved, it could be more expensive than traditional methods.

The no-fines cottage proved not only to be economic, but, given effective on site supervision and good basic design, the method was also capable of producing

No-fines concrete cottages erected at Corpach by the SSHA for Inverness County Council.

sound, varied and attractive dwellings which have subsequently stood up to the test of time. Moreover, it allowed greater reliance to be placed on direct labour for actual building rather than site servicing. Not surprisingly, therefore, the Association pressed to be allowed to concentrate on this technique while abandoning the more expensive factory made sponsored houses.

By this time the Association and councils were becoming increasingly concerned not only at the costs of sponsored houses, but also at the inferior quality now being revealed in some types. The Weir steel houses, for example, suffered from significant early deterioration in external harling and corrosion and this resulted in a protracted dispute between the company and the Association.[30] Eventually Weir decided to concentrate on Swedish timber dwellings and on its own no-fines method. This decision was encouraged when the firm won an intense competition in 1952 which resulted in 3000 or so of its timber houses being erected for various Scottish councils. Even today these houses are perhaps the most familiar wooden structures in the Scottish urban landscape.

However, confronted with increasingly clear evidence of the poor value for money represented by the sponsored houses, the government at first prevaricated on the question of continued use of such types. The minister spoke of the 'various interests' involved in the building industry 'which had to be reconciled', but he did encourage the Association to press ahead with developing no-fines and permitted it to refuse quotations for excessively expensive houses.[31]

The figures of production in the 1950s show that the SSHA made a useful contribution throughout the decade and it had certainly contributed to an easing

Weir timber house. This design won a hotly contested tender competition organised by the Department of Health for Scotland in 1952. The prize was a centrally placed bulk order and, after the above model was demonstrated at Sighthill, about 3000 similar houses were erected in various parts of Scotland.

of the worst of the post war housing crisis, particularly in the smaller towns, in rural areas and in the mining communities, but also in larger towns such as Clydebank, Hamilton and Kilmarnock, as well as the cities of Aberdeen and Dundee. It had also made a small contribution in Glasgow, at Balornock and Cadder and from 1950 it had commenced a bigger development in the city at Toryglen.

Early in 1955 the Association completed its thirty thousandth house – a long way short of Tom Johnston's intentions for it in the first decade of peace, but still a substantial contribution. On a calendar year basis, from 1945 to the end of 1954, 209,366 public sector houses were built in Scotland and, of these, the SSHA contributed 29,361, or approximately 14 per cent. According to the *Guide to Non-Traditional Housing in Scotland*, 100,000 houses of non-traditional construction were built in the kingdom over these years. That total presumably includes both SSHA and sponsored no-fines houses, since these are listed in the guide, and the 'transitional period' 'prefabs' which are also listed. Discounting transitional housing, would indicate that 70,000 permanent non-traditional sponsored houses were erected in Scotland.[32]

Department of Health Circular No.82–1954 signalled the formal end to this phase by announcing that, as from 1st January, 1955 central control of non-traditional house building would cease and that local authorities could henceforth select designs – which would no longer be classified as traditional or non-traditional – in direct consultation with the various contractors and promoters.[33] At about the same time the last of the licence restrictions on development for the private market were removed.

When the Conservatives were elected in 1951 a lively debate was under way as to the future of the SSHA. The roots of this dispute go back to George Buchanan's tenure as housing minister, for he had made it very difficult to operate a realistic rent policy and had delayed the formulation of such a policy for many months.

The Association was expected to set rents which would enable it to function ideally with no more assistance than normal Exchequer subsidies plus an allowance equivalent to the rate support given in typical local authority schemes. The Association had to consult local authorities about rent levels, had to take whichever tenants the councils nominated without regard to their ability to pay and its houses (unlike those of councils) were subject to the Rent Restrictions Acts, hence, once fixed, its rents could not be increased. Moreover, there was a very awkward contradiction in government policy. On the one hand, while the Association was instructed that, in accordance with the 'general needs' policy, public sector houses were no longer intended solely for low income households, the Treasury tried to insist that better off tenants should be excluded from houses which had a deficit subsidy. Mr Buchanan, however, would not agree to rent levels which avoided a deficit; and while he accepted the need for a rent rebate scheme for poorer tenants he rejected its introduction where the local authorities (notably Glasgow) were opposed to such a system.

This was an impossible situation and inevitably there were many months of sometimes heated negotiations. Eventually, following Buchanan's departure, Association rents were approved in the range £35 to £39 per annum in the cities and £29 to £35 elsewhere for houses of three, four and five apartments; and a rebate fund of up to £2 per house was establish to give relief if necessary and where the local authority agreed. The result of this was that Association rents were significantly higher than the rents levied by most local authorities, but, almost as awkwardly, lower than those applied elsewhere. As a consequence, there was a stream of protests from councils and several refused to factor Association houses, thereby forcing it to develop its own management structure in many parts of the country.[34]

The rent problem added to local authority hostility towards the SSHA and strained the relations between the organisation and some sections of the Labour Party. The Councils of Fife and Clackmannan Counties and of Kirkcaldy, Hamilton and Motherwell demanded that the SSHA's houses in their areas be handed over to them and several Trades Councils urged the Secretary of State to transfer all Association houses to the local authorities.[35] The matter was thereafter taken up in 1951 by the Parliamentary Party. However, the government chose to defer its decision until after the election of October, hence the issue was left to the verdict of the incoming Conservative government.

In a memorandum of 13 November 1951 the position was succinctly summarised for the new minister. Arguments in favour of retaining the Association were that it provided an important source of financial assistance to weaker councils; it enabled the Scottish Office to pursue a 'housing policy affecting national as distinct from local interests'; the Direct Labour Organisation was useful as was the Association's work on non-traditional houses; and the Association was an alternative builder for authorities confronted by excessively high tenders. On the other hand, it was recognised that the Association was disliked by some councils which regarded it as 'usurping their functions', that where its rents were higher there was particular resentment, that it competed with councils for scarce resources, and that there would be a saving to the Exchequer as a result of winding up the organisation.[36]

Galbraith also had some reservations about the Association, drawing attention to a complaint from a contractor who had protested about what were regarded as the Association's unnecessarily high standards in houses being built for forestry workers. However, officials, including Sir George Henderson and Craig Mitchell, fought hard to retain what they obviously valued as a mechanism which enabled the Department to intervene directly in housing throughout Scotland, hence by the end of November the Minister had been persuaded to allow it to continue operations. Even then, however, the matter was not entirely settled for several months later Lord Home, the Minister of State, asked for further clarification. A memorandum of April 1952 explained to him that criticism of the Association typically came from two main sources –

a) from left-wing Councils who favour a low rent policy and dislike the Association because of the higher rents (it) must necessarily charge;
and
b) from private builders who see in the development of the Association's direct labour organisation a possible threat to their interests.[37]

Given its commitment to increased house production, there seems little likelihood that the new government seriously considered scrapping the SSHA and the memo to Lord Home more or less ended the episode. Thereafter under the succession of Conservative administrations the Association gradually returned to a position of influence in the development and discharge of Scottish housing policy. Despite the fact that controls on the private builders were relaxed through the 1950s, in the period 1950–59 the SSHA comfortably outstripped the entire Scottish output for private purchase, producing 35,676 houses against just 29,075. Peak years for the Association were 1952 to 1955. These figures, of course, were far below the 232,640 houses built for Scottish local councils in the same period.

That rent levels were a source of tension between the SSHA and certain local authorities is not at all surprising. As was indicated in the opening chapter, Glasgow had a long tradition of low rents in the private rented sector and this situation had become a virtual fixture from the First War as a consequence of the Rent Restrictions Acts. However, the same phenomenon had taken firm root in respect of much of Scotland's local authority housing. The 1935 Housing (Scotland) Act had, with little or no restriction, allowed councils to subsidise their Housing Revenue

Accounts out of local rate borne taxes. As Miles Horsey has expressed it, at a time when rent controls and the liability of private landlords for rates were combining to push Glasgow's privately owned older tenements deeper into decay, 'local authorities were converting the legacy of polarised pre-war landlord-tenant relations into a political power-base of low-rent housing for middle and working classes alike'.[38] In other words, a system of low council house rents supported by rate borne subsidy was a key element in the post-war housing policies of Glasgow's Labour group. Factors such as the true costs of maintaining decent housing were ignored with, inevitably, grim consequences for housing quality and for the lives of subsequent tenants.

It is perhaps worth reflecting further on this political dimension to attitudes towards housing. In one sense the ideology involved may have meant that some socialist politicians of the day were concerned to produce housing which was identifiably 'working class' in character, and which would thereby encourage communal attitudes or solidarity of political outlook and behaviour. In these terms council housing had perhaps to look 'industrial', to be uniform in appearance, to be accessible by a wide section of the community and to be obviously associated with a low rent philosophy. The trouble was, however, that this was precisely a formula for rapidly turning 'working class' housing into bad housing. And, of course, its articulation gave some form of political respectability to the absurd notion that reasonable housing could be made generally available at little personal cost.

As Horsey indicates, a part of the background to the problem was the muddled relationship between rents and rates which then existed in Scotland whereby the rates were fixed in accordance with the rent level attached to a property and were payable partly by the occupier and partly by the owner. In these circumstances, private landlords, with their rents controlled, were in an almost impossible position, being quite unable to recoup the rate burden by raising rents. Moreover, although local authorities were not subject to the Rent Restrictions Acts, the connection between rent levels and rateable values made it impossible simply to increase rents without also increasing rates. The upshot of this was that (as was pointed out in the annual report of the Department of Health for Scotland in 1952) whereas the average rent of a council house had risen from £18 17s 7d in 1938 to £23 16s 1d in 1951 (an increase of 20%), in the same period the cost of building material had increased by 200% and the growth of earnings in the building industry was 130%. Similarly, the average annual rent of a pre-war council house rose from £21 2s 6d in 1949 to £23 8s 2d in 1956, an 11% increase, at a time when the general index of retail prices had grown by 38%. Clearly, the economic base of public rented housing in parts of Scotland was progressively losing touch with reality.

It was in an effort to resolve the problem that the government introduced first, the Housing (Repairs and Rents) (Scotland) Act, 1954 which allowed owners of controlled houses to increase rents by two-fifths on condition that the properties were in good order; and second, the Valuation and Rating (Scotland) Act 1956, which separated rateable values from actual rents and abolished owners' rates. When this was done the ridiculously low real levels to which many local authority rents had sunk was clearly revealed, for the average council rent in 1957 was shown to be a mere 5s 6d per week. It is hard to escape the conclusion that these economic considerations provide an important explanation for the progressive decline in the quality of much urban council housing.

The government issued a circular in June, 1956, pointing out that whereas in 1938 rent had accounted for 10.5% of average earnings, by 1955 the proportion was only 4.5%. Accordingly authorities were urged to review their rent levels on the basis that –

> a) subsidies ought not to be given to those who did not need them:
> b) no one in genuine need of a house should be asked to pay more rent than he can reasonably afford.

From then on the government repeatedly exhorted local authorities to put their rent levels on a more reasonable footing and this marked the start of a period of considerable tension between central and local government.[39]

The main problem, of course, was that too great a proportion of the housing budget was having to be borne by the ratepayers and, in addition to objecting to this in principle, it was the government's view that high rates were damaging Scotland's ability to sustain a healthy economy. A government circular to local authorities in 1962 stated the case. 'A policy of keeping rents artificially low is unfair to rate payers with low incomes who are not in council houses and is prejudicial to the long term interests of the area and indeed the country as a whole'.[40] A little earlier the Secretary of State told MPs; 'experience shows that the low rent tradition ... stamps an area as industrially and socially old-fashioned, so that new industry tends to hesitate before seeking new investment and providing new employment in such areas'.[41] Writing of this period John Gibson concluded that council rents 'were often much too low to the detriment of the town or county council's ability to embark on other services or on work which should have gone hand in hand with new housing as, say, the building of community centres and other amenities'.[42]

If the problem was general, unsurprisingly it was particularly acute in the case of Glasgow. Following successive comments by the auditor on Glasgow Housing Accounts for 1955, 1956 and 1957, and a complaint to the Secretary of State from a councillor, a formal enquiry was held under the chairmanship of Mr C.J.D. Shaw, QC, (later Lord Kilbrandon) into the city's failure to review rents under the Housing (Scotland) Act of 1950. His report found that the Corporation had failed to discharge its statutory duties, and in 1959 city rents were increased from an average of 5s 2d per week to 8s 5d (or £21 17s 8d per annum).[43]

Inevitably the SSHA was caught up in the rent conflict between the government and local authorities. The Association had been freed from the terms of the Rent Restrictions Acts in 1954 and, in 1958, it announced its intention to increase rents to £33, £36 and £39 per annum for three-, four- and five-apartment houses respectively, and to introduce an improved rent rebate system for those in hardship. These were general proposals which could not be fully implemented because the government would not sanction specific increases greater than 7s 6d per week, but it nevertheless insisted that in the minority of cases where local authority rents were higher the Association should, as far as possible, match their levels.[44]

The Association's increases provoked uproar among certain councils and stimulated a serious rent strike with thousands of tenants, particularly in the Glasgow area, declining to pay. (The rent strike, of course, had a deep-rooted place in the mythology of working class Glasgow.) When the Association's chairman, Sir Ronald Thomson, was confronted by a delegation from Glasgow Corporation he rejected their request to cancel the proposed rent increases. He explained that half of the cost of Association houses was already being met by Treasury subsidy and that the burden of debt was increasing. He argued that the new rents were fair and realistic and that when rents and rates were both taken into account the cost to Glasgow tenants compared very favourably with the situation of tenants in other parts of the country. He indicated for example, that the

> total outgoings of a tenant of a three-apartment house in Birmingham were 35s 5d per week, in Carlisle, 28s 6d per week, and in Coventry, 37s 3d per week, as compared with 30s 7d in Glasgow under the Association's proposal and 21s under the Corporation's present rent policy.[45]

This episode stimulated a fresh outburst of local authority hostility towards the Association and among the many complaints came one from Saltcoats Town Council demanding to buy the 260 Association houses in the burgh. (Around this time Saltcoats claimed to have the lowest council house rents in the country.) Other councils reacted by declining to factor houses on behalf of the Association or refusing to collect the additional rent, but this only succeeded in encouraging the Association in a rapid extension of its own Housing Management division under the leadership of the admirable Jean B. Pollock.[46] Several court battles were fought (with Midlothian County Council among other authorities, and against tenants to recover rent arrears) before the increases were imposed. Thereafter, the rent strike gradually collapsed. But it was a long battle, for as late as April 1960 1,270 of the Association's tenants (most in the Glasgow area) were still refusing to pay. By the following October, however, the last of the tenants had given up the struggle.[47]

Examination of the Association's accounts over the period gives an interesting indication of the effects of the changes in rent policy. A striking feature is the operation of the new rent rebate scheme. Tenants in receipt of help are shown to have increased from a mere 4 in 1957–58 to 8,344 two years later and the total amount given in relief to Association tenants increased in the same period from just £23 to £103,393. However, a key consideration is that the new rents enabled the Association to increase sharply the amount spent on the maintenance of its houses from £271,252 in 1957–58 to over £389,000 in 1959–1960. Finally, it does seem that the move to direct management for the bulk of properties brought a significant initial growth in management cost per house, although, with the increase in rents, as a percentage of rent receivable, management costs are shown as having reduced.[48]

As has been explained, one of the key contributions made by the SSHA in the early 1950s was its recovery and further development of the no-fines process of house building. Association technical officers extended their knowledge of the system by studying its use in both Holland and Germany.[49] Interestingly the Germans in particular had turned to the method in the immediate post-war period to assist in the speedy and cost-effective reconstruction of their war-battered towns and cities. Not only did no-fines concrete produce rapid results from an unskilled labour force, it also enabled much of the rubble and waste material of bomb damaged buildings to be recycled as aggregate.

In Scotland, properly used, the system produced satisfactory and economic houses and these comprised an increasing component of output in the first half of the 1950s. However, a constructional method which had been seen by the SSHA as a means of rapidly erecting cottage type houses proved itself to be readily adaptable for the purposes of building three- and four- storey tenement blocks of flats and even multi-storey buildings of up to ten storeys in height. The latter were never built in very large numbers (although curiously those that were built have subsequently proved to be well-liked by tenants), but the former were enthusiastically seized upon by those authorities which aspired to high density developments.

In the very early 1950s the Association remained committed to the cottage, but the 1952 replacement of A.G. McBain as chairman by Sir Ronald J Thomson may have introduced a gradual change in attitude. Certainly senior technical staff had argued for some time in favour of flats, both in order to encourage the Association's inclusion in building operations in Glasgow and other cities as well as in the interests of the presumed prestige associated with the creation of high rise buildings.[50] However, McBain and his senior colleague, Thomas Paterson of Ayr, both appear to have led the Council of Management opposition to the trend. With McBain's departure (appropriately, he became a member of East Kilbride Development Corporation) the position seems to have changed and flats rapidly became favoured in the attempt to increase production and to reduce costs in the Conservative's housing campaign from 1952.

The Association first turned to three- and four-storey no-fines tenements at Glasgow's peripheral Arden development, at the huge Faifley estate above Clydebank and around the edge of Fintry to the north of Dundee. In retrospect, this was a disaster, which was to produce some of the worst houses constructed by the Association throughout its entire history. At Arden and Faifley the buildings descended to the levels of the poorest contemporary council estates, while at Fintry the position was particularly poignant. There, the SSHA had constructed a large, but reasonable development involving various house types and laid out on what Charles McKean has characterised as *bastard garden city* principles.[51] Now, however, there appeared around the rim of the estate a rank of grey, ugly four storey tenements backing almost obscenely into the green belt countryside beyond the city boundary and inevitably depressing much of the character of the place.

Concrete tenements built at Faifley, Clydebank.

Fintry, Dundee.

If, in the second part of the 1950s, the SSHA began to produce some of its least effective housing, this merely tends to illustrate the way in which this highly professional central government controlled organisation was drawn into the disaster which now overtook much of Scottish public sector housing. Before describing the events and significance of the later 1950s and 1960s, however, it may be appropriate to recall the context against which housing policies of the period should be considered.

Despite the repeated economic crises experienced by governments and a gathering sense of unease at the way in which the economy was being outstripped by progress in other countries, the quarter of a century following the end of the war was a time of considerable prosperity during which the wealth of the U.K. virtually doubled. World trade grew rapidly; a host of technological advances – jet propulsion, radar etc – stimulated by war could now be exploited for peaceful commercial purposes; the Korean War and the onset of the long-drawn 'cold war' provided an ongoing military/technological stimulus – including, until 1962, employment for young men in the form of conscription; and, of course, the building programmes promoted activity in many parts of the economy. Overall, these years were characterised by sustained growth (roughly 2.5% per annum), by full employment (at certain times and in certain industries verging on chronic labour scarcity), and by relatively low rates of inflation for most of the period. The principal beneficiaries were working people – particularly clerical, semi-skilled and unskilled workers – who gained most from the high levels of employment and the developed system of social security. Real earnings of this group increased more than for others so that there was a general narrowing of income differentials between professional and manual workers, between skilled and unskilled. In addition, the buoyant labour market and wider access to education produced a marked growth in employment opportunities for women and an increase in the tendency of married women either to remain in paid employment or to return to employment after having their children.

By 1961 Scotland's population had almost stabilised at about 5.2 millions and, after the brief upturn between 1940 and 1959, average family size began once more to decline.[52] With more people living longer, the average age of the population began to rise, while the divorce rate increased sharply from the 1960s. One consequence was a gradual and long-run increase in the number of Scottish households.

The characteristic features of this era, perhaps encapsulated in Harold Macmillan's 'never had it so good' slogan for the 1959 general election, were a massive growth in consumer spending and steadily rising living standards for much of the population. In the years 1961 to 1973 consumer expenditure in real terms increased by 39 per cent, and growth in spending on household durables was particularly spectacular – up by 119% on electrical goods and 50% for other household items. Increasingly the demand was for equipment such as automatic washing machines, spin driers, vacuum cleaners, refrigerators, food mixers, television sets and so on, all of which tended to enhance the convenience and quality of household living. Nothing, however, was more remarkable than the growth in demand for motor vehicles, the number of licensed vehicles in the U.K. increasing from 4.3 millions in 1951 to 16.5 millions in 1973.[53]

The impact of these developments on the housing requirements of consumers was inevitably considerable. The motor car, for example, enabled an increasing number of people to live further and further from their places of employment and this increased the ability of sections of the population to move away from the old urban centres. In the 1990s we are, of course, conscious of the traffic congestion and pollution problems associated with a large commuter population, but the factor which enabled its development in the years since the war is fundamentally the exceptional efficiency of the personal motor vehicle in moving individuals precisely from a multitude of points of departure to a multitude of destinations. The blunt fact is that the motor car dramatically changed the physical mobility of much of the labour force in a manner far beyond the scope of even the most advanced form of public transport.

In these years, therefore, economic and social developments were gradually producing what came to be called the 'consumer society', and as the wealth and independence of individuals and households tended to increase, so many of the older social and traditional ties and groupings began to weaken and disintegrate. For example, the size of the labour force in a typical work place decreased dramatically. Large heavy industrial factories, mines or shipyards with overwhelmingly male employees became less and less common while the real growth areas in employment tended to be either in light engineering such as electronics or, even more, within the service sector, where gender divisions in the nature of work were increasingly blurred and where the work forces were often relatively small. Individual outlooks, individual qualifications and prospects and individual or nuclear family interests tended to be enhanced by such developments while wider community or group attitudes or activities were slowly eroded. In particular, the collectivist attitudes and solutions which had been favoured immediately after the war gradually became more difficult to sustain, increasingly being regarded as inefficient, restrictive and frustrating to individual aspirations.

By the mid 1950s it was becoming clear to central government that the worst of the post war housing crisis had been resolved and, as we have seen, from 1955 it ended its support for factory made sponsored houses. At the same time it relaxed the controls which had restrained building for the private market and Scottish output in this sector jumped from 2,608 houses in 1954 to 6,529 by 1960. In England and Wales the comparable returns are 88,000 and 162,000 houses respectively. South of the border completions in the private sector exceeded those of the public sector by 1958 when 124,087 private houses were built as compared to 117,438 council houses.[54] Thereafter, while public construction remained overwhelmingly dominant in Scotland the lion's share of provision to the south was in the hands of private developers and for the next two decades there was a progressive divergence in the nature of housing output north and south of the border.

Slum housing in the Gorbals in the mid 1950s.

In Scotland the government chose to continue to rely heavily on the public sector and mainly on local authorities providing for 'general needs'. Part of the reason for this was connected with a continuing recognition of the problems which still confronted some of the cities, and particularly Glasgow.

> Glasgow's congestion in 1956 was unparalleled in the United Kingdom: 700,000 people were living in the centre of the city … Housing standards in these areas were unbelievably low: 43 per cent of all houses in the city were of one or two rooms, compared with only 5 per cent in London and 2.5 per cent on Merseyside; 30 per cent of Glasgow's families shared toilets compared with 2.6 per cent in London and 1.1 per cent on Merseyside.[55]

It was this situation that persuaded the government to designate Cumbernauld in 1955 and to pass the Housing and Town Development Act of 1957 which set out the procedures by means of which the 'Overspill' programme would be carried forward. Under this scheme other towns and cities – initially in the Clyde valley, but later all over Scotland – were encouraged to accept some of Glasgow's citizens. To assist this process, the SSHA was authorised to build half the required houses in the new locations and grants were made available to provide shopping centres, enhanced sewage services and to enable Glasgow businesses to relocate to provide jobs for the migrating workers.[56]

So far so good, and the policies indicated above did have many good effects. Cumbernauld, as with East Kilbride, proved to be an economic growth point, although both new towns also provided for the residential needs of a burgeoning commuter population which continued to work in Glasgow. Unfortunately to speed progress in its early years the Cumbernauld Development Corporation deployed some of the contemporary high density structural forms and this was to leave it with a significant legacy of poor housing. However, this phase passed and the town soon came to play its useful part in the redevelopment of central Scotland.

Similarly, the overspill programme resulted in developments in many towns such as Irvine, Kirkintilloch, Grangemouth, Johnstone, Arbroath, Whitburn, Bathgate, Hamilton and even Fort William. As far as the SSHA was concerned, the peak year of activity in this area was 1963 when it completed over 1,000 overspill houses.[57] As with Cumbernauld, some of the early buildings were far from ideal – notably in Grangemouth – but most developments were good and generally blended indistinguishably into the host communities.

In 1962 and 1966 Livingston and Irvine respectively were designated as new towns and activities in these locations thereafter proceeded under development corporation guidance. However, the overspill programme seems to have resulted in about 20,000 houses being built in various parts of the country, just over 10,000 of these being provided by the SSHA. This was almost certainly much less of an achievement than was originally hoped, but a key problem inhibiting the success of the venture was always the failure of industry to migrate successfully to the new locations.

On balance, therefore, it may be argued that both the new towns and, to a lesser

The first no-fines 10-storey high rise buildings being constructed at Toryglen, Glasgow in 1956.

extent, the Overspill programme can be regarded as useful and forward looking initiatives of the 1950s. However, what the government failed to address at that time were the problems associated with the growth of a local government dominated housing system. Indeed, in December 1954 the government took the fateful decision to make available to both the local authorities and the SSHA an additional subsidy of £10. 10s per house for flats built above the ground floor level and, in so doing stimulated the trend towards high density high rise building.[58] Glasgow had produced its first 10-storey tenement at Moss Heights at Cardonald by 1953 and now the SSHA was specifically encouraged by the minister, Commander Galbraith, to push ahead with developing its own smaller scale ten storey no-fines blocks at Toryglen and at Dryburgh in Dundee.[59] These pointed the way ahead to much higher structures built by different techniques. If introduction of the new subsidy was, in retrospect, to prove an unfortunate move, even more serious was the failure by government to re-examine the problems being created by the local-authority-based 'general needs' housing policy.

Toryglen as completed.

As was described in the previous chapter, the war-time planners at the Scottish Office led by Tom Johston had intended that local authorities would build roughly half the required houses in a post-war programme extending over a specific period limited to ten years from the end of the war. In fact, of course, mainly as a result of the policies pursued by George Buchanan and his colleagues, councils had been enabled largely to dominate output to 1955.

Completed Houses Scotland 1945–1955

Sector	Total Output	% Output
Private Sector	17,330	6.7
Local Authorities	195,240	75.9
Combined Public Sector	239,912	93.3
Total	257,242	100

At the end of the ten year period a major review of the emerging situation might surely have called forth a degree of caution, but since Harold Macmillan had been willing to make full use of the councils in his initial housing drive, presumably his promotion first to the office of Chancellor and then to the premiership in 1957 ended the immediate prospect for any reconsideration of the fundamental strategy. It is, of course, true that the government expected and intended that more and more of the housing requirement should be met by private enterprise and that public authority housing should increasingly be only for those who could

A 10-storey block at Dryburgh, Dundee.

'neither afford to buy or pay economic rents.' However, while general needs subsidies were initially reduced, under the Acts of 1956 and 1961 increased subsidies were made available for housing built in support of slum clearance or approved municipal developments. In England while some urban authorities shared the Scottish enthusiasm for council housing others were happy to allow the private sector to forge ahead, hence as we have seen, in England the balance increasingly favoured private building. By contrast in much of Scotland the post-war trend was confirmed.

Clearly the need to tackle the problems of Glasgow was a key factor as far as Scottish ministers were concerned, but also very significant were the problems of the house building agencies which had been built up since the war. As the production figures for the mid 1950s show, public sector output slowed down in the second half of the decade, falling from 36,245 in 1954 to 27,325 by 1956, and stabilising about that level before dipping again to 23,061 in 1959. These were the years by which time the land shortage facing Glasgow had become most acute and before full momentum had been gained by both the Cumbernauld and overspill programmes. This slow-down caused acute problems for the managers of public sector building divisions and throughout the period, for example, members of the SSHA's Council of Management and their senior officials were repeatedly urging on ministers the need for new building programmes if their labour force was to be maintained.[60] In fact, the development of high rise no-fines techniques was encouraged principally to enable the organisation to become significantly involved in building activities in Glasgow and the Association's participation in Overspill was fundamentally in answer to pleas in respect of the need to justify the administrative and building labour staffs then employed. Indeed, at the very end of the decade – in the run into the general election of 1959 – the Association was given an additional programme of houses which was specifically intended to promote employment. This 'unemployment programme' was eventually calculated to have created directly 720 additional jobs in Lanarkshire and one or two other areas where there was relative job shortage while indirectly it presumably secured a number of other positions.[61]

What was true for the SSHA was clearly also true for the other public authorities which, in the post war period, had assembled huge house-building bureaucracies and an army of operatives. At the height of its activities in the 1950s the Association employed roughly 5600 workers on its operations and about 2000 of these were typically engaged by the Building Department (direct labour).[62] As was noted earlier, Glasgow provided building work for even greater numbers and, of course, the other large local authorities also had become major building employers.

Moreover, it has to be recognised that the wider construction industry had also developed major interests in the business of house production for the public sector in the post war years. For example, on a date taken at random in 1950, the SSHA had contracts under way for a total of 3780 houses on 25 basic locations (since 1000 are listed for the county of West Lothian, the true number of actual sites was much greater) and, in addition to the SSHA's own architects and surveyors, the

15-storey tower blocks under construction at Clydebank.

organisation was employing no fewer than forty independent professional firms.[63] In addition, of course, many local building contractors were being fully employed in a system which removed from them all the risks associated with speculative building for private sale. A guaranteed contract from a public authority made profitable financial sense to many building and related companies all over Scotland.

As can be seen, therefore, the system which was being created fed on itself and called for ever increasing stimulation. To give another example, as more council houses were built, so waiting lists extended as people queued for access to the cheap accommodation and this pushed particularly the cities into a 'catch your tail' cycle. Between 1945 and 1961 Glasgow Corporation completed more than 62,000 dwellings, yet the waiting list, which was already 90,000 in 1949, continued to increase every single year.

In these circumstances it is certain that the SSHA was not alone in bringing pressure to bear on Scottish ministers to address the decline in output in the later 1950s and to re-stimulate public sector building. Whereas a more rational central policy would surely have involved a serious step back and review of the conse-quences of continuing to develop a public sector dominated housing system, the measures taken in the period 1954 to 1957 disastrously boosted the process within the cities, and within Glasgow in particular. In other words, what might have been acceptable as a temporary recourse brought about by immediate post-war needs, was translated into something which, in certain parts of the country, approached a full blown Eastern European style state housing system. Government attempts at an alternative strategy amounted to little more than the partial U.K. wide decontrol of rents in 1957 in the vague hope that this might lead to some recovery in private renting.

Even at this stage the nature of what was being produced in many of the peripheral estates was becoming clear and a serious objective review might have been expected to result in a slow down or halt being called. But, as we have seen, ministers responded to appeals to re-stimulate activity not only by sensibly sanc-tioning Cumbernauld and Overspill, but by confirming council activity through enhanced subsidies for flats and giving clearance for further local authority-led rebuilding in inner city areas. By 1954, 95% of the output for Glasgow council was already in the form of tenement flats, and now it and other urban authorities were being given an additional incentive to favour such types as well as, of course, high rise blocks.[64]

The first result of these decisions was, inevitably, that work on Easterhouse and the other major peripheral estates went ahead to completion at full speed. Green belt land was taken up, densities were increased far beyond 100 persons per acre and at Darnley and Summerston 41,000 dwellings of very poor quality were produced in the following decade.[65]

In addition, however, attention now turned to renewal operations in slum districts of the cities. In Glasgow three initial redevelopment areas were identified and the first of these was in the Gorbals-Hutchesontown district, not far from the city centre, but south of the Clyde. There virtually all of the older houses were to be demolished to make way for a new development modelled on contemporary projects undertaken by the London County Council (which was, of course, greatly preoccupied by its need to deal with the replacement of war-damaged housing). The population of the district was to be reduced from about 26,000 to 10,000 persons, the latter being rehoused in a mixture of high slab blocks and tenements.[66] Some of the most distinguished architects of the day were involved, including Sir Robert Matthew and Sir Basil Spence, the latter designing extraordinary 20-storey concrete slabs with inset communal balconies. Moreover, the plan indicated that 'shops were to be reduced from 444 to 57 in line with corporation policy, public houses from 46 to 9 and industry was to move out altogether'.[67]

Work commenced at Hutchesontown in 1957 and this project was intended by Glasgow's planners 'to substantiate their next, most daring proposal, the .. *Report on the Clearance of Slum Houses, Redevelopment and Overspill*, published in the same year. This advocated that all building in the city be concentrated on 29 Comprehensive Development Areas under council control. These areas would all get the Gorbals treatment with everything being flattened to make way for new municipal housing as well as new roads. '100,000 houses, a third of the city's stock and half of all property not already owned by the corporation, would be demolished after compulsory purchase, to be replaced by municipal housing'. Basically the plan was to destroy at a rate of 4500 dwellings per annum through until 1980. Mercifully, there were many delays which impeded this massive programme of destruction and by 1969 only nine of the intended C.D.A.'s had been approved by the Scottish Office. However, much of the clearance did go ahead and it seems to be the case that in the period 1954 to 1979 no less than 76,914 of the houses within Glasgow were knocked down. Indeed, if the destruction which took place from 1945 to 1954 is included, the total of post war demolitions in the city to 1979 exceeded no less than 95,000 dwellings.[68]

The 1957 report proposed that only 40,000 new council houses would be built within the city, the remainder of the requirement arriving via overspill and the new towns. However, partly under the stimulus of the new subsidy arrangements, the flatted developments which now appeared in various parts of the city quickly increased the prospects for the corporation. Moreover neither a housing convener such as David Gibson (1961–1964) nor professionals such Lewis Cross, senior engineer in the Corporation's Department of Architecture and Planning and responsible for overseeing sites and contracts, were prepared to confine their activities to the declared C.D.A.'s. Gibson, 'bringing the uncompromising intensity of (his) I.L.P. tradition to bear on the particular issue of slum conditions' favoured the use of high rise structures wherever land was available, hence buildings soon began to grow upwards in odd corners of the city, in gap-sites as well as on strange places such as in and around the old inter-war cottage developments at Knightswood.[69] In accordance with the C.D.A.'s, of course, major developments occurred at Pollockshaws, Royston, Govan, Anderston Cross, Woodside, Laurieston-Gorbals, Cowcaddens and Townhead. The upshot was that as early as 1972 a further 48,000

High rise housing built at Broomhill, Glasgow 1967–68.

council houses had been built inside the city boundaries and other C.D.A's were pending at Shields Road, Kinning Park, Elderpark, Springburn and Sighthill.

In this period Glasgow's 'Housing Committee unleashed the most concentrated multi-storey building drive experienced by any British city, with high flats accounting for nearly three quarters of all completions in 1961–1968'.[70] Output of council

Another view of the Broomhill high flats showing the dramatic contrast with the surrounding tenements.

houses in the city reached a rate of over 4,000 per annum by 1964, by which time the SSHA was also operating vigorously within the city. An agreement of 1960 gave the Association a programme of 3,500 houses to be built at Maryhill Barracks (Wyndford), Hutchesontown/Gorbals Area D and Broomhill and these were intended to be completed in annual instalments of 1000 houses.[71]

At Wyndford the Association actually completed one of the most successful developments of the period. The specified density was 61 houses per acre (or roughly 200 persons per acre) which was far beyond the level that the Association had previously believed to be acceptable. However, under the guidance of the Chief Technical Officer Harold Buteux, the task was attempted. His design provided for about half the dwellings in the form of three- and four-storey blocks of mixed flats and maisonettes and the remainder in tall or very tall buildings. The layout was an open planning arrangement forming a series of interpenetrating squares and a variety of architectural finishes was introduced to give each square or neighbourhood its own individual appearance. The result was, by the standards of the day, a remarkably successful development from which many lessons could be derived.[72]

320 high rise blocks of flats were constructed in the city, 58 being built for the SSHA and 262 for the Corporation. Moreover, the council was not content with producing such structures in inner city sites, and by the late 1960s they were appearing on the remnants of land in the peripheral estates, pushing densities there also up to the 200 person per acre level. Blocks ranged from 8 to 31 storeys in height and contained houses of one-, two-, three-, or four-apartments. In

Glasgow, however, the majority of the larger houses (presumably intended for larger families), were included in the 120 or so higher buildings of from 20–31 storeys.[73] Perhaps the most dramatic of the city's developments in this period was at Sighthill where 2,500 dwellings were provided between 1963 and 1969 in a scheme made up of ten huge 20-storey slab blocks and a number of tower buildings.

The trend towards high rise building was further stimulated both by the construction industry and central government. In general terms from the 1950s many of the U.K.'s architects and planners were enthusiatic for high construction for it was so much easier for professionals to build reputations from designing dramatic landmark structures. Steel and reinforced concrete may be said to have provided the technological means by which they could express some of their most ambitious urban planning concepts. In fairness it also has to be noted that many of the attitudes in question were merely a reflection of the views of the general public. To a generation of cinema goers (and increasingly television viewers) the film images of the towering buildings of American cities seemed to be almost visions of the future. Moreover, since the inhabitants of this film world seemed to live opulent lives in superbly appointed apartments, by the early 1960s few people doubted the sophistication or quality of life offered by high-rise living or stopped to reflect on the factors which were necessary to achieve such an outcome. For instance, when the SSHA opened its first ten-storey block in Dundee in January 1960 no fewer than 25,000 people came to examine the flats and this gives some indication of the contemporary level of public interest.[74] The fears expressed by Jean Mann and others in the war years had been long forgotten by professionals and public alike.

The industry in general encouraged the trend since, of course, it enabled many of the factories and concrete users which had lost from the cessation of support for sponsored houses to make a recovery. Load-bearing no-fines high rise (an on-site method of construction) could not be used safely beyond about twelve storeys, hence the desire to build much higher buildings led to the increased use of 'industrialised' methods whereby panels and sections were made in factories and assembled on site. This process was encouraged by the Emmerson Report of 1963, a *Survey of Problems Before Construction Industries* prepared for the Ministry of Works. Sir Harold Emmerson pointed to the need for large scale contracts if the costs of industrialised buildings were to be reduced. It was already clear that, when measured in terms of cost per dwelling, high flats were considerably more expensive than ordinary houses, but the report seductively urged local authorities to think in terms of big contracts or to combine in order to process large projects to enable average costs to be reduced.

In the prevailing circumstances, the construction industry clearly saw the possibility of extremely profitable activity in operations for urban councils and they developed a 'package deal contract' for multi-storey flats. These offered a combined planning, design and construction service to the local authorities and this proved very attractive to many councils since it appeared to hold out the prospect of the maximum number of dwellings from a given budget and all delivered with the minimum of effort on their part. By the mid 1960s the offices

Wyndford nearing completion.

of city councils all over England and Scotland were being 'besieged by contractors' representatives touting multi-storey blocks in much the same way as door-to-door salesmen sell vacuum cleaners ... These representatives simply requested that a site – any site, however inappropriate – be allocated to them and all would be well'.[75] Not surprisingly, councils often fell into the trap, sometimes ignoring even the most basic requirements of financial and professional prudence. (Douglas Niven estimated that by the mid '60s as much as 50% of total municipal house production in Scotland was being carried forward on this type of 'package deal' basis.[76]) To some extent councils were egged on by the newly formed Scottish Development Department, but in 1960 the Scottish Office had at least established a Joint Development Group to study the practical outcome of high density building and ultimately to offer some guidance on the various structural methods and designs.[77]

The figures for Scottish house production in the 1960s are as follows;

Date	Local Auth's	New Towns	SSHA	Other Housing Assoc's	Govt Depts	Total Public Sector	Private Sector	Total
1960	17913	1519	2071	127	433	22063	6529	28592
1961	16823	1265	1453	53	489	20083	7147	27230
1962	16245	1576	967	65	124	18977	7784	26761
1963	17699	1649	1816	32	399	21595	6622	28217
1964	24814	2608	1734	12	341	29509	7662	37171
1965	21823	2996	1765	154	825	27563	7553	35116
1966	21343	3870	2302	118	526	28159	7870	36029
1967	27092	3941	2189	181	557	33960	7498	41458
1968	26756	3207	2048	288	970	33269	8720	41989
1969	27497	3656	2779	183	187	34302	8327	42629
1970	28045	2790	3525	244	302	34906	8220	43126

As can be seen, public sector activity as a whole did slow down at the beginning of the decade although it jumped noticeably in the election year of 1964. However, when Labour returned to power that year and was confirmed in office with a good majority in 1966, soon support for an enhanced public programme of building was forthcoming. The sharp increase in council output in 1967 is obvious and it is interesting to note that new town (now officially including Irvine and Livingston) and SSHA production both also grew significantly. Indeed, the SSHA was urged by the minister to reach an annual output figure of 5,000 houses in a rolling five year programme, but that proved just beyond its capacity since it was again somewhat excluded from Glasgow in the late 1960's.[78]

By this period much of the activity was in response to the government's planned approach and specifically to the White Papers, *The Scottish Housing Programme 1965–1970* and *The Scottish Economy 1965–1970*. These built on an initiative of the previous government to try to link new house production to what were called economic 'Growth Areas'. At first these were connected with ventures such as the development of the petro-chemical works at Grangemouth or the Rootes Group

A model of an 'Overspill' development to be constructed by the SSHA at Johnstone Castle.

car factory at Linwood, but this activity was now formalised for the Association into what was called the 'Economic Expansion' programme. Under this programme the SSHA built some 20,000 houses through until the early 1980s and, as the name suggests, these were typically for workers moving to areas experiencing economic growth.[79] Much of this was to prove interesting and useful. However the fundamental thrust of policy throughout the 1960s tended to further stimulate inner city destruction and high rise building and extension of the local authority housing system.

For example, one initiative of the Wilson government was the introduction of Selective Employment Tax. This tax was a payroll tax which was intended to discriminate in favour of certain industries and types of employment preferred by the government. In many ways it was yet another attempt by Labour to protect heavy industry at the expense of commerce and services. All employers were liable to pay the tax, but firms in particular industries or localities had the money refunded or were given an additional premium as a bonus. In the case of the building industry the tax operated to the advantage of users of concrete and against brick builders – presumably as a deliberate means of discriminating in favour of the municipal builders who tended to rely more on concrete than private building companies, the latter obviously depending more on traditional bricks and mortar.[80] In addition, city localities like Glasgow or Dundee were favoured at the expense of operations in what were perceived to be more prosperous areas. It was a strange and very ill-considered departure and it certainly stimulated a fresh surge of dubious building in Scottish cities.

Many of the industrialised high-rise 'system' buildings were poorly constructed. The edges of precast panels were often damaged so that joints made bad and leaky connections, wall-ties were sometimes inadequate, omitted or abused by workers rushing to maximise piece-work payments and supervision and inspection was frequently not nearly good enough. As a result defects were evident before long and problems of damp penetration, condensation and insect infestation were soon common. Fears in respect of poor quality were dramatically confirmed, of course, with the partial collapse of a block of council flats at Ronan Point at Newham in London in 1968. This ultimately began to force a greater degree of caution in respect of tower blocks.[81]

There is nothing intrinsically wrong with high rise buildings in an urban setting. Any inspection of high flats in North American cities provided either by private companies, or by condominiums for rent or for private ownership, will show that this form of housing can be very acceptable and will be attractive to a significant proportion of the population. Moreover, the structures in question are often much higher and more dramatic than anything built in Glasgow or other Scottish cities.

For example, a forty-storey block in a Toronto suburb was recently visited by the author. His hosts were a young couple and their year-old son. They live on an income which is certainly not above average, but they had chosen to purchase their two bedroom flat. The residents own the interior of their apartment and a space in the underground car park. Everything else is owned and managed by a condominium and this includes external walls and roof, lifts, and the communal facilities such as gymnasium, solarium, swimming pool and tennis courts, and the organisation also provides a full concierge and security service. For these services the condominium charges a very reasonable $130 per month. Three small shops were located on the ground floor and, needless to say, the whole atmosphere of the building was bright, clean and secure. The young couple both considered that the neighbouring privately owned and managed blocks gave an even better service – although at a higher charge. In these cases the swimming pools, for instance, were internal and the management also made available a pre-school facility. I saw nothing to suggest that these arrangements were untypical of dwellings in urban Canada.[82]

Two points seem evident. First, high-rise can provide a perfectly reasonable solution which, if properly offered, will be chosen by a significant proportion of households. Second, to make this life-style genuinely attractive much more than the basic living space is required. North American organisations which operate such buildings (typically for profit) understand that it is necessary to attract residents by providing a range of additional services. Accordingly, they arrange to lay on the sort of facilities outlined above, and when this is done the residents move in by choice.

In the U.K. and in Scotland high rise accommodation was provided exclusively by local authorities and the dwellings were allocated rather than chosen. It was never a question of attracting residents and, as has been shown, the attempt was typically made to produce the maximum units from a given budget. Inevitably, therefore, none of the additional elements which make such a life-style pleasant were provided. Apparently in Glasgow the original intention was that high flats should only have childless adults living above the fourth floor, but this restriction was soon abandoned and higher flats were allocated to families with young children as well as to others who simply had no wish to live in such a way. The lack of security led to vandalism particularly to elevators and in many cases the immediate external environment, typically of grey concrete, rapidly became hostile and harsh, particularly where high buildings were built too close together, thus compressing air flows and producing almost perpetual high winds.

Not all Scottish high rise buildings were failures and some, such as the blocks at Callendar Park in Falkirk, provide good accommodation and are popular with tenants. There, good management arrangements, careful selection of tenants and a pleasing external setting, seem to have produced success. But this was not typical. Elsewhere disillusionment frequently set in; isolation became a major problem for some tenants; young mothers often found it very difficult to cope; and psychoneurotic disorders were common. The Glasgow development which attracted most criticism was at Red Road which contained the tallest building in the city completed in 1965. Within a very few years the repeated vandalism to lifts and other problems, had driven the community to distraction so that virtually every tenant wanted to be rehoused and by as early as 1978 two of the buildings were condemned as unfit for habitation.[83]

Fundamentally local authority provision discredited the whole concept of high-rise living, hence an urban life style which plays a key part in almost all modern cities across the world is, in the U.K., and in Scotland in particular, associated in the minds of consumers and private developers alike with poor quality and low standards.

As was noted earlier, the period under discussion was one of generally rising living standards for many sections of the community and one result of this was an increasing demand for houses for private ownership. This trend was enhanced by tax relief on mortgage interest payments, by the Labour government's introduction in 1968 of the 'option mortgage' system for lower earners and by the home improvement grant system (introduced in 1959 and improved in 1969). In England from the late 1950s the already large stock of privately owned houses was growing at a much faster rate than the public sector and even in Scotland there was significant growth through the 1960s, output in the peak year of 1968 reaching 8,720 houses, or almost 21% of the Scottish total. However, because of the urban obsession with public sector housing, those seeking private home-ownership had an ever increasing incentive to move out to the suburbs and beyond, swelling the ranks of the commuters.

For example, denied the opportunity to build houses and confronted by an increasing rate burden to support council housing, the middle classes of Glasgow progressively fled to places such as Bearsden, Milngavie, Lenzie, Bishopbriggs,

Newton Mearns and beyond to the surrounding towns and villages. It is a remarkable fact that throughout the years from 1960 to 1970, despite all the land being cleared by demolition, only 1742 private houses were built within Glasgow's boundaries, with a mere 57 being constructed in 1966.[84] At the same time some 43,933 public sector houses were built in the city. No wonder many of those who could afford to do so fled to the commuter belt. Basically they were driven away. And wherever they settled, almost invariably they acquired detached or semi-detached cottages with gardens.

However, it was not only the professional middle classes who took flight. Increasingly the skilled workers and higher wage earners joined in the process, often queuing to move to the new towns or as part of overspill. Inevitably the population of the city went into steep decline, falling at a rate of about 25,000 per year, the process removing, at least from residence and often completely, many key participants in the city's economy. A population which had been 1,140,078 in 1961 had shrunk to 850,000 by 1973 and there was no end in sight to the descent.

Progress in the Comprehensive Development Areas was patchy. In a few cases operations pushed ahead vigorously while in others there were many delays. The peak periods for demolition and destruction were, therefore, not actually reached until the years 1968–1974. However, the havoc which was created was on a monumental scale.[85]

Clearly no one can argue that many of the slums which were swept away merited anything else. They were often rotten, provided hopelessly inadequate accommodation and were incapable of restoration. Moreover, there is also no doubt that the long years of rent control had left the properties of many private landlords in a condition which was intolerable. In any event, therefore, major demolition and

Typical 1960's 'Overspill' housing at Irvine.

Comprehensive destruction. Scenes of Glasgow in the mid 1970s.

replacement in one form or another was both necessary and inevitable. However, the way this task was conducted from the mid 1950s to the mid 1970s was desperately lacking in imagination and understanding.

In certain parts of the city the social cost of the destruction was devastating with population levels plummeting and whole communities being displaced and dispersed. The long time lag between compulsory purchase, demolition and reconstruction meant that even those intending to return were for years exiled to peripheral areas. 'Whole territorially based communities, with deep historical roots, were destroyed as the massive C.D.A. onslaught tore the heart out of the city' and 'vital areas' such as Govan, Partick and Springburn were desolated.[86]

The city also paid a phenomenal price in terms of its architectural and urban heritage as many fine buildings, well capable of effective restoration and renewal, were swept away along with the dross. As late as 1971, Lord Esher was describing Glasgow as Britain's finest Victorian city, ironically at a time when the indiscriminate bulldozing was at its most ferocious, and when much that was potentially valuable was being lost forever.

Looking back at this episode, what seems most remarkable is the sheer lack of appreciation of the damage which was being done to the economic structure of the city. From the mid 1950s many of the large traditional firms involved in shipbuilding, locomotive engineering, metal manufacturing and other heavy engineering were shedding jobs or closing down. In many cases this was part of a long run process arising not simply from lack of international competitiveness, but from advances in technology, particularly associated with large jet powered aircraft, diesel electric locomotion and super-tanker shipping, all of which left Glasgow's traditional manufacturers at a disadvantage.

Such a decline was long-run and indicated before the war, hence the management of economic change was an inevitable task of the post war years. However, in their obsession with heavy engineering those responsible for the affairs of the city seem almost completely to have lost sight of other key elements of economic activity. In declaring the C.D.A.'s, for example, the municipal authorities sent a clear signal to businesses that the populations would be moved out – at least for a time – and this can only have provided a major disincentive to any thought of investment in new firms in these parts of the city. Moreover, as the demolition advanced so many small enterprises were either swept away or saw their local markets disappear with the departing population. Glasgow had a great tradition of shops on the ground floor of tenements along street frontages, hence inevitably loss of the residences was accompanied by disappearance of the shops and the jobs of those whom they had employed. Similarly, many back-court firms, employing the tradesmen who had serviced the needs of local residents, were simply wiped out. As Andrew Gibb expressed it, '.. serious in its consequences was the death of hundreds of small enterprises whose low levels of capital and low overheads, in brick backyard or railway viaduct premises (were) destroyed by demolition, (and) denied .. the possibility of relocation'.[87] In these circumstances it is not at all surprising that persistently high levels of unemployment dogged the city (over 11%

Castlemilk photographed in 1991 before renewal activities had commenced.

in 1973 when the U.K. level was 4.6%) and this general decline fed the outward migration of the population and accelerated the trend far beyond anticipated levels. Fundamentally, it has to be suggested that by the early 1970s the whole process had run out of control.

Moreover, other chickens were now coming home to roost in the peripheral estates and, indeed, in several of the much more recent rebuilding developments in intermediate and inner city areas. As economic decline took hold so, of course, the inhabitants of the great estates which now existed around the edge of the city were at an increasing disadvantage arising both from their physical remoteness and from the lack of incentive for businesses to invest in such places. Inevitably unemployment rates soared in these locations. Almost as night follows day vandalism and more serious crime flourished. Part of this trend was no doubt related to increasing levels of relative poverty, but it has to be suggested that such problems also resulted from the damage done to family and social ties as a consequence of the massive council driven relocation of the population. Moreover, cheap, shoddy housing and the typical relentless grey environment were presumably also factors. As early as 1972 an Easterhouse minister was reporting Easterhouse, Barlanark and Garthamlock to be among the most disadvantaged areas of Glasgow while more than a third of the residents were already 'wanting out of Easterhouse'.[88] By 1977 council house areas at Drumchapel, Castlemilk, and Pollock were also recording annual transfer request rates of the order of 30%, and many blocks of flats were standing empty simply because applicants to the council were refusing point blank to accept tenancies in such localities.[89] Void buildings and their companions of vandalism, graffiti and trash fed an atmosphere of decay and poverty.

Much of the forgoing discussion has centred on the course of events in and around Glasgow and that is inevitable given the city's size relative to Scotland and the significance of trends in that area. However, where Glasgow led, again others followed. Policy decisions could not be applied exclusively to one city hence subsidies in support of high rise building, slum clearance or urban development were also dangled in front of other authorities and seized with greater or lesser enthusiasm in the expansion of the council housing system from the 1950s to the 1970s.

Edinburgh had been fairly cautious immediately after the war, but from the late 1950s it too plunged into peripheral development, area renewal, slum clearance and high density building. At Oxgangs, Gracemount, Moredun and later Hyvot on the southern edge of the city, large council schemes were constructed. At Niddrie/ Craigmillar grey tenements and high flats made their appearance, and a truly awful estate of deck access flats was developed at West Granton, achieving the remarkable feat of being even more distressing and miserable than the neighbouring estates of Pilton and Muirhouse.

Mercifully Edinburgh Corporation was at least restrained by the unmistakable merits of some of the superb 18th and 19th century buildings of the new town and the city also had the advantage of a large stock of inter-war and older private housing, hence there was nothing on the scale of the demolition programme

A West Pilton, Edinburgh tenement in the early 1980s.

followed elsewhere. However, parts of the south side and Leith were cleared to make way for rebuilding and in the period 1962–1965, under the leadership of Pat Rogan, Edinburgh Corporation Housing Committee removed many of the post-war prefabs to make space for more than 9000 (mainly) high flats. Developments at Leith Fort and Muirhouse were completed at this time. As part of this operation in the mid 1960s a massive development was launched on a 116 acre site on the west edge of the city at Wester Hailes where the council planned to house 18,000 people cleared from older areas.[90] Although commenced relatively late in the day almost all the errors and blunders evident elsewhere – and particularly in Glasgow's peripheral estates – were repeated. Grey groups of bleak tenements, massive slab blocks and high flats were the dwelling forms, while the other fundamental requirements of a community were typically noticeable by their absence. Within a very few years Ian Adams identified Wester Hailes as

> a dormitory town without a soul. What do people do? Work, entertainment and recreational facilities are elsewhere. There is no choice of shops and secondary school. Where are the nursery schools, the tearooms, small sheltered parks, workshops for small craftsmen or repair shops? What life is here for an old person … or for a young mother walking her pram or toddler across acres of windy open space?[91]

Dundee was only surpassed by Glasgow in the extent of its municipalisation of the housing stock in the 1950s and 60s. High rise buildings flourished in comprehensive redevelopment and some very poor estates were built, notably at

Deck access housing at West Granton, Edinburgh. The last of these dreadful blocks has now been demolished.

Ardler where six massive 17-storey blocks were constructed; but perhaps the very worst scheme was not developed until the early 1970s. Yet again lessons by now obvious elsewhere were blissfully ignored as the Whitfield estate was constructed to the north of the city on the very edge of the green belt. Not only contemporary examples were neglected, but also forgotten were the war-time warnings against deck-access tenements.

Not surprisingly, therefore, it was not only the Glasgow estates which rapidly came to display the symptoms of decline and decay.

Lower Whitfield was built over the period 1968 to 1975 and consisted of about 2,500 homes on a 37 acre site and composed of a mixture of flats, cottages and maisonettes. At the western edge of a landscaped area four high rise blocks were built in 1969, providing 360 flats. But the most extraordinary part of the scheme was to the north at Whitfield Skarne where a further 2,500 dwellings were constructed in 1971–72 in the form of 135 deck-access blocks of four and five storeys. These were system built in grey concrete and arranged in an inter-connected honeycomb of eleven 'crescents' each containing up to 424 homes.[92]

The typical process of decline described above rapidly followed and when, in 1988, the area finally became the subject of a special 'Partnership' initiative led by the Scottish Office, a devastating estate profile was indicated.

Whereas the planned population of the estate had been of the order of 12,000, less than fourteen years after completion the actual number of residents had fallen

Whitfield, Dundee photographed in 1991.

to 9,000, and 24% of the houses were standing empty – 879 in Skarne and 132 in Lower Whitfield. Seven new vacant houses were appearing each week; and there was an astonishingly high rate of turnover, with the occupants of one third of the houses moving out each year. Increasingly those taking up tenancies were in the younger age ranges and many were single parents with few alternatives, but, of course, now looking at the prospect of rearing their children under the very worst of circumstances. Male unemployment in the estate was 40%, more than double the city figure of 16.9%. Unemployment among the 17–29 age group was over 50% and of those who were unemployed, most had been in this predicament for more than a year. Not surprisingly almost three quarters of tenants were receiving housing benefit.[93]

The deck-access maisonettes were clearly the least popular dwelling forms and part of the reason for this was their vulnerability to crime. Inevitably, criminal activities and vandalism were widespread and the deck-access and inter-connecting towers made the estate almost impossible to police with people being able to enter or leave at many different points. Drug dealing was a real growth industry.

What was true of Whitfield was in essence true of many of the huge single tenure council estates which had appeared round Scotland's cities from the 1950s to the 1970s. Whitfield was not noticeably worse than Castlemilk, Wester Hailes or Ferguslie Park, the other schemes selected for Partnership treatment, and it should be understood that these estates were not inferior to several others which might just as easily have been given similar priority. (Anyone who doubts that might reflect on the fact that by the end of the 1980s not only was the housing of Drumchapel of hopelessly poor quality, but the level of male unemployment in the estate was almost 35% and the mortality rate was 16% higher there than for the city as a whole. Drumchapel was, therefore, at least as deserving of immediate attention as any other area.)

The real point is, however, that estates of this type illustrate and embody the very heart of Scotland's urban predicament in much of the period since the late 1950s.

Now, of course, it is true that councils have provided good housing for many thousands of citizens all over the country and it is undoubtedly the case that over the years a host of decent, well-intentioned, caring professional officials and councillors have successfully delivered effective housing services to many of their tenants. Moreover, it would be wrong to condemn a system merely on the basis of a few of the worst examples. However, the problem was not simply confined to a few examples. If Glasgow had its Castlemilk, Drumchapel, Easterhouse and etc, Edinburgh its Wester Hailes, West Granton etc and Dundee its Whitfield and other huge 'hard to let' schemes, so virtually every sizeable town in Scotland had its problem estate(s). Perth had Fairfield, Stirling its Raploch, Paisley its Ferguslie Park, Kilmarnock its Longpark and it would be easy go round each town and city and point to similar estates. In every case, long before the late 1970s, such schemes were notorious and obvious concentrations of poverty and deprivation, hence what we are here concerned with are not isolated phenomena, but rather typical products of a system. The local authority housing system not only provided good

Urban renewal at Castlemilk. In these 1991 photographs activity has commenced in the Windlaw area of the estate.

Housing in Ferguslie Park, Paisley, in 1991.

housing for some people; it also created an ecosystem which trapped thousands of others into poverty and hung a massive millstone around the neck of the Scottish economy. These estates were effectively huge engines for generating and perpetuating poverty.

Part of the problem was the monopolistic position which council housing had gained in respect of rented accommodation in certain parts of the country. All of the huge estates discussed above were characterised by their mono-tenure and lack of choice; but in several Scottish towns this was not just a question of one or two schemes. As recently as the early 1980s in both Motherwell and Monklands virtually 80% of the entire housing stock was council housing and this was also true of several smaller towns and villages.

Since the end of the cold war an increasing number of students have turned their attention to Eastern European housing to investigate the housing output of communism, but also to consider the extent to which housing played its part in the collapse of the communist system. In particular, some, such as Bertrand Renaud for the World Bank, have had to reflect on changes which require to be made in housing arrangements to facilitate the economic recovery of countries such as Poland or the former soviet republics. It is instructive to consider a little of Renaud's analysis.[94]

Under communism housing, often, but not always supplied through municipalities, was regarded as a commodity which was the property of the state and allocated in accordance with state rules. These typically involved a points system which attempted to identify priority by measuring 'need'. Housing was seen as 'social consumption' alongside pensions, health care, education and so on. Investment in housing was determined by the state and subsidies were typically very large. The system was supply driven with no consumer choice. Decisions as to where and when to provide housing were made by bureaucrats and were often based on the need 'to facilitate industrial housing production', and the quality of the dwellings produced was usually poor. 'Rents are normative and have little to do with the economic cost of providing housing services'. Rents in the Soviet Union were effectively frozen from the 1920s.

> Both the consumption of housing services and the production of new units are heavily subsidised. This creates excess demand for housing and significant intermarket spillovers. Simultaneously there is excess consumption and permanent shortage.[95]

The forms and types of housing selected by bureaucrats inevitably tended to be communal, discouraging of individuality, capable of mass production and theoretically achieving the maximum number of units from budget.

The consequences of such a system include such points as –

> Because housing is heavily subsidised, there is chronic excess demand and a permanent housing shortage.
>   The housing stock tends to be very poorly utilised …
>   Because subsidised rents and utilities are proportional to the size of units, housing subsidies are highly regressive.

Communist housing in Warsaw.

Housing mobility rates are very low, which impedes labour mobility.

… The incentive to own housing will remain weak as long as rental housing is more heavily subsidised.

Since rents do not cover maintenance costs, the housing stock is poorly maintained and housing production has to be subsidised.

In 1992 the author and some of his colleagues were given the opportunity to consider this matter first hand by examining housing in Poland. Of all the Polish cities visited, Poznan was probably the most advanced and progressive. Yet on my return I wrote that there the housing co-ops have a stock of 382,000 dwellings and a waiting list of 110,000 applicants. Within the city itself the 184,000 apartments are located in 2,500 (mainly tenement) blocks and the current occupation figure is 1.8 families per dwelling. The city Director of Architecture estimated that 632 blocks of flats were in need of refurbishment, but that resources were available to repair only about 30 blocks per year.

The problem in Poznan described above is almost a summation of the problem of Poland as a whole. Over the years of the communist regime the task of providing accommodation was systematically transferred from households and families to the state acting through the municipalities and housing co-operatives. Ultimately the possibility of households working out their own economic solutions was almost eliminated. Meanwhile, the burden on the state became progressively insupportable.[96]

This is not the place for a full account of our examination of Polish housing, but part of my conclusion was as follows.

The lessons from Poland were, sadly, very obvious and the parallels with the Scottish public sector housing system in some areas were impossible to seriously dispute. Many of the huge municipal estates which were built in Scotland from the 1930s to the 1970s are in truth microcosms of the same system which has trapped and impoverished the people of Poland. Of course in Scotland we are only talking about certain localities, such as Castlemilk, Drumchapel, Wester Hailes etc rather than whole cities – indeed whole nations. But the system is the same. Effectively the people of Poland were embedded in a communal method of housing which made it profoundly difficult for individuals to promote the economic growth of themselves, their households and communities. Individual initiative, enterprise, opportunity, choice and control were effectively excluded as responsibility for housing was subsumed by the state via the municipalities and giant co-operatives. Under such circumstances even the most energetic and responsible citizens were reduced to helpless impotence and literally thousands of people held in poverty. Moreover, any semblance of flexibility was driven out of the system, hence economic decay became almost inevitable. But in addition, the sheer inefficiency of the communist housing system is breathtaking. The crushing burden taken on by the state became impossible to sustain and now what is left is widespread poverty, miserably low standards of accommodation and a legacy of what we would regard as homelessness which is simply appalling. And all this in a country which is potentially wealthy.[97]

Obviously there is a limit to the extent to which comparisons can be carried between Poland and Scotland. However, the fundamental housing system which did so much to impoverish Poles also contributed to the impoverishment of thousands of Scots as Scotland developed proportionately the largest state housing system of any non-communist country. Moreover, the excessive development in Scotland of the municipal housing system played its part in ensuring that the Scottish economy dragged behind the rest of the country for many of the post war years.

Finally, one of the most remarkable features is the depth of the silence which descended on discussion of Scotland's urban housing predicament. Certainly frequent attention was drawn to specific housing problems, but the way in which the Scottish media, politicians and academics avoided getting to the essential principles is more than strange. Given the Labour Party's historic commitment to

More Polish housing? No! This is council housing at Hyvot in Edinburgh, 1995.

public sector housing, one can readily appreciate part of the difficulty. But why others should have ignored the subject is harder to understand. As recently as 1994 and in the context of a discussion of the 'outer estates' Duncan Maclennan, Professor of Urban Studies at Glasgow University was to write –

> There is a further important question which Scottish research and policy has ducked......the Scottish question which must never be spoken is whether household choices shape the outcome. Scottish cities, and their run-down areas, have appalling health records in relation to drink, eating and smoking related disorders. Educational performance, truancy and illegitimacy are at their worst in such areas and drug abuse has reached dangerously high levels. Why?[98]

The root of the answer to his question lies in the public housing system which spawned these estates and the silence which reigned on this topic is a disgrace.

CHAPTER FIVE

The Turn of the Tide

*T*HE 1970s were a difficult decade in economic terms. These years marked a period where management of the national economy became extremely arduous and where there were major surges in inflation. There was a serious international energy crisis and the problems of many of Britain's key industries which suffered from poor levels of productivity and a lack of competitiveness tended at that time to become critical. In addition, there were frequent and vicious industrial disputes (particularly in 1973 and again, in the 'winter of discontent' in 1979) and the country gained an unenviable reputation for poor industrial relations. In 1976 a sterling crisis forced the government into the arms of the International Monetary Fund and thereafter there were increasing efforts to curb public expenditure. Among the areas to be restricted was spending on public provision of housing.

Scottish housing output figures for the decade illustrate the latter situation.

Date	Local Auth	New Town	SSHA	Other Housing Assoc's	Govt Depts	Total Public Sector	Private Sector	Total
1970	28,045	2,790	3,525	244	302	34,906	8,220	43,126
1971	23,125	2,394	3,058	332	260	29,169	11,614	40,783
1972	16,335	1,519	1,739	413	151	20,157	11,835	31,992
1973	14,432	1,589	1,328	245	224	17,818	12,215	30,033
1974	13,016	2,099	1,067	480	435	17,097	11,239	28,323
1975	16,086	3,636	3,062	766	402	23,952	10,371	34,323
1976	14,361	3,980	2,813	1,152	517	22,823	13,704	36,527
1977	9,119	3,167	2,042	546	314	15,188	12,132	27,320
1978	6,686	1,510	1,711	1,127	282	11,316	14,443	25,759
1979	4,755	2,018	1,084	544	206	8,607	15,175	23,782

In general terms, the dramatic slow-down in public construction was easy to justify. Crudely, Scotland's stock of dwellings was now more than sufficient to match the numbers of households. Actually, this had been the case from the late 1950s on and thereafter the gap between numbers of dwellings and households had steadily widened – despite the massive destruction of older urban properties. By the early 1980s there were approximately 2,000,000 dwellings as against 1,786,000 recorded households.[1] However, as the government's Green Paper, *Scottish Housing*, noted in 1977, it did not 'follow automatically from this that Scotland has too many houses'. When allowance was made for second homes,

Typical SSHA housing of the years around 1980. This estate is at Stenhousemuir.

empty houses waiting for modernisation, houses officially classed as sub-tolerable, and the problems of shortages and surpluses in different localities, it was argued that 'a simple comparison between households and houses is only the first step towards an assessment of housing need'.[2] While this line of argument had validity, the fact remained that it was becoming impossible to maintain that there was a general housing shortage in Scotland.

Another factor which tended to validate the sharp contraction of new public building was the increasingly obvious trend towards private home ownership. From 1973 to 1978 the proportion of Scottish home owners increased from 32% to 35% (the equivalent figures for England are 54% and 56%) and it was reasonable to expect more private individuals to want to own their own houses in future.[3] By contrast with the slow down in public building, output for the private market jumped in 1971; and in 1978, for the first time since 1925, private sector builders erected more houses in Scotland than the combined public sector.

The trend of tenure patterns in Scotland in the decade can be seen in the following table.

Dwelling Tenure	1971	1976	1981
owner occupied	31%	33.6%	36%
public rented	52%	54.2%	52%
private rented[*]	17%	12.2%	10%

[*] includes housing associations

As far as the four Scottish cities are concerned, by 1981 the proportion of tenure taken up by the public sector in Glasgow was 63%, in Dundee 57%, Aberdeen 48% and Edinburgh 31%, illustrating the way in which Edinburgh's experience throughout the century had been significantly different from the others.

The true private rented sector (excluding housing associations) was declining rapidly during these years and not the least reason was the demolition process in the early 1970s, described earlier, when the properties of many urban private landlords were swept away in the general programmes of destruction.

As was noted in Chapter 3, the 1944 survey for *Planning Our New Homes* had indicated that almost half the Scottish population had wanted to buy their own homes and were confident that they could afford to do so. However, the policies pursued in Scotland from the war years on had drastically slowed down the trend in such a direction. Part of the explanation for this was the low cost of council housing in many parts of the country, but it should be noted that the demolition programmes, particularly in the cities, added to the problem by systematically removing many of what might have been cheap houses, thus destroying the bottom rungs of the home owning ladder.

Nevertheless, as the 1960s and 1970s progressed so the attractions of home ownership became harder to resist. As we have seen, urban council building in these years became more concentrated on flatted dwellings of one kind or another, hence those who aspired to a new house and garden often had to look beyond the cities and to consider home ownership. Not the least criticism of the council housing system in this context is that by tending to defy the essential consumer choice of housing form it made the divisions within society increasingly obvious in physical terms. Moreover, it widened the gap between Scotland and the rest of the country. By the early 1980s, whereas only 18% of U.K. residents lived in a flat, the equivalent Scottish figure was 41%; and while 82% nationally lived in a terraced or semi-detached house, that form was available to less than 60% of Scots.[4]

However, it soon became clear to many home owning households in these years that they could use their homes directly to increase their wealth. In the period in question house prices consistently rose faster than the rate of inflation. While much of the cause of this was attributable to national factors, the reality is that the level of demand for houses tended steadily to outstrip the available supply thus pushing prices ahead. In part this was a consequence of government action. The Finance Act of 1974 limited tax relief on a new loan to buy or improve a residence to interest on a ceiling of £25,000, but at the time that was more than enough to provide a strong incentive to purchase for many Scots. (Indeed, this system put Scotland, with her high proportion of public sector tenants, at something of a disadvantage relative to the rest of the country since the bulk of Scottish households obviously could not enjoy the advantages of tax relief.)

Moreover, in an Act of 1969 the Labour government introduced major changes to the home improvement grant system. By this point there was a gathering awareness that many fine older buildings were being lost both through public demolition and from neglect and the Act tried to address the problem by making larger grants available both to public agencies and to private individuals. For private housing standard grants to assist in the replacement of basic facilities were increased up to £200 and discretionary payments of up to £1,000 were made available to fund other repairs. Even larger amounts could be obtained to assist property conversions.[5]

The result of this was that many individuals soon developed an eye for a property which could be purchased, improved with the help of grants and then later sold on at a considerable profit. This lucrative domestic business flourished particularly in suburban communities and in commuter belt country areas, and here Scotland seems to have been particularly successful. Professor Maclennan estimated that although Scotland contained only 9% of the British stock of pre-1919 houses, some '23% of repair and improvement grants spent in GB between 1975 and 1985 were used in Scotland'.[6] Of course, not all of this was spent on private accommodation, but many households did benefit from the system.

But even with much more modern dwellings, it was possible for families to enhance their wealth. In a society becoming increasingly mobile – particularly in physical terms through the spread of the motor car, but also because of increasing volatility between jobs – the tendency was for people to change their homes with greater frequency, perhaps also reflecting the fundamental life cycle. Anticipating changes in residence, people learned increasingly to trade in their dwellings. This process involved adding value to the property, perhaps by installation of improved heating, or double glazing, or by loft conversion, building an extension, or sometimes simply redecorating or upgrading the external appearance. The subsequent sale almost always resulted in a larger than proportionate enhancement in the price and typically not all of the benefit was tied up in a replacement purchase.

This process, which can be described as a form of domestic capital formation (ie investment in personal domestic property) became a substantial method of wealth generation to home owners. It has been estimated that at the UK level, whereas land and dwellings accounted for only 23% of personal wealth in 1960, by 1980 the figure had risen to about 50%.[7] This did not, of course, encourage particular rejoicing in government nor among large firms and banking institutions, since households tended increasingly to engage in domestic investment rather than in the purchase of company shares and securities. Nevertheless the system did massively stimulate the economy and dramatically enhanced consumer power. The growth of D.I.Y. businesses indicated one means by which consumers were developing their properties. Moreover, as the pace of property exchange increased, so demand for household goods – furniture, fitted kitchens, white goods and so on – was maintained and expanded and much of this type of consumption had about it at least an element of investment.

At one level this situation merely enabled home owners to protect their savings from the worst of the bouts of inflation of the period; but, at another, it also brought real capital growth. However, a key point is that the above processes of enrichment and personal economic development are precisely those which were denied to the tenants of the great council estates, hence the true economic gap between sections of the community widened. In their hearts most professionals understood exactly what was happening, which is why most of them did not personally rent public sector housing, but rather moved swiftly into the ranks of the home owners.

It was an increasing awareness of this situation and a desire to curb public expenditure on housing which persuaded the government to consider the question of selling public sector houses to tenants. The Conservative government 1970–74 made the first significant moves towards a sales policy by giving housing authorities permission to introduce sales schemes. Few Scottish councils seem to have indicated much interest, but the SSHA after overcoming its initial reluctance, carried out several surveys of tenants to determine attitudes and thereafter evolved a limited sales programme.[8] At first several pilot schemes were introduced and it is interesting to note that one of the first of these was at the old Sighthill experimental estate in Edinburgh where several members of Association staff promptly seized the opportunity to buy their houses. Essentially the policy at that time was to try to encourage sales within suitable selected areas, but to decline to sell houses such as multi-storey flats or maisonettes, where particular management problems were thought likely. Elsewhere, tenants could also buy houses if they applied, but they were given no particular encouragement and had no right to buy outside the specified areas. At the time the terms of sales were either at full market value or with a twenty per cent discount if a five year pre-emption clause was accepted, and at all times the agreed price had to be sufficient to offset the outstanding debt on the house. Inevitably the latter condition meant that the newer houses in particular were bound to be as expensive as an equivalent house purchased from the private sector.[9]

In fact there was a good degree of interest from tenants[10], but with the demise of the Heath government the momentum quickly petered out, particularly since Association policy was not to sell houses in areas where the local authority were not in sympathy with the idea. 204 Association houses were sold in 1973 and 161 in the following year, but by 1975 the number of sales had dropped to a mere six.[11]

As a matter of interest, Scottish ministers in the Conservative government of the early 1970s were still somewhat ambivalent and paternalistic in their attitudes to housing policy. In these years the North Sea oil industry was beginning its development and straining the infrastucture of the north east of the country. A Houses for Industry Committee suggested an economic expansion programme of 14,000 houses to be provided in the area by the SSHA between 1973 and 1977. The government determined on more modest figures, but remarkably it authorised the Association to buy up new privately developed houses which, instead of being sold, would then be made available as part of the Association's stock for rent. That workers in a booming oil industry might be well able to buy their own houses seems to have been ignored and some 676 houses were thus taken out of the private sector.[12]

This episode perhaps illustrates one of the problems with Tory ministers of the day. In many cases they seem to have seen housing policy much as a laird might view managing estate workers cottages. From this perspective, selling the housing stock was like 'selling the family silver' and effectively relinquishing control of an asset. That housing might lie at the heart of household finance; might be central to a household's ability to control its own affairs and exploit its own assets; might in this way be a key element in personal and national economic development, seems still not to have been recognised.

Nevertheless, the case for a sales policy did not disappear so easily. In 1977 Professor Cullingworth and his colleagues returned to the subject in the government Green Paper *Scottish Housing*. They pointed out that the supply of houses for sale in Scotland was unequal to the potential demand and with tenure dividing 54% to 33% between public rented accommodation and owner occupation, the distribution in Scotland was markedly out of step not only with England and Wales, but with the rest of Western Europe and failed to match the growing aspirations of a significant portion of the population. Their argument was that 'if access to home ownership is to be widened then other sources of supply are required from the existing stock of other tenures'. They emphasised that 'the public sector ... contains a large pool of second-hand houses of varying ages from inter-war to modern in a variety of types of environment. Their market values would accordingly vary widely but a good many would be valued at a price sufficiently below the price of new housing to bring home ownership within reach of many people who cannot afford it at present.' The conclusion, therefore, was that the sale of some public sector housing seemed a 'reasonable instrument of a sensitive and varied local housing strategy, directed at making better use of the existing housing stock to provide the kind of housing which people want'.[13]

Given the hostility of many councils towards the sale of their houses, it is not surprising that the Labour government found it difficult to support a sales policy and the recommendations in the Green Paper were deliberately vague in this respect. However, Cullingworth himself developed the case in his *Essays on Housing Policy*, published in 1979. He again pointed to his claim that the problem in Scotland was the inability to obtain a 'filtering' process into home ownership because of the small size of the private stock and particularly because of the lack of houses which could be afforded by relatively low income families. 'What is needed is an increase in the supply of cheap, satisfactory houses for owner-occupation. One way of achieving this is by the sale of older public authority houses'.[14] Discussing the Scottish position in particular he stressed that there was a chronic gap between 'nasty old housing and good (but expensive) new housing' confronting the potential buyer of modest means and this in fact forced most Scots to become public sector tenants.

> In short, housing choices are distorted by supply. If households are to be given the real opportunity to choose the tenure they prefer, then considerable adjustments are needed in the pattern of real alternatives available to them. This cannot be achieved simply by new building: this is inevitably relatively expensive and, in any case, can only make a small marginal contribution. There is thus a strong case for infusing the supply

with good quality, older and cheaper housing: in short, the sale of public sector houses. There is no other way in which the 'missing rung' of the ladder can be provided.[15]

Cullingworth cautiously favoured a selective sales policy biased according to local conditions and concentrating on older houses. The incoming Thatcher government in 1979, however, had no such inhibitions and moved swiftly to implement the seminal Tenants Rights' (Scotland) Act of 1980 which gave public sector tenants an enhanced range of rights including greater security of tenure and the legal right to purchase their houses with substantial discounts related to length of occupation. Initially the minimum discount was 32% after two years of tenancy. Later, from 1987 the discount level was improved up to a maximum of 60% of market value for houses and 70% for flats, sales of which had proved more difficult to effect. Discounts become available at a rate of 44% after two years and thereafter they accumulate by 2% per year until the ceiling is reached. From 1990 an additional Rent to Mortgage sales scheme was introduced (although so far this latter method has proved less successful than the basic system).

Inevitably such incentives made home ownership available and attractive to many public sector tenants, even if they had relatively modest means. The outcome to the sales policy is indicated below.[16]

Sales of Public Authority Dwellings in Scotland

Year	Local Auth's	Agency New Town	SSHA/ Scottish Homes	Dwelling Houses	Flats	Sales to others	Total Sales
1979	185	815	10	880	130	393	1,403
1980	2,615	2,070	1,417	5,552	549	401	6,503
1981	6,934	1,797	1,929	9,426	1,082	510	11,170
1982	10,904	1,289	1,933	12,376	1,701	1,029	15,155
1983	12,711	2,209	2,919	15,736	2,103	476	18,315
1984	11,680	1,784	2,444	14,213	1,875	1,151	17,239
1985	10,967	1,507	2,463	10,921	1,950	706	15,643
1986	10,306	1,615	2,073	9,945	1,976	294	14,288
1987	13,813	2,141	3,015	11,894	4,060	1,155	20,124
1988	22,629	2,572	6,455	17,393	7,807	755	32,411
1989	29,182	4,017	6,041	21,729	11,467	304	39,544
1990	26,943	2,743	3,056	17,237	12,449	245	33,120
1991	18,755	1,899	2,221	11,925	8,483	631	23,506
1992	20,096	1,448	2,497	12,915	8,365	799	24,840
1993	16,544	1,351	2,212			402	20,509

These figures trace the basic success of the sales policy. Up to 1993 27% of the former public sector stock was sold through the Right to Buy mechanism. Sales accounted for 24% of local authority housing, 43% of the houses of the five new towns and 45% of the stock formerly owned by the SSHA.[17] These latter figures illustrate the greater propensity of tenants of new towns and the SSHA/ Scottish Homes to purchase their houses when contrasted with local authority tenants. Part of the reason for this is almost certainly the fact that Scottish local authorities have a significantly higher proportion of their dwellings in the form of flats of one kind or another and the table clearly shows the much lower levels of sales of flatted dwellings. Again this emphasises the ongoing general consumer preference for cottage type houses. While the improved discounts for flats did bring about a sharp increase in sales of such properties from 1987 they have never reached anything like the levels in respect of conventional houses.

Another reason for the comparatively lower sales of council houses may be that local authorities were, particularly initially, somewhat slower at processing sales. The SSHA had not waited for the 1980 Act to become law, but had in June 1979 – with a little encouragement from the Scottish Office – introduced its own voluntary plan, which was rather more restrictive than the government scheme in that it attempted to exclude certain types of dwelling. Some local authorities made a half-hearted attempt to persuade the Association not to implement sales in their areas, but it rapidly became clear that many tenants were eager to buy. By September 1980, a month before the Act became law, the Association's council learned that approximately 4,500 applications to buy had been lodged and that missives had been concluded for no less than 946 houses.[18]

As the table illustrates some of the new towns were even faster off their mark than the SSHA, but it has to be suggested that several councils did not move on the matter with great eagerness or enthusiasm. Applications to buy tended to surge ahead of levels of completed sales, reaching a peak through 1987, 1988 and 1989, when the totals were 39,426, 59,996 and 47,376 respectively.

Obviously over recent years the sale of public sector houses has produced a dramatic change in the tenure pattern of housing in Scotland. By December 1993 there was a total of approximately 2,190,000 dwellings in the country. 55% of the stock belonged to owner occupiers; 35% to public authorities; 6% was owned by private landlords and a little over 3% was the property of independent housing associations.[19] Clearly, this breakdown itself indicates something of a revolution since 1979.

One consequence of the sales policy has been the generation of additional resources for the improvement of Scottish public sector housing. In England, the desire of government to restrain public expenditure has meant that (typically) English local authorities have been tightly restricted in spending the capital receipts produced from the sale of their houses. By contrast, in Scotland no such controls have been applied, hence both the councils and the SSHA/ Scottish Homes have been able to redeploy the funds to finance major upgrading of much of their stock. There is no question, but that a large proportion of the improvement works which have been carried forward on Scottish public sector housing over the past fifteen years has been made possible largely as a result of money drawn in from sales.

What the sales policy has meant in terms of investment in Scottish private housing may be indicated by the fact that in 1993 private sector investment was estimated to be some £2.3 billions. Approximately one third of the total (£774 millions) was accounted for by the provision of new housing, but the remainder of private expenditure (£1,527 millions) was calculated to be in the form of repair, maintenance and improvement, and it was recognised that this figure 'will have been augmented, possibly considerably, by do-it-yourself action and unrecorded activity by workers avoiding VAT'.[20]

As far as the provision of new houses is concerned, whereas in 1979 public building made up 34% of all new Scottish dwellings, housing associations 2% and the private sector 64%, by 1993 public sector new construction had shrunk to less than 5%, housing associations had increased their share to 8% and the proportion made up by new building for the private market had jumped to 87%. Total new completions had declined from 23,780 in 1979 to 20,420 in 1993 and this was almost all explicable by the fall in public sector output. The number of new private sector houses built has averaged around 15,000 per year.

It is obvious from these figures that many additional home owners have been able to join in the processes of household investment or wealth generation mentioned previously. Moreover, it is certainly true that families have eagerly seized the opportunities provided by the system. There is, for example, evidence that even elderly public sector tenants, who, comfortable with the ways of the past, previously might have been reluctant to purchase, have increasingly tended to take advantage of their (usually maximum) discounts. Sometimes a reason for doing so has been to provide a capital nest egg as security against the problems of very old age; but it seems clear that other buyers have enjoyed the opportunity to

Sheltered housing for the elderly at Sutherland Street, Edinburgh, 1983.

develop legacies for their off-spring. Given the length of tenure in many cases, it seems very reasonable that this type of benefit should have been gained. However, once acquired, it is certain that families make every effort to protect, develop and augment the capital asset for whatever purpose.

What this means in community terms was brought home to the author when, shortly after his return from Poland he took a party of students to consider two former SSHA estates, the one at Faifley, above Clydebank and the other almost directly across the Clyde at Erskine. Both communities have roughly similar economic advantages in terms of location. Only two or three miles apart via the Erskine bridge, they have easy access to the heart of the greater Glasgow conurbation, to the businesses on both sides of the river and to Glasgow airport hence, all other things being equal, both communities should have roughly equivalent economic prospects.

Erskine was visited first. As part of the Glasgow overspill programme, this estate was built from 1970 on a site originally identified in the Clyde Valley Plan of 1946 as being suitable for a new town. Charles McKean commented that the size of the Erskine project and the initial comparative isolation of the site forced the Association to build what was essentially a new town.

> In architectural terms, the specifications used at Erskine were very similar to those used by Glasgow District Council in the construction of their equally large peripheral housing estates in Drumchapel, Easterhouse and Castlemilk: the vital difference was the considerable effort made by the SSHA to give Erskine an identity and coherence of its own, something the other large housing estates lacked.[21]

One might also add that in Erskine there is not a tenement or high-rise block to be seen and the town is a garden city in fully modern guise which was quickly popular with its Glasgow overspill tenants. Of course it was built at a slightly later date, by which time some of the damning lessons of the earlier period were obvious (although apparently not to some of the designers of contemporary estates such as Whitfield or Wester Hailes). Yet the fact remains that in concept, location and initial execution the creation of Erskine can be said to be fully representative of the ethos and outlook of the early SSHA and its Scottish Office friends. Even the 1970s style cottages were constructed of no-fines concrete using methods developed from those devised in 1939 and which the Association was prevented from using in the early post-war period. In a very real sense, therefore, Erskine represents the concept proposed by the SSHA, Tom Johnston and the Clyde Valley planners in the war years.

When, as a new member of the Association's Council of Management, the author was taken in 1980 to look at Erskine he was informed by staff of the great difficulty being experienced by many of the very low income tenants who, of course, had only recently been moved out from some of the slum areas of Glasgow. They apparently were experiencing great difficulty in paying their rents and staff were concerned for the future.

In May of 1992 as I looked at the town with my students I asked them to give me

No-fines cottages in Erskine.

their impressions of the economic health of the community. They were unanimously of the view that this had to be a fairly prosperous place. Gardens were neat and pretty, and there was absolutely no sign of void dwellings, still less of vandalism. On the contrary, it was obvious that many houses had been bought and adapted. Cars were parked throughout the town and there appeared to be many two car families. Moreover, private development projects were pushing ahead on various sites around the community. Subsequently we learned that of the 3391 houses built at Erskine by the SSHA some 2219 or 65% had been bought by tenants.[22] It was thus perfectly clear that in little more than ten to fifteen years this community had been transformed into a thriving go-ahead town with every prospect for the future. And this had been achieved mainly by allowing control and ownership to pass into the hands of the residents. Moreover, the dominant cottage-style buildings had made the process easy to effect.

We then crossed the bridge and, in a few minutes arrived to reflect on Faifley. This estate consisted originally of 2,373 dwellings, three quarters of which were owned by the SSHA with the remainder belonging to Clydebank District Council. It was built largely in the 1950s to provide replacement accommodation for houses lost through bombing. The Association's stock was made up of 476 cottages and 1,310 flats in three- and four-storey tenement blocks. By the mid 1980s it had been clear that this estate was in some danger of significant decline; access to parts of the estate had become 'easy', and apparently something of the order of seventy per cent of the applicants for tenancy nominated to the Association were single parents. In 1986, therefore, a major investigation of the community had taken place and the findings and proposals were encapsulated in the document *A Future for Faifley: A Strategy for a Problem Estate.*[23] Eventually a major programme of renewal had been commenced, partly under the leadership of the tenant led Faifley Housing Association which had acquired 320 of the District Council houses.

By the time of our visit many of the tenements had been modernised or, in some cases, demolished and a considerable transformation accomplished. Work was ongoing but clearly much remained to be done, and the students had little difficulty in identifying continuing problems. They concluded that poverty probably was still a serious factor here and assumed a continuing relatively high concentration of unemployment. Visible signs of personal household development were much less obvious and, for example, the level of car ownership appeared much lower. Given the predominant communal housing forms, far less seemed to have been achieved through the sales policy.

However, to my eyes the signs of progress and improvement in Faifley were clear and I had little personal doubt that the prospect for the community was becoming much brighter. This was subsequently confirmed when recently it was learned that 892 (41%) of the Association's houses have now been purchased, indicating a rise in the morale and wealth of residents and a commitment on their part to the future of the area.[24] What has to be understood, however, is that this satisfying progress will only have been achieved after four decades and massive reconstruction via a huge injection of public resources. By contrast with Erskine, where one generation has been sufficient to transform the economic situation of many residents, Faifley proved much more difficult and expensive to revitalise and liberate. But the two communities do provide a highly illustrative comparison between an effective housing system and one which had inhibited household development over many years.

Part of the success of the Right to Buy policy is connected with the contemporary change which has taken place in rent levels within the public sector. As was explained earlier, many local authorities traditionally maintained low rents by means of subsidies from rates and Housing Support Grant from government. For example, in 1960 Glasgow obtained only 31.6% of its housing revenue from rents (in contrast with equivalent figures of 68.2% for Birmingham, 47.1% for Liverpool and 54.8% in Manchester) and this was a major factor in both the poor quality of the buildings and inadequate maintenance.[25] Attempts by the Heath government in the early 1970s to tackle the problem were quickly quashed by the following Labour administration. Under Mrs Thatcher, however, strict controls were imposed on rate fund contributions and councils which breached the limits forfeited capital allocation. Rate borne subsidies were, therefore, effectively squeezed out of the system and Housing Support Grant was sharply reduced, and this tended to force up council rents.

Moreover, the housing benefit system also made an impact. Since a high proportion (now almost 80%) of council tenants qualified for housing benefits provided by the D.S.S., many councils realised that a major element in any rent increase would actually fall on central government rather than on tenants. Councils, therefore, tended to see rent rises as a method of drawing additional housing income out of the government. The tenants who did not qualify for housing benefit were obviously most adversely affected by rising rents, and for such individuals the increasing expense of renting from the public sector has acted as a considerable inducement to exercise their right to buy. This, of course, was not a trend which was greatly relished by some authorities, hence in more recent years some Scottish councils may have been more cautious about rent setting.

One final point worth making on this subject is that the 'Right to Buy' policy seems to have had a particularly beneficial effect on attitudes among residents of many estates. Where significant numbers of properties have been purchased, and where new owners have invested in their houses, it would not be surprising if the general level of local interest and care taken of the surrounding environment has tended to strengthen. Moreover, it may also be suggested that awareness of value for money issues has improved among both owners and tenants alike and this has been to the advantage of very many communities.

If the sales policy has attracted much interest the other major change of the past two decades is undoubtedly concerned with the move away from the former urban demolition policies to rehabilitation and renewal activities. In the early 1970s the destruction of buildings in old city areas reached something of a crescendo, but it became impossible to ignore or avoid the damage which was being done and, in particular, to Glasgow. Population figures showed not only the collapse of the communities in certain localities, but that the retreat from the city was almost out of control. The 1960 development plan had assumed a fall in the city's population from 1,055,000 at that time to about 997,000 by 1970. In fact the reduction was twice as great as anticipated. By 1973 the population was down to 850,000 and about 25,000 people were leaving each year. Moreover, many of those departing were skilled workers and professionals and many were leaving not just the city, but the region.[26]

At first planned overspill was blamed for this situation and the recently designated new town for Stonehouse was promptly cancelled. However, it was subsequently estimated that overspill accounted for only about 22% of the loss of population in the period 1961–72.[27] It was inescapable, therefore, that economic decline was at the root of the problem and that the wholesale destruction of great chunks of the city could not continue. In addition, public anxiety at the loss of fine older buildings became harder to avoid and there was increasing opposition to radical transport plans which would require further devastation.

It was under these circumstances that the Comprehensive Development Area approach was abandoned in the early 1970s and the Town and Country Planning (Scotland) Act, 1972 and the Local Government (Scotland) Act 1973 required District Councils to prepare local plans for all of their districts and these soon had to take account of wider Regional structure plans. Such programmes required consultation and co-operation with local communities and tended to encourage retention, preservation and renewal.

Towards the latter part of the 1960s the SSHA had turned its attention increasingly to the modernisation of older buildings typically on behalf of urban authorities and its activities in this direction were dramatically stimulated by the havoc done in January 1968 when a huge gale left a swathe of stripped roofs and damaged buildings across central Scotland. Many older tenements in Glasgow and Stirling were severely affected and the association responded to requests for assistance from various quarters.[28] Repairs and improvements carried out at this time helped to demonstrate the possibilities of modernisation and by 1970 the SSHA had developed a major programme of rehabilitation and conversion which included a total of more than 30,000 older houses.[29]

At about the same time the Government introduced the 1969 Housing Scotland Act which authorised the designation of small scale Housing Treatment Areas each of which extended to a locality of about 100–400 homes. In such places preferential grants became available. In addition municipalities were empowered to purchase and improve houses built before 1919 and it was estimated that some 4,000 units, most in Glasgow, were improved by such means.[30] This was an interesting pointer to the future, but the initial low level of achievement does indicate something of the reluctance of urban authorities to change their basic tack.

The shift towards rehabilitation was also encouraged by the rise of the housing association movement. As the annual figures for house-building will have illustrated a tiny number of houses each year had been provided in Scotland by small charitable housing associations. It will also be recalled that during the war

Tom Johnston had been among those keen to see an extension of housing association activity and had called for local authorities to give active support to such a development. His pleas had been substantially ignored and, indeed, the massive operations of local authorities had effectively relegated associations to an almost insignificant background role. By 1964, however, the Housing Corporation had been established to co-ordinate and promote the work of associations and its main function initially was to encourage the formation of housing societies to build cost rent and co-ownership schemes.

For the next decade very little seems to have been achieved in Scotland by the Housing Corporation, but in 1974 its powers were significantly improved. It was given the ability to provide capital and revenue grants to local housing associations engaged in the rehabilitation and improvement of property. In addition, under the 1974 Housing (Scotland) Act local authorities were empowered to declare Housing Action Areas (similar in scale to the previous Treatment Areas) where the housing and physical conditions were unsatisfactory and required major refurbishment. These initiatives established the legislative framework for the major involvement of associations in rehabilitation programmes.

To begin with the switch of policy in favour of renewal rather than demolition and replacement, posed great difficulties for some local authorities. Not only were their building divisions typically unsuited to the type of work involved, but their use of compulsory purchase and other methods tended to be resented by property owners. Work was often, therefore, significantly delayed.

However, by the end of the 1970s the community based housing associations were increasingly being seen on many sides as key agents for future urban redevelopment. Part of the credit for the initial success of the housing associations in Glasgow has to be attributed to the activities of Raymond Young and some of his architectural colleagues at the University of Strathclyde. Young, then a postgraduate student, obtained the support of residents in Govan to form the Tenement Improvement Project which in turn developed into ASSIST, a university-based architectural practice which specialised in advising community groups on rehabilitation and renewal. In 1974, when the powers of the Housing Corporation were being augmented, it was decided to raise the profile in Glasgow by opening a branch in the city with Young in charge. In addition, by agreement with the Scottish Office the Corporation gave priority to investment in rehabilitation within the city and thereafter associations gradually gained ground, the example set in Glasgow slowly being followed elsewhere in Scotland.

The general trend in this direction was also stimulated by the 1977 Green Paper *Scottish Housing* which stressed that new building would be restricted and the emphasis henceforth placed on renovation.

To begin with associations were seen by some councillors and officials as potential rivals, but gradually that attitude gave way as they began effectively to harness local communities to the processes of improvement. Typically they were run by committees of local residents, often either retired or unemployed individuals who were eager to use their skills and experience to the benefit of their neighbourhoods. Sometimes the committees included a number of local business people or professionals, and they also attracted a strong involvement from local women who may have found them an effective means of developing personal skills of organisation and administration. In addition, their access to government funds proved an enormous inducement to the local authorities since, not surprisingly, major rehabilitation was not cheap. By 1990 about thirty local housing associations were active in Glasgow while generally the movement was developing across urban Scotland.

The methods deployed by such associations tended to involve an agreement being reached with the District Council about the association's territory, which usually extended to somewhere between 500 and 2000 dwellings, and this location would then be underpinned by designation as a Housing Action Area. Thereafter private developers would be chosen to carry out work on small batches of proper-ties. On completion, the dwellings would then be rented out (until 1989) under the terms of the Fair Rent regime then applied to the private rented sector. Management and maintenance costs and loan charges were set against rental income and Housing Association Grant was used to cover the inevitable deficit. In addition, as rehabilitation operations gained momentum so further backing came via environmental grants made available by both local and central government.[31]

Another factor which tended to strengthen the popular view of housing associations was their involvement in special needs housing. In this case the associations were of a rather different type, tending to be national and charitable in character and concentrating their efforts on a particular category of client. However, with an increasing elderly population the need for specialised sheltered or, in some cases, disabled housing was broadly understood and the eagerness of associations to provide the required accommodation helped to win the respect of the public. If organisations like Hanover, Bield, Kirk Care or the Abbeyfields were not directly involved in urban renewal, their operations nevertheless helped immensely to generate confidence in the housing association movement. More-over, this was well understood by many of the area based associations, since they frequently included special needs housing in their own programmes while some-times the national associations were brought in to develop one of their units as part of a wider project.

Following the return of the Conservatives in 1979, after a short pause in spending, support for housing association-led regeneration increased. No doubt, the government was enthusiastic for local community participation, but it was also gradually becoming obvious that the activities of associations were stimulating additional private sector investment and the return of a degree of confidence to formerly run-down urban areas. Increased resources were channelled into repair and improvement grants and local authorities were able to manage these so that they were made available in the vicinity of housing association operations. Thus the emphasis swung from housing rehabilitation to area regeneration.

In addition, as the appearance of older properties was upgraded so new building on vacant neighbouring 'brown field' sites became more attractive and this gradually tended to proceed with housing association and private developer operations in close proximity. 'In Glasgow alone, by the end of the 1980s, associations had improved 15,000 BTS units, improvement and repair grants had been used on over 120,000 units and 13,000 new private units had been completed'.[32]

Glasgow, fundamentally because of its appalling condition in the 1970s, enjoyed priority in the resources deployed in Scotland and it typically attracted 50%-60% of the funds provided to Scottish housing association programmes throughout the 1980s. However, in other locations, such as in Leith, community based associations also made a major contribution.

Such was the extent of the devastation to parts of Glasgow by the mid 1970s, however, that it had then seemed necessary to organise at least one major multi-agency initiative to address the problem. This was the Glasgow Eastern Area Renewal (GEAR) project which was announced by the Secretary of State in May 1976.[33] It was concerned with a large area to the east of central Glasgow comprising Bridgeton, Dalmarnock and Shettleston and it contained some of the most wretched urban conditions in the western world. At the time such was the scale of decay, destruction and despair, that there were many who doubted that a viable solution would be found. In 1978 Ian Adams had this to say.

> 'Physically shocking', 'like going through a bombarded city' and 'dreadful' were some of the comments made by delegates from the European Parliament at the sight of the East End of Glasgow in 1976 ... It is a daunting challenge for the area is suffering from *planning dementia*, a species of planning blight, a condition which is the result of earlier notions of planning which have themselves created more problems than they have solved ...[34]

Indeed the GEAR area illustrated precisely the nature of the folly of the previous flatten and rebuild policies. It had contained seven of the designated Comprehensive Development Areas and the systematic destruction had reduced its population from around 145,000 in 1951 to about 45,000 by 1979.[35] Despite this clearance, however, the area still contrived to contain some 42,000 jobs, (55% manufacturing, 37% services and 6% construction) hence it was critical to the economy of the city.[36]

Initially there were thoughts of placing the problem in the hands of a development corporation along the lines of new town management, but that may have been just too radical a solution to swallow for the government and the newly reorganised local authorities. Leadership of the GEAR project was, therefore, given to the (also new) Scottish Development Agency and it was tasked with co-ordinating a multi-agency comprehensive modernisation programme involving Strathclyde Regional Council, Glasgow District Council, the SSHA, the Health Board and the Manpower Services Commission. Before very long, the impact being made elsewhere by housing associations could not be ignored, hence the Housing Corporation was quickly drawn in and community associations established.

G.E.A.R.

Such was the scale of the GEAR project that it undoubtedly had major implications not just for the morale of the communities directly involved, but for the city as a whole. Judged purely in terms of housing a great deal was achieved and apart from anything else the physical appearance of the area was transformed. Qualitatively much of the work done by the SSHA, housing associations and private developers was excellent and the mere fact that (albeit comparatively small) numbers of private houses were being constructed in such a part of the city indicated significant progress. The GEAR plan provided for 20% of the houses to be for owner occupiers and the 134 houses commenced at Dalveen Street in 1979 made up the first private housing scheme to be commenced in the East End since the second world war.[37]

All told just under £1 billion (1994 prices) was committed to the project and to some degree this co-ordinated multi-agency approach to area regeneration was replicated in the early 1980s in the Maryhill Corridor in Glasgow, in central Dundee and in Leith. In each case the SSHA was heavily involved through its designated Redevelopment Assistance Programme (RAP) and these in fact represented the last of the Association's major development initiatives. Under its RAP heading, from 1978 to 1986 the Association built 4,675 new houses and acquired

New housing in the G.E.A.R. area.

and modernised 3027. In GEAR during this time it produced 1209 new houses and rehabilitated 2049.[38]

A final evaluation of the GEAR project has been made, but never published, hence the cautious conclusions expressed have perhaps not been very widely considered. However it appears that, despite its scale and public resources, it failed, at least initially, to stem the population loss and to halt the economic decline. The training and employment measures were not very successful and, for example, housing investment was not linked to employment creation within the area. Apart from by means of housing association activity it seems that the project secured little community participation or involvement. Moreover, while social, health and education facilities were improved the impact of this on the community was not assessed effectively. Only the housing and environmental measures appear to have been regarded as successful at a basic level.[39]

Such gloomy findings inevitably must have made for a degree of caution in government and clearly established the massive and complex nature of the task of recovery from the disastrous policies of the 1960s and early 70s. However, not withstanding the validity of the criticisms, it has to be suggested that GEAR and the simultaneous work conducted in the Maryhill Corridor remain vital initiatives as far as the wider well-being of Glasgow is concerned. Decline in key parts of the heart of the city was visibly being addressed in a manner which obviously renewed the physical fabric of the areas. Seeing the transformation which was being accomplished made it possible for Glaswegians to start believing in the city again. In the author's opinion, whatever their imperfections, GEAR and the Maryhill projects marked a crucial turning point in the contemporary history of the city. Indeed, in some ways they were perhaps symbolic of more general changes which were of significance to Scotland as a whole.

CHAPTER SIX

A Housing Revolution

*I*T will be clear from the foregoing discussion that by the mid 1980s a considerable change had been effected in the approach to housing in Scotland, and the Right to Buy policy in particular had introduced the first major challenge to the consensus which had underpinned the development of the Scottish public sector housing system since the war. Moreover, it was noticeable that while the Scottish public continued to disclaim any great sympathy for Mrs Thatcher's government, applications to buy tended to shoot up in election years and opinion polls confirmed a strong latent desire in favour of home ownership.

One modern historian in his book *No Gods and Precious Few Heroes: Scotland 1914–1980* (1981) has deplored the quality of many of the ministers who have been responsible for Scottish government in the period since the First War.[1] However, irrespective of political allegiances, in Malcolm Rifkind, the Secretary of State (1986–1990), and Michael Ancram, Minister for Home Affairs with responsibility for housing (1983–1987), it must be arguable that the Thatcher administration produced two of the sharpest ministerial intellects which have applied themselves to Scottish housing policy.

Ancram turned his attention increasingly to the problems of the great monopolistic council-owned peripheral estates. Labour local politicians were still often very reluctant to admit the folly of earlier policies and that the distress in such areas might be as serious as in inner city locations; but the ministers did not mince their words. Rifkind pointed to low rent policies as a primary factor which had 'damaged the housing stock almost irretrievably' and had eventually produced a situation where many council tenants could now expect only a 'second class service'.[2]

Addressing the Convention of Scottish Local Authorities Ancram acknowledged that in view of their (then) possession of half of the Scottish housing stock, councils were bound to have a large future part to play. However, he saw no reason why they should continue to own and manage such huge amounts of property. He contrasted the massive sums of local authority expenditure on housing with the very poor living conditions for tenants which had often resulted and he placed the responsibility firmly on the councils themselves. Authorities had built up 'over-large council empires'; the very size of the stock in some cases was making efficient management almost impossible, and he pointed to the example of the 12,000 council houses throughout Scotland which were then lying empty. He also drew attention to the state of the great urban council schemes, including the notorious

peripheral estates where 'mistaken social planning and poor subsequent management have contrived to create a frequently depersonalising and alienating
environment'.[3]

At that time the minister was on particularly strong ground for Glasgow District
had itself commissioned an inquiry into the state of the city's housing and the
investigating committee, led by Professor Sir Robert Grieve, had published its
report in 1986.[4] In many ways Grieve was sympathetic to the council, but the dire
nature of some of the housing problems was clear. All told 15% of the city's houses
were reckoned to be below the tolerable standard and more than 40% required
major repair work. Almost £3 billions of investment would be needed and no less
than two thirds of that would have to be found for improvement or replacement
work on the council's own stock. Drastic action was urgent.

But the investigating committee did not restrict itself to questions of physical
condition and resources. It pointed to the adverse economic and employment
effects of lack of tenant choice in certain communities. Absence of rent differentials penalised those expected to live in poorer areas and the finding was that the
council's monopoly over much of the rented housing was responsible for lack of
choice, lack of mobility and poor housing standards. The committee's conclusion
was that the council had to reduce its role, with approximately 25% of its stock
(and particularly in the peripheral areas) being transferred to co-operatives,
housing associations and to private sector firms in order to produce a healthier
social mix and to open the way for some genuine choices.

Much of this message was heretical from a Scottish local authority point of view.
Now, however, it was coming not just from a Conservative government, but from
sympathetic independent enquirers.

Rifkind was already emphasising his desire to move away from monopoly council
estates and to encourage diversification of tenure. Big estates should be broken
up so that more and more control and authority was transferred in one way or
another to smaller communities of interest. He reasoned that people should be
able to take more responsibility for the management and ownership of their homes
and favoured an extension of housing associations and co-operatives of various
kinds into the communities in question. In addition, private investment had also
to be attracted to such areas; and he had no doubt that councils should relinquish
much of their stock.

Rifkind, however, also saw the opportunity for significant further initiatives on
the part of the government. In 1988 many of his views were indicated in the White
Paper *New Life For Urban Scotland*. It drew on much of the experience which had
been gained in GEAR and elsewhere and set out the lines of the government's
approach to the requirements of regeneration in the peripheral and other big
council estates. A co-operative partnership approach was required from the various
official and private agencies and the need to improve the economic prospects of
residents had to be grasped. While housing was important so too were a host of
other amenities and commercial services. Central to the approach to housing
would be variety of tenure forms so that future communities had genuine choices

and home ownership would be encouraged. Similarly new methods of manage-ment and ownership of rented housing would be fostered. To give practical expression to these ideas the Secretary of State targeted four of the most problem-atic estates in the country for Scottish Office led formal Partnership initiatives and these were aimed at Castlemilk in Glasgow, Ferguslie Park, Paisley, Whitfield in Dundee and Wester Hailes on the edge of Edinburgh. In each case the full range of policies would be deployed and demonstrated, to regenerate the communities, but also partly to give visible encouragement to others.

To create formal Partnerships all over the country was obviously impossible, impractical and unnecessary. However, some form of co-ordinated leadership probably was required if Scotland was to develop a fully modern and healthy system of housing in the years ahead. As early as 1979 Douglas Niven had called for the establishment of a Scottish Housing Board

> to administer a coherent and hopefully an appropriate housing policy for Scotland. The organisation would be staffed by people with a commitment to the idea of helping the people of Scotland to help themselves to better housing. The existing bureaucratic process would be progressively dismantled .. (to encourage) .. a freer attitude to housing policies and to housing design.[5]

Such a board would, Niven argued, develop an accurate flow of information in respect of Scottish housing and would foster the conditions under which citizens could satisfy their preferences from a full range of 'reasonable housing options'.

Both Rifkind and Ancram agreed with these opinions. In 1986 the SSHA was subject to one of the quinquennial reviews during which the performance of a public organisation is assessed and evaluated. On this occasion the Association came out of the examination very well, but in his foreword to the review document the Secretary of State wrote

> In considering my response to the main findings and recommendations of the *Policy Review* I have been conscious of the need to look at the role of the SSHA in the wider context of overall housing activity in Scotland, over which government exercises control. While each of the main bodies concerned has its own distinctive approach and contri-bution to make to the housing needs, there is common ground and some overlap in their activities. There have also been significant changes in recent years in the pattern of housing tenure, provision and management as a direct result of the successful pursuit of this government's housing objective.[6]

Accordingly he instituted an investigation of the possibility of a merger between the SSHA and the Housing Corporation in Scotland. In this ministers were supported by John Richards, Chairman of the Scottish Committee of the Housing Corporation from 1982 and a distinguished architect. Richards backed the idea because he approved of a decentralisation of autonomy to the Scottish level. This was a sentiment shared by some senior officers at the Scottish Office and particu-larly Harold Mills, who contributed largely to the drafting of an appropriate White Paper and thereby turned the idea into a praticable proposition. There is no doubt that one of the attractions was that such a merger would result in the transfer of public funds for housing associations from the budget of the Department of the Environment to the Scottish Office block. That in turn, of course, would enable a much more strategic approach to be taken to the identification of Scottish housing priorities and to the subsequent channelling of resources.

The possibility of concentrating central housing funds in the hands of the Scottish Secretary was very attractive. In addition, however, it was realised that there was a certain inconsistency in an argument which advocated dispersal of local authority housing stocks to smaller, more community orientated and efficient organisations on the one hand, while, on the other, continuing to maintain a large number of public sector houses under direct central government control via the SSHA. Moreover, since the Association's management track record was good and its staff were extremely professional, the condition of most of its houses was quite reasonable, and not surprisingly its level of house sales to tenants was high. Before long, therefore, some change in its nature was inevitable. Finally, if diversification of tenure was to be encouraged, the possibility of using SSHA stock to nurture the growth of housing associations and other possible future landlords had to be considered.

The re-election of the government in 1987 hastened the pace towards a merger of the SSHA and the Housing Corporation in Scotland and, despite apparent doubts on the part of the Prime Minister – perhaps instinctively uneasy about an institution which was bound to be somewhat interventionist – Rifkind was able to bring about the creation of the new organisation, Scottish Homes, under the terms of the 1988 Housing (Scotland) Act. Effectively what was created was a national housing development agency and it was provided with a wide range of powers and competence. Indeed, perhaps the most surprising feature of the legislation was the breadth of the scope of the new organisation and the lack of restriction under which it was required to operate. Whereas the focus of much of its future operations would necessarily be through the housing associations, Scottish Homes, unlike the Housing Corporation, was enabled to develop a truly national remit in respect of Scottish housing and to look to the health of all sectors and localities. It was specifically instructed to foster housing research and information generation on housing matters and on the state of Scottish dwellings. It was expected to develop policies concerned not just with the great council estates, but with towns and villages as well. It was empowered to assist the activities not simply of associations, but of private developers by means of grants called GRO-grants; and, if need be, it could deploy a proportion of its resources for environmental and other non-housing purposes.

The establishment of Scottish Homes from April 1989 was a genuinely radical departure and without any real parallel elsewhere in the U.K.. The agenda which it would be expected to develop was clearly complex, requiring to strike a balance between the Government's general desire for market orientated solutions with the need to intervene in many run down and impoverished parts of the country. The fundamental object of the exercise would be (so far as it was possible for housing policy), to promote conditions wherein households would be enabled to maximise their own economic potential and where qualitative dwelling standards would be raised to acceptable modern levels. In particular, the housing choices open to many consumers would have to be transformed. In the words of the White Paper – *Housing: The Government's Proposals for Scotland* (Nov 1987) the

> unreasonable and unnecessary deprivation of many people's opportunity for any choice or control over such a vitally important aspect of their lives has impoverished the quality of those lives and hindered Scotland's capacity to respond to economic problems and challenges.[7]

The essential purpose of Scottish Homes was to address precisely that problem.

A crucial task in the establishment of Scottish Homes was the identification and appointment of appropriate leadership. Michael Ancram had been rewarded for his efforts by being voted out of his Edinburgh South constituency in 1987 and he agreed to serve for a time on the Board, but indicated his desire for an early return to politics. (In fact he was soon selected for Devizes and his subsequent election enabled his appointment to the Northern Ireland Office where he has won golden opinions as a key participant in the current moves towards peace in the province.) His place on the Board, therefore, was seen as transitional and probably temporary (he actually withdrew in 1990) and he was not a candidate for the important chairmanship.

To fill the position, Rifkind turned to Sir James Mellon, a career diplomat who was about to retire from the diplomatic service. Mellon at that time was Consul General in the United States where he was responsible for trade promotion and thus in contact with the Scottish trade minister, then Ian Lang. The Northern Ireland Office was at that point keen to secure the future services of Sir James, but Rifkind, tipped off by Lang, moved swiftly to divert him into the position at the head of Scottish Homes.

The son of a Paisley schoolmaster, Mellon had been brought up in Glasgow as part of a large family. A graduate of Glasgow University he had undertaken post-graduate study in Denmark, before joining the Department of Agriculture of the Scottish Office. Thereafter he had transferred to the Foreign Office and developed his career as a diplomat, moving through various overseas positions, but typically retaining an interest in development economics and trade promotion. He combined a first class intellect with a breadth of international experience and he had the inestimable advantage of being able to relook at his native Scotland from a genuinely objective perspective. In many ways he was an inspired choice and he agreed to take the job partly because he welcomed the chance to bring back his knowledge and experience and apply them to a key area of Scottish life.[8]

Inevitably, Mellon was not well known in Scotland and the initial reaction to his appointment in many parts of the Scottish housing establishment was to question his lack of a background in the subject and his lack of contact with recent Scottish affairs. In fact, however, he brought a breadth of vision and grasp which was, from the outset, both challenging and refreshing. He understood housing in terms of a complex system which impacted on, and was a critical part of, the economy. He understood that the U.K. (and, of course, Scotland) was moving into increasingly international economic conditions and that it was essential to look at Scotland's housing arrangements within that context. Fundamentally the housing system had to become much less rigid and, far from acting as a drag on household and regional economic performance, it had to be sufficiently flexible and efficient as to facilitate and encourage economic well-being at all levels. Choices in housing had to be capable of promoting rather than restricting the potential of households and communities.

This was a language and an analysis to which very few people in Scotland were accustomed and it stemmed largely from his Whitehall and international experience. An appointment in East Germany had made him conscious of the strains imposed by eastern European housing policies. Equally, however, he was aware of the effect which non-interventionist open 'single' market conditions had had on down town city areas in the U.S. – south side Chicago, the neglected poor wards of Atlanta or in the Bronx of New York. And he was concerned to ensure that Scotland was much better equipped to thrive in the developing single European economy.[9]

Sir James's appointment was announced in the autumn of 1988 and, in addition to Ancram, he was joined on the original Board of Scottish Homes by Frances McCall, the dynamic founder of the Calvay Housing Co-operative in Easterhouse; Heather Sheerin, a successful Inverness business-woman and chair of Albyn Housing Association; Duncan Maclennan, Professor of Urban Studies at Glasgow University and a leader in the field of housing research; and Norman Lessels, chairman of the Standard Life Assurance Company and a director of various firms including the Bank of Scotland. From the Housing Corporation in Scotland came the former chairman John Richards (he was to serve as deputy chairman of Scottish Homes from 1991 to 1994); and the SSHA supplied both its former deputy chairman, Charles Snedden, convener of the Central Regional Council, and the author. (In 1990 Ancram was succeeded by Daphne Sleigh, a shrewd and amusing Edinburgh District Councillor and a year later Charles Snedden was replaced by Cameron Parker, Managing Director of Lithgows.) The final member of the new board was the chief executive, George Irvine, a Scot who came to the position after a career in the building industry in England.

The appointment of a chief executive from the private sector stemmed perhaps from a desire to ensure that Scottish Homes developed in a manner which was in keeping with the government's general approach to business. The new Board commenced work in the late autumn of 1988 and took over its duties from its predecessors in April 1989.

Inevitably, in the early stages many of the internal organisational and administrative tasks took precedence and the problems involved were often complex and difficult. Not only were the cultural backgrounds of the staff quite different, but numerically they were unbalanced. The Housing Corporation in Scotland had required only a small complement of central staff since it had operated through the housing association movement. By contrast the SSHA had still retained more than twelve hundred employees. Moreover, the latter, excellent people, were pre-eminently dedicated to managing and maintaining a large stock of houses or had been employed to carry out the direct production of dwellings either through new build or rehabilitation. To a great extent they were unused to and untrained in the kind of indirect intelligence gathering and development approach through which the new organisation was expected increasingly to operate in future. In addition, many of the staff had understandable worries about their personal careers if the shedding of stock was about to accelerate and the Secretary of State had responded to such concerns by promising job guarantees. Management of major change is never easy. But in the circumstances just described, the welding together of an effective organisation with clear aims and objectives, efficient methods of operation and an enthusiastic, committed staff, was no lightweight matter.

George Irvine was a thoroughly decent gentleman who was soon well liked by many of his colleagues. However, he was never entirely at ease with his role. He was perhaps not comfortable with the type of wide strategic thinking inevitably associated with his position, nor was he accustomed to some of the requirements of public methods of administration and control. It was not, therefore, surprising that he soon decided to return to England. This eventuality was a matter of disappointment to his friends and it may be suggested that he was to some extent squeezed between a Board which was impatient to move on with the broad agenda, and a senior staff who were rather more concerned with operational difficulties.

The Board decided to be cautious over the appointment of a replacement chief executive and during much of 1991, therefore, the day to day leadership of the organisation was taken on by Ian Penman, a senior Scottish Office official who was about to take early retirement from the civil service. Penman in fact did an excellent transitional job before handing on to the present holder of the position, Peter McKinlay.

McKinlay in many ways proved to be the ideal foil for Mellon. The son of a Campbeltown fisherman, McKinlay had also been a career civil servant and therefore, the two men were easily on the same wavelength.[10] Much of McKinlay's career had been in the Scottish Development Department and he had most recently distinguished himself in the role of chief executive of the Scottish prison service. A big man in every way, he quickly established his authority and, after appropriate investigation, commenced to reorganise his resources.

Initially, McKinlay was concerned to obtain a clearer direction for the organisation and to take the steps necessary to improve staff morale, confidence and sense of purpose. This he addressed through structural changes and by improving information flows. He also soon identified the degree of tension between the Board and senior staff and set about readjusting the latter in order to get people into the right places. Soon an effective team including Raymond Young (Research), Bob Millar (Strategic Policy), Jim Hastie (Development), John Breslin (Finance), Andrew Fyfe (Operations) and Richard Burn (Housing Management) had been assembled or repositioned, and, under their leadership, many younger, able members of staff began to make an increasing impact. Moreover, steps were taken to produce a much clearer level of understanding between Board and Executive as to the nature of the programme to which they were working. This latter task was partly addressed by joint seminars and workshops to fashion a common under-standing of the strategic thrust of policy and perhaps a key turning point for the organisation was such a weekend 'jackets off' session at a Perthshire hotel in December 1991.

Before examining the thrust of the emerging policies, it may be as well to reflect briefly on the background events of recent years.

First, it may be suggested that the departure of Mrs Thatcher from the Prime Ministership, taken together with Malcolm Rifkind's move to the Ministry of Defence, may have relieved some of the intensity of the pressure for radical change. To a certain extent, by 1990 this may have been no bad thing for it allowed a degree of breathing space for Scottish Homes to prepare itself and to take the time to properly work out its programme. Similarly, the new Secretary of State, Ian Lang and his junior minister with responsibility for housing, Lord James Douglas-Hamilton, were able to concentrate on consolidating policy within the new structure.

However, an important contextual consideration of the period from 1987 concerns the remarkable contemporary developments in home ownership markets (particularly in England). From 1987 the movement towards European Monetary Union began to impact increasingly on monetary policy and this was to have a major effect on housing markets. Monetary union implied promotion of a degree of convergence in the economies of the various European Union countries and the first stage for Britain, according to the European enthusiasts in both the government and opposition parties, was for the U.K. to move towards the Exchange Rate Mechanism. To prepare for entry, from March 1987 the then Chancellor of the Exchequer, Nigel Lawson, commenced a policy designed to maintain an exchange rate ratio of approximately £1 to 3 Deutsche Marks.[11] In order to achieve this outcome he used interest rate changes. Effectively, what this meant was that interest rates were now being adjusted not in response to demand and supply pressures for borrowed money, but rather in order to maintain the external value of the currency.

Unfortunately for the Chancellor, the government and the U.K. housing mar-ket, sustained manipulation of interest rates to meet exchange rate considerations took insufficient account both of consumer borrowing habits and of the nature of the type of property owning society which Britain had become. Through much of 1987–1988 interest rates were maintained at relatively low levels to prevent the pound appreciating, despite the fact that inflationary pressure was evident. In addition, the Chancellor gave four months' warning of his intention to end the practice whereby partners living together had been able to combine their entitle-ment to mortgage tax relief so as to create an effective ceiling of £60,000 rather than £30,000. The consequence of giving advance warning of this change, taken together with unrealistically low interest rates, was a massive surge in English housing markets through the summer of 1988. With readily available cheap mortgages, people sought to change their homes and house prices rocketed.

Boom is perhaps inevitably followed by slump, and in 1989, for almost the first time since the inter-war depression, property prices began to fall. In that year the pound tended to sink below its desired Deutsche Mark level, hence, to defend it, interest rates rose higher than might otherwise have been expected. Inevitably, a high price for borrowed money reduced the demand for mortgages and subsequently deflated the housing market.

However, the problem now became mechanised from 1990 as Britain joined the European Exchange Rate Mechanism. For the next two years unrealistically high interest rates were maintained in an effort to keep within the agreed exchange rate margins. This had the benefit of continuing heavy downward pressure on inflation, but it also meant that domestic interest rates were much too high given the needs of depressed British markets. From the point of view of U.K. home-owners, the situation was little short of disastrous and many English families saw a

UK Housing Markets 1978-1993

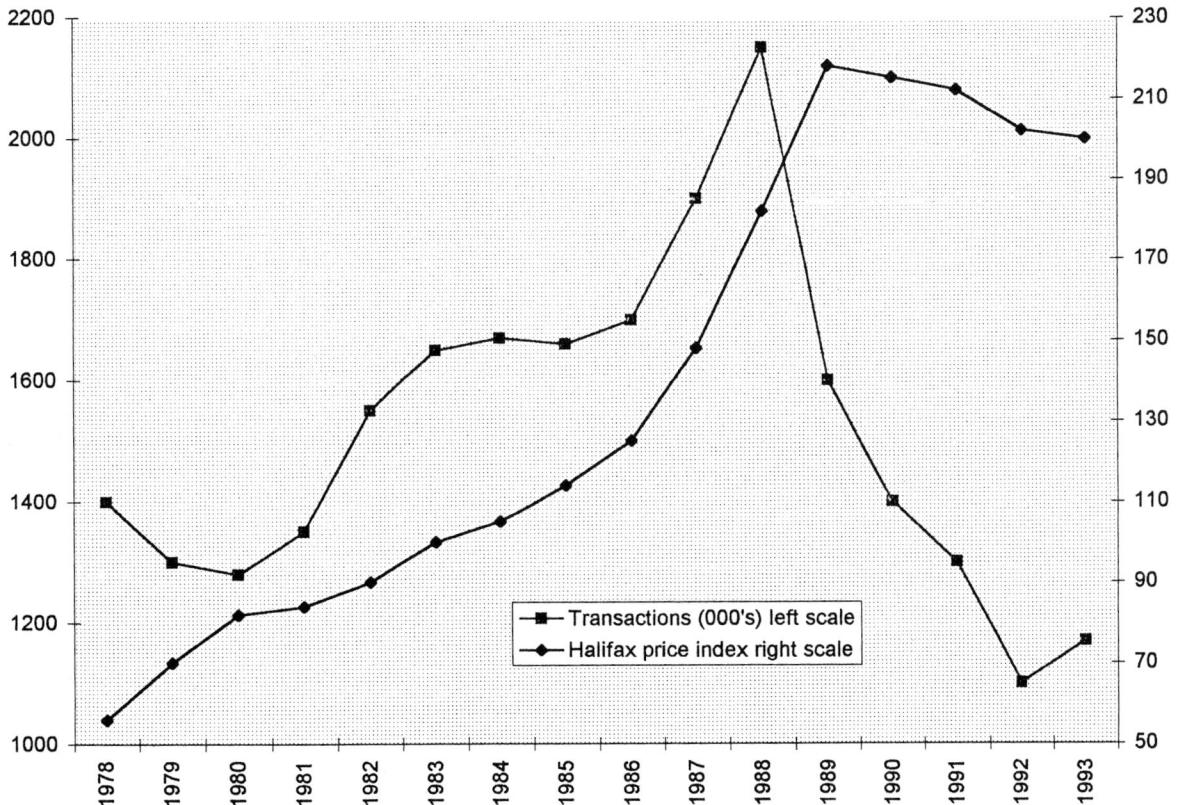

Source : Halifax

quarter or more of the value of their property being wiped out as house prices plummeted. The phenomenon of negative equity became common whereby home owners selling their property could not obtain a price sufficient to offset the outstanding mortgage debt. Those most vulnerable, were obviously people who had only recently purchased at the top of the market when prices had been high and who were thus carrying the largest amounts of debt. In this situation, many home-owners, not surprisingly, became very reluctant to sell if they could avoid doing so, hence activity on the market slumped. The inevitable follow-on result was that demand for household products – furnishings, white goods and so on – fell away and this intensified what had by now become a debt driven recession.

In September 1992 a financial crisis and international pressure on the pound drove Britain out of the ERM and interest rates thereafter returned to more viable levels and became more responsive to the requirements of the U.K. economy. A much more competitive pound slowly brought recovery with the happy combination of low inflation and export-led growth. However, it has proved very much more difficult to restore confidence to housing markets in England and, at the time of writing, house prices in much of the country remain far below the levels of the late 1980s while general consumer confidence has been very slow to recover. The government inevitably paid a huge price in terms of lost popularity as a result of these events.

Reflecting on the episode, two points are perhaps worth making. First, those who advocated the prolonged use of interest rates as a means of maintaining the external value of the currency were ignoring the realities of a society in which the public held much of their wealth in household property. The government was subjected to heavy pressure from the U.K. banking community to participate in the ERM as a step in the direction of a common European currency. However, such moves paid insufficient attention to the implications of the very different tenure forms of the various European partners and particularly Britain and Germany. After the war the West Germans gave little priority to home ownership and relied on private landlords or housing associations backed by subsidies to supply the vast majority of their housing. By 1987, therefore, only 38% of German households owned their homes and typically private house purchase was contemplated only by middle-aged individuals at the height of their earning powers. The Germans have not evolved the type of extensive property trading system developed in the U.K. and this means that housing plays a much less central part in the operation of their domestic economy. Moreover, inevitably Germans have not tended to develop the mortgage and other borrowing habits of the British and general consumers are, therefore, much less vulnerable to interest rate pressures. All of this should have been understood by Lawson and his colleagues in the late 1980s, but unfortunately institutional pleading carried rather more weight than the interests of domestic property owners.

Second, Scotland weathered the economic stresses of the episode somewhat better than many other parts of the country. There were several reasons for this. As has been made clear throughout this narrative, the Scottish private sector was significantly slower to develop than was the case in England and this means that even today there is a scarcity of supply of certain types of dwelling in various parts of the country. A consequence is that even in adverse economic conditions there is a tendency for demand to exceed supply in specific parts of Scotland and for particular types of housing, hence prices under such conditions still tend to drift upwards. Again, because so many Scottish home owners of the contemporary period have purchased their former council houses at discount, the level of debt carried by typical Scottish mortgage holders is relatively low. For both of these reasons general house prices in Scotland did not crash and few Scottish families suffered severely from negative equity. (It is interesting to note that, having traditionally lagged behind, Scottish house prices have in recent years gradually closed the gap with prices elsewhere, so that they are now more or less on par with the U.K. average. Over the decade to 1992 Scottish prices rose by no less than 132%; and in 1993, while U.K. house prices were still falling by 2.5%, prices in Scotland continued to rise by a further 2.6%.)[12]

In addition, the Scottish social rented sector from 1987 to the present was declining steadily, but still remained around a comparatively high 40% of the total stock. This means that a large portion of the population was not particularly adversely affected by high interest rates and the pressures on the market for domestic property. They were, of course, affected by the general economic downturn. However, while the construction industry suffered severely through the slump in housing markets, its problems seem to have been much less acute in Scotland. Part of the reason for this is explained above, but another factor was certainly the continuing high levels of public expenditure, particularly on redevelopment and rehabilitation work in the Scottish cities. (One major builder admitted to the author that without the activities of Scottish Homes in the period 1990–1993, his firm would have been in serious difficulty.)

An obvious lesson from this episode is that those who wish to promote closer European integration should give greater attention to the important differences which exist in the various economies and particularly in the cultures of the people concerned. Changes need to be thought through properly before they are attempted. Moreover, it is unwise to place too much weight on sectoral interests, even when they are as powerful as the leaders of the banking community.

Another lesson, however, is that a healthy housing system is one which is both balanced and flexible and which does not encourage over-borrowing. While home ownership is properly important to a modern sophisticated society a good, efficient and high quality rented sector is also necessary. Easy movement within and between sectors (depending on household circumstances and local conditions), is central to the effective operation of a housing system. These are lessons which contemporary Scottish housing policy makers have to keep firmly in mind.

Returning to the development of the strategic approach of Scottish Homes, a key obstacle to progress was the lack of understanding of the broad nature of the task both within and beyond the organisation. As far as the public were concerned, too often housing policy was viewed in traditional simplistic output terms – ie numbers of houses produced. Rarely did journalists or other commentators talk or write about housing as a system, hence systemic failures evident in Scotland were discussed only crudely. This was a problem to which Mellon addressed himself and he was aided by a steadily improving flow of information. One of the most important contributions came from the massive Scottish Homes organised Scottish House Condition Survey of 1991 which indicated that approximately 113,000 dwellings were standing empty and that almost half of the vacancies were in properties owned by local authorities. At the same time there was concern about the growth to over 35,000 in applications to councils under the terms of the Homelessness legislation. Taken together, of course, the two factors – apparent homelessness in a land with empty houses – demonstrated that Scotland does indeed have a problem which is at least partly due to system failure.

Lack of appreciation of the task was not, however, merely a question of general perceptions. Within the local authorities there was considerable scepticism and suspicion and there was resentment that Scottish Homes and the housing association movement were apparently being favoured by government in terms of resource allocation. Moreover, many officials within council housing departments feared the consequences of policies favouring possible bulk transfers of council stocks. The attitude of local authorities was a critical problem as far as Mellon and his colleagues were concerned since the co-operation of councils was an essential prerequisite to the healthy evolution of policy. Future development initiatives and enhancement of housing services would depend on the willingness of councils to place much greater emphasis on their roles as strategic enablers with clear understanding and visions of the desired shape of their own communities. Mellon, therefore, gave great attention and effort to winning the confidence and trust of councillors and their staffs.

One of the methods by which this was tackled was through continuous negotiations and discussions. What has to be remembered is that despite the controls placed on them, Scottish local councils have in each recent year received permission to spend roughly £550 millions on their own housing stocks and a further £120 millions or so on the grant support of owner occupiers. This means that total public capital spending on Scottish housing is split so that approximately two-thirds comes via local authorities to one third from Scottish Homes. Moreover local councils have wide-ranging planning powers in respect of many non-housing local services. Although more than 200,000 local authority houses (25% of the original stock) have now been sold to tenants, about 30% of Scottish households still live in local authority accommodation.[13]

In these circumstances, co-operation in obtaining a coherent approach to housing policy is absolutely crucial, and Mellon therefore set about attempting to develop formal frameworks within which investment programmes could be brought together. Scottish Homes has accordingly negotiated and signed Strategic Agreements with the great majority of the country's local authorities. The principles behind such agreements are to encourage common understandings and partnerships, to obtain maximum benefit for communities by ensuring that investment plans are co-ordinated and complementary, and to set out the ways in which Scottish strategic objectives are to be met at the local level.[14]

Moreover, this trend towards co-operation has been enhanced since 1993 by the Scottish Office decision to develop an annual tri-partite planning system. This involves civil servants meeting together with officials from Scottish Homes and local authorities to discuss intentions and resource requirements. The climate in relations is, therefore, now significantly more constructive and one trusts that the current reorganisation of local government will enable further improvement.

It should perhaps also be mentioned that one of the most important initiatives of Scottish Homes in the last two years has been the development of what is called Local Housing System Analysis to assist in the preparation of investment programmes and to provide an accurate information base not just for Scottish Homes, but also for its partners. LHSA enables Scottish Homes Districts to identify the nature of housing in their areas, the effectiveness and extent of markets and the existence of various forms of shortage or misuse of resources. This should in future allow for a much more informed and appropriate deployment of funds and other assets by all concerned. It is an approach to which Scottish Homes is particularly suited since, of course, in many places housing markets are bound to cut well across the boundaries of local authorities – even of the large regional councils which are shortly to be replaced. The system, therefore, should be helpful to everyone active in housing including the new single tier councils, builders, housing associations and ultimately consumers and the immediate task must be to make the facility readily available and accessible.

The housing association movement also presented its difficulties. Many of the members of associations assumed that Scottish Homes would be no more than a Scottish version of the Housing Corporation and paid little attention to the implications of its wider remit and powers. Indeed, at first there was a tendency to deplore the emphasis which was placed on encouraging an extension of private investment and associations found it hard to understand the desire of Scottish Homes to assist private developers. Diversification of tenure was fine so long as it meant an extension of housing association activity. But it was often less welcome where it involved making space for the private sector. Too often association activists were so preoccupied with their excellent social or charitable perspectives that they tended to disparage more fundamental economic questions and were impatient with attempts to establish a more strategic approach.

Part of the early problem in relations in this case was general housing association distrust of the new arrangements initiated by the 1989 Housing (Scotland) Act. New housing association lettings were henceforth to be in the form of 'assured' rather than 'secure' tenancies and rents were to be fixed by the housing associations rather than through the Fair Rent system. Development costs not covered by Housing Association Grant would now have to be found from private borrowing rather than through public loans; and if development budgets were exceeded associations could not rely automatically on increased HAG rates.

These changes in the legal framework encouraged some unease, but gradually

Council flats built at Niddrie, Edinburgh c1967.

it was realised by associations that their operations were not being curbed or threatened. Indeed, in recent years the pace of association activity has, if anything, tended to quicken. Partly expansion has been permitted by the increase in resources available to Scottish Homes to 1994/95, but it is also true that associations have become rather more adept at drawing in private finance than many of their members may have anticipated. Obviously there has had to be some adjustment in activities and the proportion of association investment in low-cost home ownership has increased relative to spending on subsidised rental housing, but there is now perhaps more agreement that such arrangements tend to make for better balanced communities.

The confidence of the Scottish housing association movement has thus remained high and there are currently some 260 registered associations and co-operatives active in Scotland.[15] Most are general lettings and charitable associations and the largest single group are the Abbeyfield Societies which make up almost a quarter of the total. The latter are very small, often with less than fifteen units. In 1983 Scottish associations had just 16,698 houses. By 1993, despite sales to tenants and others of about 2,500, the associations' stock had risen to around 60,000 dwellings, or 3% of the entire Scottish total.[16]

In such a climate of growth there was every reason for confidence. However, even today only three of the Scottish associations possess more than 2,500 units and this

Flats at Niddrie modernised by Hunter's Hall Housing Co-operative.

raises some questions for ongoing consideration. Clearly, efficiency is to some degree related to size. Just as housing organisations can be far too large and remote from tenants, it is also true that they may be too small, with the consequence that the average cost per dwelling owned becomes very high. While formal or informal co-operation between associations can help to restrain costs, in the longer term it will be very much to the advantage of Scottish housing if a number of larger housing associations are encouraged to develop to a more optimum size – probably somewhere between 5,000 and 10,000 units. Continuing development and bulk transfers of Scottish Homes, new town and local authority stocks could well double the size of the housing association movement by the year 2000 and within this process due attention should be given to the scale of operations and cost patterns of the emerging organisations. Similarly the introduction of Compulsory Competitive Tendering for local authority housing management services should help to emphasise the potential benefits to some associations of being efficient managers and of thereby enabling themselves to enter the tender process with realistic prospects.

The mutual confidence between Scottish Homes and the housing associations seems to have improved steadily after the initial uncertainty and one would hope that a greater degree of understanding continues to develop.

At first, even within the Board of Scottish Homes there were problems which arose from the very different backgrounds and levels of comprehension of members. Moreover, as has previously been mentioned, for many months the Board and senior staff were not entirely in harmony in their analysis of the objectives which they were trying to attain or of the policy measures which they should deploy.

Mellon addressed such difficulties by using all his diplomatic skills, but he also attempted to improve the quality of debate by broadening the horizons of his colleagues. In 1991–92 he arranged for a group of Board members and senior staff to examine the housing systems of Denmark, Poland and Canada and some representatives of the housing associations – David Orr, Director of the Scottish Federation, his then Chairman, Harry Mulligan, and Craig Sanderson, Chief Executive of Link Housing Association – were invited to join in one or another of the parties.[17]

The trips were in no sense leisurely, and as indicated previously, the visit to Poland was particularly instructive and interesting. Analysing the housing system in the context of the wider economic functioning of society was especially informative, for the party found doors being opened for them at all levels of government and throughout the housing industry. The eventual job of reporting conclusions to the Polish Government and to local representatives of the World Bank ensured that participants concentrated on the task and worked hard and the result was a marvellous learning experience even for so experienced a company.

The lessons gained in Canada were more complex, but there was no doubt about the quality of much of Canadian housing and the efficiency with which housing markets appeared to operate. Consideration of the various means by which Canadians seek to intervene in housing to assist low income families without trapping them into poverty was important and helpful. Perhaps the most interesting aspect of that trip, however, was the opportunity which it provided to examine the activities of the Canada Mortgage and Housing Corporation, an organisation which has maintained a strategic role in the development and operation of Canadian housing since the last war. Even the presence of decentralised State legislatures and governments has not enabled Canadian federal governments to avoid the requirement for a national organisation dedicated to assisting in the promotion of an efficient housing system. The quality of information generation and dissemination was particularly admirable and it was interesting to speculate as to whether the CMHC was a potential role model for a future Scottish Homes.

Such activities gradually raised the level of understanding of Scotland's housing problems at the top of the organisation and, perhaps in consequence, the general strategy became more coherent. Moreover, from 1991 the Scottish Homes share of the available public budget began to increase so that by 1993 spending through housing associations accounted for almost one third of the total public investment in Scottish housing. This, of course, gave increasingly powerful leverage. An indication of the thrust of activities may be derived from the development funding programme indicated below.

SCOTTISH HOMES INVESTMENT PROGRAMME 1995/1996

TABLE 1   THE PROGRAMME ALLOCATION

	Approved Programme 1994/95 £m	*Approved Programme 1995/96 £m*
Development		
Partnership Areas	24.509	21.860
Inner City	74.190	73.049
Outer City	54.173	54.218
SURIs	24.037	32.445
Urban Areas	72.669	68.670
Rural Areas	60.419	60.883
New Towns	1.908	.780
Revenue Grants	6.050	6.050
Windlaw	2.600	2.600
Total Development	320.555	320.555
Housing Mangement		
Capital	33.396	22.202
Revenue	20.600	19.115
Technical Fees	3.366	2.080
Total Housing Management	57.362	43.397
Total Programme	377.917	363.952
Corporation Tax	4.500	–
Total	382.417	363.952

TABLE 2   DEVELOPMENT FUNDING PROGRAMME BY SUPPLIER

	Approved Programme 1994/95 £m	*Approved Programme 1995/96 £m*
Housing Associations		
Rented	233.435	230.053
Low Cost Home Ownership	33.376	34.500
Tenant Incentive Scheme	2.000	4.000
Revenue Grants	6.050	6.050
	274.861	274.603
Other Suppliers		
GRO Grants for Rent	7.477	7.000
GRO Grants for Owner Occupation	26.000	27.000
Individuals	1.638	1.360
Special Needs Capital Grant	2.000	0.859
	37.115	36.219
Environmentals	5.979	7.133
Windlaw	2.600	2.600
Total Programme	320.555	320.555

PROGRAMME OUTPUTS 1995/96

Programme	Number of Houses	Private Finance
Housing Associations		
Rented	4895	£47m
Home Ownership	1260	£36m
Other Suppliers		
Rented	375	£12m
Home Ownership	1970	£80m
Total	8500	£175m

The development programme gives an indication of where housing association funds and grants to others are being applied. It illustrates that the bulk of expenditure is still directed to the cities and, inevitably Glasgow still attracts the lion's share of resources. The programme for 1995/96 is intended to produce around 8,500 new or rehabilitated houses and to draw in some £175 millions of private investment in areas which would otherwise be neglected. 3,230 new or improved homes are intended to be provided for outright or shared ownership; 6,775 of the houses are planned to be developed in urban areas and 1,725 in rural communities; 1,850 houses will be for those with special needs such as some of the elderly, or physically or mentally impaired. Directly or indirectly 2,725 homes will be for letting to the homeless and included within this number will be 100

Longpark, Kilmarnock in 1992 illustrating the type of conditions before the area became subject to a S.U.R.I. initiative.

furnished units. Finally, the programme provided for SNAP (Special Needs Allowance Package) grants to assist with the revenue costs of 4,000 bed spaces for Care In The Community initiatives and some 700 elderly households will be assisted to stay on in their own homes through the Care and Repair system.

Of the headings under which the programme is set out, SURIs (Smaller Urban Renewal Initiatives) is interesting and it indicates a policy initiative particularly supported by James Douglas Hamilton, the junior minister responsible for housing from 1987 until 1995. Aware that smaller towns such as Alloa, Grangemouth or Clydebank were as liable to suffer from urban decay as any of the cities, Lord James encouraged Scottish Homes to develop a mechanism through which the kind of multi-agency approach adopted in the urban Partnerships could be applied in a smaller setting. At present fifteen SURIs ranging from Hamilton and Airdrie to the Vale of Leven and Kilmarnock are in existence and others may follow. Under the SURI regime major transformation is being effected in the towns concerned, and there is no doubt of the success of the approach. However, it has to be emphasised that where local authorities, Scottish Homes and their other partners have their local plans in effective harmony, good renewal operations do not necessarily have to have such an organisational framework.

One of the successful early actions of Scottish Homes was the development of a rural housing policy. A sub-committee led by Heather Sheerin and assisted particularly by Raymond Young was established to develop a strategy to address some of

Modernised housing in Longpark.

Scotland's neglected rural housing problems. Rural Scotland contains only twenty per cent of the population and it is true that some of the most prosperous Scots live in the country-side. In addition, of course, the visible signs of decay which are sometimes easy to spot within an urban environment are rarely as evident in rural communities. Perhaps for such reasons in the past it was easy to ignore rural housing problems or to assume that they are not worth serious consideration. The contrary is in fact the case. Relative poverty is common in some country communities. Some rural areas are heavily pressurised by incoming commuters, and other localities are affected by the demand of urban dwellers for holiday accommodation or second homes. As a consequence of such factors, house prices may well outstrip the resources of (particularly younger) local residents who may, therefore, be forced to migrate. Healthy communities need to retain or attract young people, hence country areas are just as entitled to support as are towns and cities.

Careful research and wide consultations, including a major international conference on rural housing at Aviemore in the autumn of 1990, led to the creation of Rural Demonstration Areas within which various potential policy measures were tested over the following three years.[18] This proved a successful way forward, showing that a partnership approach was just as likely to be effective in country communities as in urban areas. Rural housing associations were encouraged and various other innovative measures were developed and piloted and these included Rural Home Ownership Grants (RHOGs) which are targeted to assist low income country dwellers into home ownership. This ultimately all led to the evolution of the first genuine Scottish rural housing programme and, as the investment figures indicate, in the present year just over £60 millions will be directed by Scottish Homes to rural operations.

The policy which has aroused the greatest amount of public attention and controversy is undoubtedly the bulk transfer of former SSHA houses to other landlords. The Scottish Homes Board accepted that it was right for it to dispose of its stock. Partly this was to allow the organisation to concentrate attention on its wider strategic role and enabling operations, but, as previously discussed, it was also the result of the belief of ministers that the state should not seek to be a direct provider of housing in the longer term. The Board agreed that it was appropriate for it to seek to encourage a greater degree of tenant and community involvement in the control of the housing stock and it also had the broader purpose in mind of creating some genuine choices for those who seek rented accommodation.

To some degree the way in which this policy evolved was influenced by earlier decisions. The great bulk of SSHA houses were directly managed by the Association's own housing management staff. However, a small number of houses in the Borders had continued to be factored on the Association's behalf by the local district councils. Realising that future policy in respect of its stock was likely to change, the Association gave notice of its intention to terminate the management contract for the houses in question. Looking ahead members of the local authority staff who had been involved in managing the houses now took the initiative by getting together with tenants to form the Waverley Housing Trust which thereafter bid to take over the 1200 or so houses in various areas of Roxburgh, Ettrick and Lauderdale. Unfortunately local authority reaction was hostile, perhaps not understanding the objects of the exercise, resenting the actions of former employees, or simply feeling a threat to what was perceived to be a traditional province.

It was decided that Waverley should manage the houses while the new Scottish Homes, due to be established a month or two later, would work out the mechanisms and general principles which should be applied to the bulk transfer of the ownership of stock. It was agreed that the decision should rest with tenants who would ultimately either vote to accept or reject the overtures of a bidder. A detailed procedure was evolved, however, and this allowed for a reasonable time period during which tenants would be given full access to the various interested parties, would be provided with independent expert advice and information and, if necessary, would be given training. Moreover careful steps were taken to ensure that the eventual agreed price returned an appropriate value for the sale of what were, of course, public assets. These various requirements inevitably had within them the potential for a degree of conflict. Normally sale of public assets requires that they be sold to the highest bidder. However, in the case of bulk housing sales ministers had quite properly agreed that tenants should be able to decide the matter by vote. Obviously, therefore, there was the possibility that tenants would reject the landlord who was willing to pay the highest price, but support one who offered rather less. Scottish Homes had ultimately to develop a system which ensured that an acceptable price was negotiated; but it is a fact that a potential technical problem remains.

The first bulk transfer, therefore, involved the sale of the borders houses to Waverley Housing Trust in 1992 and this was agreed after a month long postal ballot which showed 71% of the voters to be in favour of the transfer.[19] Soon similar ballots in Dumbarton, Banff and Buchan, Moray and Easter Ross repeated the pattern of overwhelming tenant backing for transfers to new associations or co-operatives.

In the case of the transfer to Waverley there was considerable criticism particularly from local councillors and other politicians, but also from some tenants. (In one ballot area the tenants actually voted against the proposal and in that case the houses remained in the ownership of Scottish Homes.) As was expected bearing in mind the novel nature of the sale, the process was subject to prolonged scrutiny from the public auditor and the Committee on Public Accounts and Scottish Homes was mildly rebuked for failing to reconsider a potentially higher offer from another bidder. To Board members, this finding did not give sufficient weight to the requirement for bidders to have a realistic prospect of securing the support of tenants, but procedures were subsequently tightened in an effort to address the problem.

Much of the general criticism, however, was not soundly based. It was, for example, claimed that properties were undervalued, but this was simply not the case. While it is technically difficult to set a valuation for stock under the circumstances of bulk transfer, the problem was made particularly complex by various important considerations. For example, account had to be taken of such matters as that houses were being sold with secure tenants in occupation, that the houses would have to be retained indefinitely for the purposes of social renting and that some properties would be transferred in the knowledge that they required major refurbishment. It was never a question of selling unburdened properties on the open market and inevitably this affected prices and made them seem low to uninformed eyes. All such factors were properly and fully considered by Scottish Homes and its advisers, but conveniently ignored by some of its public critics.

In general terms the major complaints levied against Scottish Homes bulk transfer policies are that the tenants are eventually confronted by only one bidding landlord on the ballot paper – whom they may accept or reject – and that, unless under very exceptional circumstances, local authorities are not permitted to be candidates to acquire the properties in question.[20]

As far as the first point is concerned, it is essential to have a clear-cut decision. Nothing could be worse than for tenants to finish up in a situation where they are in conflict with one another over possible landlords. In reality, however, the complaint is not well founded because tenants are in fact given a full choice. In terms of the procedure, realistic bidders are given the time and opportunity to make their case fully and to have their bid evaluated by the tenants and their independent advisers. Only after this has been done are the views of tenants solicited and a choice made as to which potential landlord should be subjected to ballot. The system, therefore, combines the clear requirements of democratic decision making and choice, with the need to obtain a decisive verdict one way or the other, so that communities are not unnecessarily divided.

As to why local authorities are excluded, this may be said to get to the heart of what the policy is about. Ideally consumers seeking rented accommodation should have the opportunity to chose from contending suppliers. That ultimately is the best way through which to secure sustained improvements in standards of housing and housing services in rented sectors. In many parts of the country those attempting to obtain rented housing are confronted by a supply dominated by the local authority, hence when a proposal to transfer Scottish Homes stock comes forward a consideration confronting staff must be the nature of the local housing market. If the object of the exercise is to diversify supply so that some realistic choices confront the prospective tenants of the future, then there is absolutely no point in reinforcing local monopolies. Where local authorities have more than 50% of the stock of housing for rent, allowing them to take over local Scottish Homes houses would entirely defeat the purpose of the policy. Moreover, from the government's point of view a sale to another public sector landlord would produce no financial benefits to the public purse.

To the author a competitive market for rented housing is as important and reasonable as a competitive market for the supply of motor cars, food, clothing, televisions or almost any other consumer product. Monopolies almost always result in inferior services and that has been at least an element of the problem of the low quality of social rented housing in many parts of Scotland of recent decades. It is necessary to break out of this situation if we are to secure permanent long term improvement and that must mean creating a network of landlords who are to a degree in competition with one another and whose standards of service can be compared, thus enabling consumer choices to impact on quality. It is, therefore, right that Scottish Homes should seek to use its inherited stock of houses to encourage the emergence of alternative landlords.

At the date of writing a total of 10,543 houses had been transferred, 8,457 via the bulk transfer process described, 1,395 under the terms of the statutory 'Tenants Choice' mechanism and 691 vacant possession houses. Ballots have produced large tenant majorities in favour in 31 areas relating to 15 bulk transfer transactions. Only in three small areas involving 118 houses were transfer proposals rejected by the tenants and in each case the local circumstances were somewhat unusual for one reason or another. Ballots had also been concluded in respect of a further 4,129 houses and these too are likely to pass to new landlords in the near future.[21]

Finally, it should be emphasised that transfers have called for great loyalty and professionalism on the part of staff. In many cases housing management staff have transferred to the receiving agencies and a part of the procedure quite rightly involves consideration of the effects on local Scottish Homes employees. In some instances such individuals have themselves taken the initiative and assisted in the formation of the housing association which has thereafter taken its case to the tenants. However, staff tasked with overseeing and managing transfers are not in a position to involve themselves in the venture and, in a sense, therefore, may be considered to be working themselves out of their jobs. Inevitably, these changes must be managed properly to a successful conclusion and one hopes that the Chief Executive will look to the interests of those concerned, perhaps through a 'golden handcuff' mechanism which will allow the transition to be completed professionally and without personal fears for the future.

It is obvious that the past two decades have been a period of rapid change in Scottish housing. The situation and range of choices confronting households is becoming increasingly complex and older assumptions no longer necessarily apply. In addition, it may be suggested that consumers now have higher expectations in terms of the quality of services. It may have been recognition of enhanced public expectations that persuaded the Prime Minister to support the notion of the Citizen's Charter and as part of the process Scottish Homes was invited to develop a strategy for enhancing housing information and advice services in Scotland. To this end in 1992 a committee was established including in its membership representatives from various interested organisations such as COSLA, the Citizens Advice Bureaux, Shelter, housing associations, legal firms and so on, and it initiated some helpful research and widespread consultations. Out of this process it was eventually decided to establish 'Homepoint', a unit with a dedicated budget which would have the task of co-ordinating, extending and improving housing information and advice services across Scotland. If consumers are to be enabled to make effective choices they have to be well informed and to have access to a wide range of good quality information and objective advice. It is to be hoped that the activities of Homepoint will be fruitful in this area.

It will be clear from the foregoing discussion that the period since the early 1970s has witnessed something approaching a housing revolution. The most striking feature is certainly the growth of home-ownership, but other changes are equally interesting and may be of equal significance in the longer term. For example, there is no question but that there has been a major transformation in the physical quality of recently built dwellings for all sectors. As must have been obvious from the account given throughout this narrative, there was a marked deterioration in the standards of housing built in Scotland in the first three post-war decades, and indeed many of the public sector buildings produced in the period 1945 to 1975 have had to be replaced or radically reconstructed and the residue of the legacy of the period remains a major burden on contemporary housing budgets. The life-cycle cost of many of the buildings originally constructed in places such as Wester Hailes or Whitfield, for example, must have been horrendous. However, such is not likely to be the case in respect of the buildings of the last twenty years. Moreover, in the same way much of the recent rehabilitation work must surely have preserved many fine older buildings for use far into the future.

Another point worthy of reflection is the gradual improvement of general levels of understanding of housing and housing policy matters. Some of the lessons have obviously involved a very expensive learning process. In addition, there is no doubt that many thousands of families have paid a monstrous price for the folly of past mistakes.

Over recent years, however, a greatly improved level of knowledge has developed and perhaps one of the most significant achievements of Scottish Homes is slowly emerging from its various research programmes and from the strategic thinking which underpins much of its spending activities. Those interested in housing matters should certainly skim the annual Housing Research Review and/or obtain some of the more detailed reports and papers. Similarly, one of the most interesting documents produced each year is *Housing in Scotland: The National Context for Strategic Planning* which explores much of the background against which programmes are developed. Finally, as was mentioned previously, the *Local Housing System Analysis* technique now provides a local framework of data which is infinitely superior to anything previously available.

One of the most pleasing aspects of this development has been the greater willingness to see housing in its economic rather than purely social context. Part of our basic problem is that previous policies far too often paid little attention to the relationship of housing to household economic behaviour and to the functioning of the economy. For example, much excellent research has obviously come from the Rowntree Foundation, but it may also be suggested that the extent to which this admirable charitable institution, with its heavy commitment to social policy, has dominated much housing research has not always resulted in an entirely healthy focus on the subject. While in no sense wishing to discourage or diminish the activities of that or similar organisations, it is important that a more balanced approach to the analysis of housing matters is presented to opinion informers and policy makers. Official institutions in both Scotland and elsewhere in the U.K. should be careful to preserve and nurture research input from a variety of sources. Similarly, it has to be suggested that well-meaning organisations such as Shelter have actually been part of the problem, particularly to the extent that they have almost consistently campaigned for an extension of the state system. As an organisation Shelter has shown all too little grasp or understanding of the damage which the system has inflicted on households and communities, particularly through its propensity to perpetuate poverty.

As far as the Scottish economy is concerned, it has altered considerably in the past fifteen years or so. In the mid 1970s many of the traditional industries were still dominant, but in almost terminal decline. The characteristic feature of recent years, therefore, has been the transition towards the service sector and newer light industries. Services now contribute over one third of Scottish Gross Domestic Product. Employment grew in the years around 1990, before falling back slightly. However, by 1992 the Scottish unemployment level (9.5%) was below that of the U.K. (9.9%) for the first time since the 1920s. Even when the U.K. figure dropped to 9.2% in 1994, the Scottish unemployment position remained marginally better at 9%.

Similarly the Scottish economy has experienced better growth rates than many other parts of the U.K.. While the overall economy contracted by 2.6% during the recession of 1991–92, GDP in Scotland actually increased by 2.1%. During the subsequent recovery, U.K. export led growth reached 2.1%, but the performance in Scotland rose to 2.4%, and much of the improvement was attributed to a growing contribution from manufacturing in electronics.[22]

It will be seen from the above notes that for the first time since the First World War, the Scottish economy has recently been marginally outperforming other regions in the U.K.. No doubt much of the explanation for this has nothing to do with housing. However, as was explained previously, the recession of the period around 1991–92 was indeed largely related to housing and Scotland coped with the situation rather better than, for example, the south of England. It has to be pointed out, therefore, that the housing policies pursued in Scotland since 1979 have played a significant part in bringing about an important change in the structure of the domestic economy.

However, the process is very far from being complete and further improvements need to be made. For instance, it is to be hoped that the opportunities of local government reform and the introduction of Compulsory Competitive Tendering for housing management services will lead swiftly towards the development of genuine rented housing markets. Local authorities should concentrate on strategic and enabling services rather than provision within one sector. Rather than maintaining huge housing bureaucracies, they should concentrate on the healthy development of their towns and cities and nurture efficient and professional independent suppliers of rented housing services.

Recently the author had the opportunity to visit Berlin and to discuss with local government officials there the plans for Germany's capital city in the developing post-reunification period. The most striking feature was the grasp which all concerned had on the emerging 'vision' of Berlin in the future and of their general appreciation of the fact that their city was in economic competition with similar cities across Europe. There seemed in this to be lessons on which Scottish local politicians might reflect. The legacy which Berlin has inherited from the communist era is fairly grim to say the least, but the approach which is now being adopted is instructive. At base the city fathers are seeking answers to a simple set of questions. What type of city do we want? How do we make it a good place in which to live? How do we assist our people to better living standards by helping the businesses of our city to compete effectively under modern economic conditions? How do we make the city attractive to new firms which might locate here?

This is the type of approach which the Scots should require from their local authorities. It is 'visionary'; and it is strategic. It has nothing to do with the direct provision of housing. On the other hand, it has everything to do with encouraging and facilitating the development of high quality housing services, high standards of accommodation and a good range of genuine housing choices.

One of the most troublesome features of the current Scottish housing system is the extent to which the private rented sector has withered away. As is clear from an examination of the housing arrangements of most western countries (including both Denmark and Canada), a significant proportion of dwellings for private rent is a key element in a healthy and flexible housing structure. Many households do not wish to take on the financial burden of a mortgage. Similarly, many people require short term accommodation – migrant or short contract workers; students and other young people moving out of the parental home; those going through the break-up of a marriage or previous household arrangements, are all examples and there is no likelihood of such groups becoming less significant in future. To meet the housing requirements of these groups of people, the private rented sector is probably most suitable, but the fact is that for various reasons – and particularly the prolonged controls on rents – the squeeze on this part of the housing system has been relentless and previous attempts to restore the position have failed.[23]

One of the causes of the virtual collapse of the private rented sector in many parts of Scotland is undoubtedly the poor reputation enjoyed by private landlords. The explanation for this is historic and cultural, but it is a matter which needs to be addressed if we are genuinely to strengthen and increase the flexibility of our housing facilities. The Tenants' Choice and Bulk Transfer mechanisms give tenants the right to transfer to a designated Approved Landlord – ie one which satisfies Scottish Homes as to its professional competence. Personally the author would very much like to see this system extended, not compulsorily, but on a voluntary basis. For example, if universities and colleges undertook only to carry notices drawing attention to designated Approved Landlords, and if housing

Housing belonging to Garrion Housing Co-operative in Wishaw.

benefit was only available to tenants of Approved Landlords, it may be suggested that many of the owners of rented accommodation would move quickly to obtain recognition. If Scottish Homes can monitor the activities of housing associations, it is hard to see why it should not similarly assess the quality of services in the private sector. Taken together with some appropriate tax incentives to encourage increased supply, it must be suggested that such 'kite-mark' measures might do something to raise standards, enhance the reputation of private landlords and make their activities more generally acceptable to the public. Regrettably former colleagues on the Board of Scottish Homes were not convinced by such arguments, but perhaps the position may change in future when the crisis in the private rented sector becomes even more acute.

Similarly, housing companies or semi-commercial trusts ought to be encouraged to develop in the rented sector and to compete to manage or ultimately acquire the current public sector housing stock as well as to engage in further new development of housing for rent. As has been suggested previously, some housing associations could be very effective bidders in this area, but if we wish to develop a strong and flexible rented sector it will be necessary to raise larger amounts of finance from private sources. Again, within the local authorities there are many excellent housing management professionals who might thrive in a more business-like environment. Successful housing companies could produce both investment and innovation across the spectrum of rented housing and appropriate encouragement should be given to ventures of this sort.[24]

The other main area where reform is urgent is concerned with the housing benefit system. This takes the discussion towards national rather than Scottish policy and perhaps beyond the scope of the present book. However, in recent years housing benefit payments have become such a major element in the housing subsidy system that some comment is necessary.

In 1979 approximately £95 millions of housing benefit payments were drawn into Scottish housing. By 1993 this had swollen to £663 millions, more than two thirds going to support households in the public sector. This growth was despite falling numbers of public and private sector tenants and Social Security reforms introduced in 1988 which had the effect of reducing some benefit entitlements, particularly to young people.[25]

At base there are two problems with the current housing benefit mechanism. First, it is operated, not through those responsible for housing policy, but by the Department of Social Security. From a housing perspective this is very difficult to sustain. Housing benefit has become such a significant part of the subsidy structure that it is necessarily a central concern for those attempting to develop sensible housing policies. For example, the current benefit system does very little to encourage households to trade or to otherwise adjust their housing arrangements in order to obtain a better or more appropriate deal. The consequences are that family houses are often tied up by single people and little or no advantage is gained by households from moving from one house or area to another. In other words, unnecessary rigidities are introduced and control passes from households to benefit providers.

To address this problem it is suggested that housing benefit and housing policy should be the province of the same government Department – in this case, the

HOUSING BENEFIT

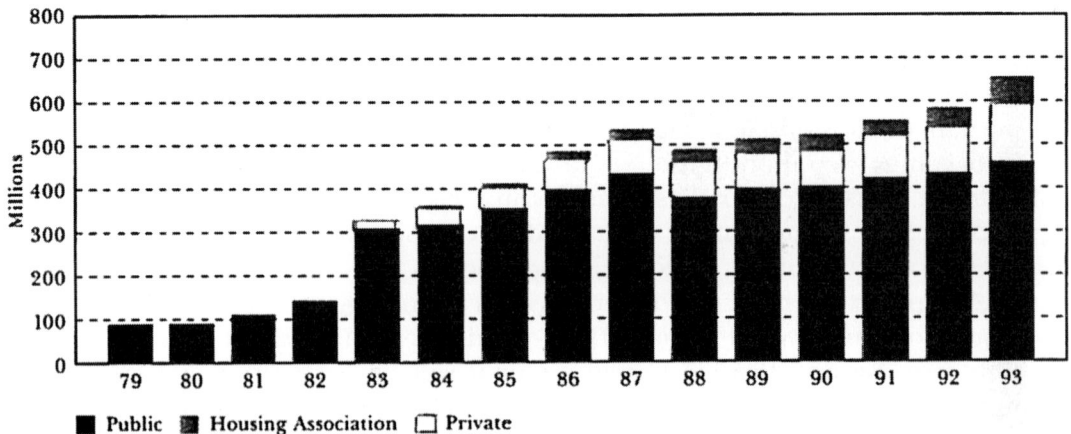

Public ■ Housing Association □ Private
Source: Scottish Homes Working Paper – Investment in Scottish Housing, D Robertson, 1994.

Scottish Office. Such a change has not found favour in recent government circles, but in the author's opinion a fully rational housing policy for Scotland will not be possible until operation of the housing benefit budget is transferred to the Secretary of State for Scotland. Actually it is hard to see why this is so unacceptable, because the truth is that the inclusion of the housing benefit system within unified social benefit arrangements is one of the factors which has made it very difficult to control the massive contemporary explosion in payments.

The second major problem with housing benefit is the contribution which it makes to the poverty trap. What this means is that as households move into employment and increase their earnings from work, so they forfeit benefits and, therefore, may find themselves working for very little marginal return. Only if they can expect proportionately high earnings will there be much incentive to seek employment and hence escape the 'poverty trap'. Consideration of this matter, would necessarily lead on almost to a second book, but suffice it to say that the problem rests at the heart of much that is wrong with contemporary social policy. In the author's view it is neither civilised, nor kind, nor efficient to maintain welfare systems which provide for immediate needs, but discourage individual initiative and self respect. A housing benefit system which enables healthy adults to shed entire responsibility for contributing to their housing costs is desperately unwise. Far better that every household should contribute something – perhaps a minimum of one fifth of the rent – so that they have some incentive to seek self betterment and to accept a degree of responsibility for their personal well-being.

All that said, however, the worst reaction which the Government could adopt to

1990s upmarket housing at Hillpark, Edinburgh.

the current growth in housing benefit payments would be to respond to the problem purely in cost cutting terms. Clearly the fundamental principle is correct of providing a measure of subsidy to low income people in need rather than attempting, one way or another, to supply housing on the cheap.

Such matters are perhaps for debate elsewhere. Meanwhile it is worth returning to the progress made in recent years and to acknowledge that a major improvement is being accomplished. Comparisons with housing in other countries will confirm that many Scots have excellent accommodation – some as good as anything to be found virtually anywhere in the world. Similarly, general standards are rising and many qualitative improvements will be recognised by even a cursory glance over most of our cities, towns and villages. On the other hand, concentrating the poorest members of society into run-down public sector estates cannot any longer be considered to be acceptable. Ghettos for the poor should have no place in modern Scotland.

Commentary

In conclusion, a brief reflection on some of the main themes which characterise the development of housing policy in Scotland throughout the twentieth century might include the following points.

In the early years of the century the desire to draw the state into involvement in the provision of housing stemmed fundamentally from a concern with the poor and insanitary living conditions experienced by many working people. Overcrowding was a key problem and the persistence of the low rent culture slowed the rate at which improvements were accomplished. Such problems masked the better standards which were actually being enjoyed by a growing proportion of the community and encouraged impatience with the rate of progress being achieved through growth.

The advent of the First World War was decisive in that it compelled the state to intervene in housing. The traditional dislike of economic rents of sections of the Glasgow industrial population provoked unrest during the war and stimulated passage of the Rent Restriction Acts in 1915. This proved difficult to remove and effectively legalised opposition to economic rents with the consequence that the private rented sector, which had hitherto dominated housing provision in Scotland, was driven into long-run decline, while standards of care and maintenance in traditional Scottish properties became less and less adequate. In the long term this resulted in the deterioration of many buildings and tended to undermine the credibility of private landlords.

At the same time the Government was induced to provide the funding to enable local authorities to become mass providers of housing for working people. As a temporary expedient in the immediate aftermath of the 1914–18 war this was a helpful and praiseworthy initiative. Similarly the Chamberlain subsidies to the developers of property for private ownership were highly successful and together with low mortgage interest rates in the inter-war period stimulated the growth of home owning through a widening section of the community. Even the Wheatley measure of 1924 would have been regarded as an unqualified success as a short term expedient. However, in the longer period the Wheatley Act (taken together with the inter war slum replacement policies) has to be considered a very doubtful blessing since it began the process of developing in Scotland a derigiste system of housing in which control was increasingly assumed by local politicians and bureaucrats. This in turn encouraged the evolution of political and industrial attitudes which were deeply damaging. Moreover, in keeping with their political purpose, increasingly the houses being produced had to conform to an appearance which was readily identifiable as industrial working class.

The period immediately after the Second War was, in retrospect, a disaster for housing in Scotland. In these years the local authority system was hugely strengthened, both by controls which inhibited private development and by the extension of a general needs subsidy mechanism which was intended to produce housing for the mass of the population. This meant a major boost was given to the political ideology of low rented managed housing through the municipalities. The direct consequence was the creation of a low quality, industrial housing system which retarded the economic development of thousands of Scottish households and the communities in which they lived. Inevitably the insistence on low rents and on houses which were uniform and proletarian in appearance resulted in enormous economic waste and the continuation of social and health problems. This contributed to the relatively poor performance of the Scottish economy when contrasted with other regions of the U.K..

Of all the claims made about the worst of the great public sector estates to be found in most of our larger towns and cities the most wretched calumny of all was that the residents of such communities were somehow or another themselves responsible for the predicament in which they became trapped. As has been argued earlier, these estates often proved to be little more than engines for generating and perpetuating poverty and the miracle is that so many households contrived to make decent lives for themselves despite the circumstances. Often, however, escape was the only real solution, hence the steep decline in the populations of (say) Castlemilk or Whitfield long before the contemporary, hugely expensive, renewal initiatives. But no-one should now be in any doubt that hopelessly misguided municipal housing and planning policies were fundamentally at the root of the problem.

The mid-twentieth century creation of a housing system which depended on publicly owned mono-tenure estates with houses being allocated according to a combination of often obscure rules and the patronage of local officials or politicians, was a profoundly damaging and unfortunate aberration in the country's social and economic development. Arguably it happened only because the successive world wars created the conditions under which extremist state solutions could flourish.

There is no doubt that the post-war planners of the 1940s were well intentioned and it is tempting to believe that the subsequent situation for Scotland would have been very different had Tom Johnston and his colleagues remained in control and had their carefully nurtured plans been implemented. The great virtue of their proposals were that they were radical yet, at the same time, moderate. They realised that short term emergency measures would be required immediately after the war. However, they also recognised and addressed the need for major urban and industrial changes in west central Scotland where most of the population and decaying industries were centred; and planned a diversified approach making full use of the private sector, housing associations and the SSHA as well as the local authorities. New towns, with all that the word town implies, were preferred to great

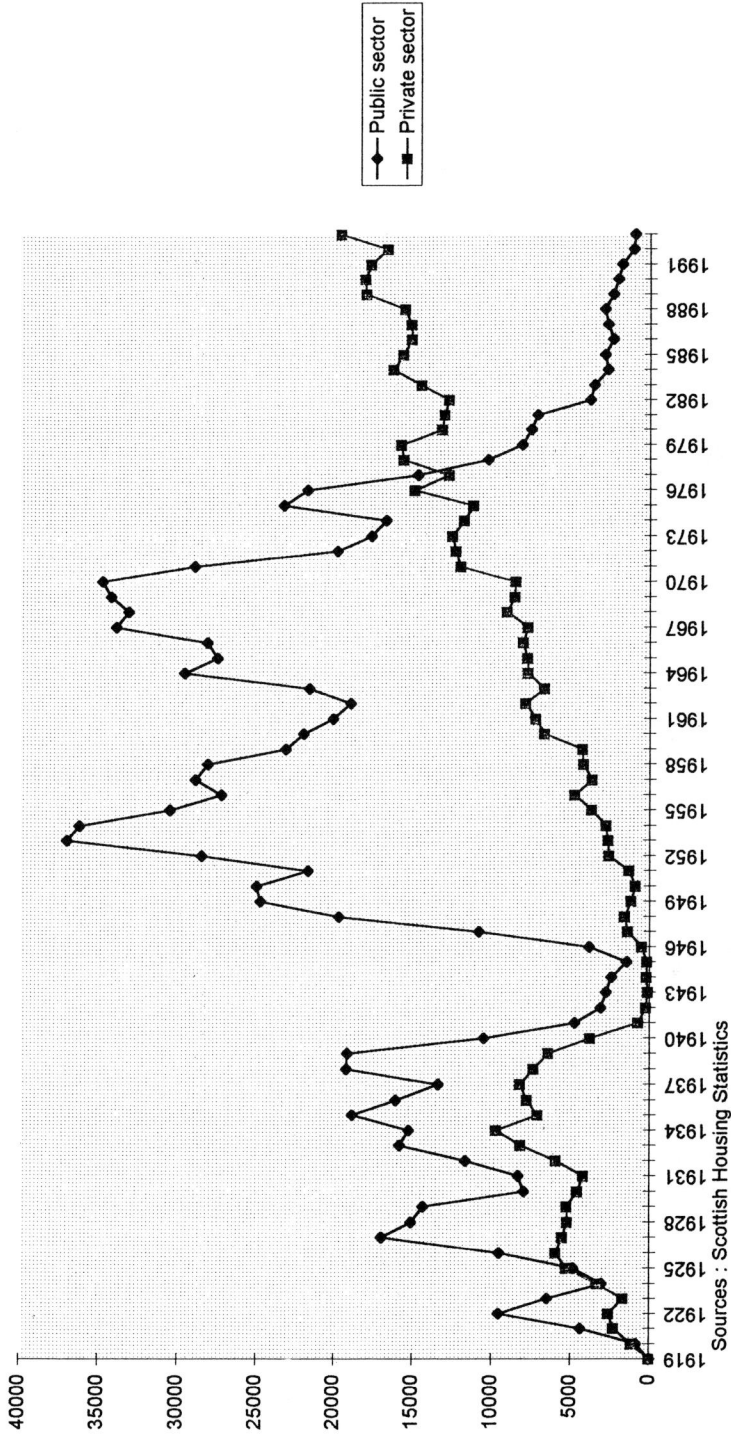

Scottish Housebuilding 1919-1993

Sources : Scottish Housing Statistics

Public Sector = Local authorities, SSHA and New Towns

Private Sector = Private and Housing Associations

Public sector
Private sector

municipal estates, and on green field sites the cottage house rather than tenement flat was the favoured dwelling form. And while population dispersal was thought to be necessary, it might have been matched by urban renewal at more sustainable community levels.

Sadly, of course, confronted by the extreme left wing policies insisted upon by influential sections of the Labour Party Johnston was effectively driven from office in 1945. Whether Johnston's plans were just pipe-dreams or practical proposals, the fact is that the drive towards a local authority based solution got more or less out of control, first in the post-war period and again in the 1960s, and the blunt fact is that much of the contemporary thrust of housing policy has been concerned with repairing the damage. Buildings can be repaired or replaced, but the personal havoc wrought on the lives of thousands of individuals and households is another matter altogether.

The failure of the Conservatives in the 1950s lay in their inability to challenge the developing housing system and, indeed, in their willingness to continue down the same route.[1] Perhaps it was a necessary political compromise, but it cannot be said to have won them the support of the Scottish population. Indeed, popular backing for the Conservative Party in Scotland actually began its decline from the mid 1950s.

The second great wave of public sector building in the 1960s was in many ways the result of the need to feed the public housing bureaucracies which had been built up since the 1940s. Some of the greatest damage was done to Glasgow at the end of this period and some of the worst estates, such as Wester Hailes or Whitfield were not completed until well into the 1970s. It has to be said also that this surge of activity was partly stimulated by good, but misguided intentions. The t.v. film *Cathy Come Home* (1966), for example, tended simply to encourage the belief that it was merely a question of throwing in more public resources.[2] Indeed the combination of the political climate engendered by this powerfully emotive film and the use of Selective Employment Tax to discriminate in favour of system building with reinforced concrete was largely responsible for the disastrous spasm of municipal building in the years around 1970.

As mentioned previously, during a visit to Poland the author and his colleagues discovered that under communism Poznan was left in a position where there were roughly 1.8 households per house. In other words almost 90% of households have to share accommodation; or, to express it yet another way, about 44% of households have no independent residence and could be considered to be homeless. Moreover, decades of low rents have left buildings in disrepair and there are no resources to sustain an adequate maintenance programme. While we were discussing this situation in municipal offices one older official, obviously a relic from the previous regime, commented, 'Our problem is that the government does not give us enough money to do the job properly'. There was a momentary pause and a kind of collective sigh from from the other Poles. 'Excuse my friend', whispered my neighbour. 'There are some of us who still don't understand that our people have to be able to make wealth if they are to have good houses'. I reassured him that the same attitudes were to be found in Scotland and remarked that housing policy provided the perfect illustration of the old saw that the road to hell is indeed paved with good intentions.

From the later 1950s on the underlying trend towards owner occupation steadily built up momentum. Partly this was a result of a desire for higher standards than were being provided by the municipal system and the wish to obtain the preferred types of cottage housing; but the trend was also stimulated by government policies in the form of tax concessions and improvement grants, both of which encouraged the view of the privately owned house as the centre-piece of domestic, household investment. With the passage of time such investment widened the wealth gap between home owners and public sector tenants. As the advantages of ownership became more obvious so it eventually provided the basic electoral support for the sale of public sector houses and opened the door for a major challenge to the state housing system.

The great demolition programmes of the late 1960s and early 1970s to make space for further public building activity also generated an element of disillusionment and unease at the damage which was being inflicted on older urban areas, particularly in Glasgow. But perhaps it also has to be said that the inflationary surges of the 1970s may, in this context, have been something of blessings in

Peter McKinlay (centre back row) and friends, at Logie Gardens, Dundee in 1994. Peter was opening a Cleghorn Housing Association development which provided a mixture of family housing and sheltered housing primarily for elderly members of the Dundee Chinese community.

disguise since they forced the government of the day to curb its expenditure on direct house provision.

In the contemporary period the motive behind Scottish housing policy is fundamentally the desire to stimulate social and economic regeneration. At a very basic level it is obvious that the Scotland of the future will look increasingly to high technology light manufacturing industries (probably employing a small proportion of the population) and a fully developed and sophisticated service sector. The labour force will have to be increasingly well educated and trained (the education sector will be large) and leisure and tourist industries will be important. To compete in these terms Scotland has many advantages, particularly its splendid scenery and recreational endowment, good communications and marvellous legacy of historic places of interest.

That fundamental economic formula more or less sets out the context for much of current and future housing strategy. Our buildings have to look good and to offer excellent urban and rural environments and the over all impression should convey a high quality of life. While modernity is desirable it is very important that we preserve our heritage of fine older buildings. People have to want to live and work in Scotland and to visit Scotland and the kind of wealth creating profile which we will have to follow in increasingly open international market conditions requires us to strive to develop houses, villages, towns and cities which provide good living and working conditions and are pleasant on the eye.

If that is indeed our housing future, then we have to carry on the business of modernisation and improvement; we have to accept and manage the terminal decline of the public housing system; and we have to ensure that all our citizens have reasonable and realistic, but genuine choices and opportunities from which to select their housing option.

References

In the preparation of this book extensive use has been made of various official sources, but especially of the archives of the Scottish Special Housing Association. The Minutes of the Council of Management, Monthly Reports and Annual Reports are contained in bound volumes and, in most cases, the pages are numbered. For this reason reference has been made to the appropriate volume and page number rather than the original reference number, since the latter would be much harder to track down. Abbreviations are recorded as follows:-

Minutes of the Council of Management – MCM (date)
Monthly Reports – MR (date)
Annual Reports – AR (date)
Minutes of Ordinary and Extraordinary
General Meetings – MOEG (date)

From 1948 the Association published an Annual Digest providing a summarised view of activities for the year and these are noted in the form AD (date) No.

The archives of the SSHA are now held by the Scottish Record Office, H.M. General Register House, Edinburgh.

References to other Scottish Record Office files are prefixed SRO and the file number is recorded. Official papers and reports are indicated in full.

Chapter 1

1. Scottish Homes, *Scottish House Condition Survey 1991: Survey Report*, (1993).

2. Among the best works on the economic history of Scotland would be included S.G.E. Lythe and J.Butt, *An Economic History of Scotland 1100–1939* (1975); R.H. Campbell, *Scotland Since 1707* (1985); B. Lenman, *An Economic History of Modern Scotland 1660–1976* (1977); A Slaven, *The Development of the West of Scotland 1750–1970* (1975).

3. Again, there are many examples, but see J.H.Muir, *Glasgow in 1901*, (1901); Shadow (pseud A. Brown) *Glasgow, Midnight Scenes and Social Photographs* (1976) or for a modern account S. Chapman, (ed) *The History of Working-Class Housing* (1971), essay by John Butt *Working-Class Housing in Glasgow, 1851–1914*.

4. Anthony S. Wohl, *The Eternal Slum – Housing and Social Policy in Victorian London* (1977), pp84–91. F. Berry, *Housing: The Great British Failure* (1974), p17. Interestingly, Berry regards the Cross and Torrens Acts as 'of little effect' and considers the Public Health Act 'profound' in improving housing standards.

5. I. H. Adams, *The Making of Urban Scotland*, (1978), p160.

6. M.J. Daunton, *House and Home in the Victorian City - Working Class Housing 1850–1914*, (1983), pp 288–9 quoting W. Thompson, *The Housing Handbook* (1903).

7. See Frank Worsdall, *The Glasgow Tenement: A Way of Life* (1989), pp110–115 for a description of Glasgow City Improvement Trust developments.

8. J Butt in S. Chapman, op cit, p63.

9. John McKee, *Glasgow Working-Class Housing Between the Wars 1919–1939* (1977), M.Litt Thesis, University of Strathclyde, p1.

10. Jean Kay Young, *From 'Laissez-Faire' to 'Homes fit for Heroes': Housing in Dundee 1868–1919* (1991), PhD Thesis, University of St Andrews, pp71–272.

11. R.L. Reiss, *Municipal and Private Enterprise Housing* (1945), p13

12. Anthony S. Wohl, op cit, p260 and W. Ashworth, *Genesis of Modern Town Planning* (1954), p85.

13. J.K. Young, op cit, see pp299–303 for example.

14. Ibid, p302; see also Miles Horsey, *Tenements and Towers: Glasgow Working-Class Housing 1890–1990* (1990), p4.

15. J.K. Young, op cit, p301.

16. See J McKee, op cit, Chapter 2 for an interesting discussion of the process of construction, acquisition and renting in the Polmadie district of Glasgow in the years around the turn of the century.

17. J.K. Young, op cit, p303.

18. G. Gordon and B Dicks, (eds) *Scottish Urban History* (1983) essay by J. Butt, *Working-Class Housing in Scottish Cities, 1900–1950*, p235.

19. R.H. Campbell, op cit, pp226–233, S.G. Checkland *The Upas Tree, Glasgow 1875–1975* (2nd Ed 1982), p23.

20. J. Melling, (ed) *Housing Social Policy and the State* (1980), essay by Melling on *Clydeside Housing and the Evolution of State Rent Control*, p143. See also Martin Doughty, *Building the Industrial City* (1986), essay by Richard Rodger on *The Victorian Building Industry and the Housing of the Scottish Working-Class*, pp180–181.

21. F. Worsdall, op cit, p6. See also M. Doughty, op cit, essay by Rodger, pp153–157 on tenements.

22. J. McKee, op cit, p1.

23. *Report of the Royal Commission on the Housing of the Industrial Population of Scotland Rural and Urban*, Cmd 8731 XIV, p346.

24. Census of Scotland 1911, reproduced Rodger, op cit, p48.

25. Marion Bowley, *Housing and the State* (1945), pp261–262.

26. M. Doughty, op cit, essay by Rodger, p153.

27. See Royal Commission Report, Cmd 8731, op cit, Chapter 3.

28. Ibid, pp8–9.

29. M. Bowley, op cit, p262.

30. Royal Commission Report, Cmd 8731, op cit, p292.

31. J. Melling, op cit, has an interesting discussion of the various movements in Glasgow.

32. See for example, Arthur Marwick, *Britain in the Century of Total War* (1969), including pp121–122.

33. In culling much of the literature on housing in the First World War era I could not help being struck by how little real feeling for the war experience emerges from much of the work in question. David Englander, *Landlord and Tenant in Urban Britain 1838–1918* (1983), for example, includes much that is interesting, but his Chapter 11, under the title, the *Impact of War*, is so intensely pre-occupied with class struggle that it succeeds in conveying no real sense of the wider impact of the war on society. The same criticism could be levied at many similar recent works on the period.

34. For example, Mark Swenarton, *Homes Fit For Heroes* (1981); Laurence F. Orbach, *Homes for Heroes: A Study of the Evolution of British Public Housing 1915–1921* (1977); David Englander, *Landlord and Tenant in Urban Britain 1838–1918* (1983); and Marion Bowley, op cit.

35. Ebenezer Howard, *Garden Cities of Tomorrow* (re-issued 1986).

36. Michael Simpson, *Thomas Adams and the Modern Planning Movement; Britain, Europe and the United States, 1900–1940*, (1985), pp53–54.

37. M. Swenarton, op cit, p11.

38. Ibid, pp17–18.

39. Ibid, p189.

40. M. Simpson, op cit, pp54–55.

41. Ibid, p54.

42. J.K. Young, op cit, p542, quoting (BPP (1914) XLC7327, pIXXV).

43. M. Simpson, op cit, p58.

44. J.K. Young, op cit, p556.

45. M. Swenarton, op cit, p45, quoting PRO T1/11838/25107 no. 7665, (Admiralty to Treasury, 8 April 1914).

46. Interestingly, however, at the time some of the workers moving into Rosyth were less than impressed and dismissed it as 'a very cheap gimcrack version of middle-class Letchworth'. David Englander, op cit, pp265–266, quoting *Workers Dreadnought*, 9 August, 1919.

47. Ibid, quoting *Municipal Journal*, Vol XXVI, (11 May 1917), pp447–448.

48. J.K. Young, op cit, p641.

49. M. Swenarton, op cit, p95.

50. F. Berry, op cit, p34.

51. M. Swenarton, op cit, p190.

52. Sidney Pollard, *The Development of the British Economy 1914–1950*, (1962), p88.

53. Asa Briggs, *Seebohm Rowntree* (1961), p134.

54. P. Johnson, *Land Fit for Heroes*, (Chicago, 1968), p59.

55. J.R.Jordan, *Homes for Heroes* (1971), MA Thesis, University of Kent, p35; Lawrence F. Orbach, op cit, p56 agrees.

56. J. R. Jordan, op cit, p37.

57. Ibid, pp61–62 for example.

58. Ibid, p49

59. M. Swenarton, op cit, p31, passim.

60. H. Richardson and D. Aldcroft, *Building in the British Economy Between the Wars* (1968), p137.

61. M. Swenarton, op cit, p77.

62. *The Times*, 13 November 1918, quoted in B.B. Gilbert, *British Social Policy 1914–1939* (1970), p19.

63. Martin Gilbert, *Winston S Churchill, Vol IV 1917–1922* (1975) pp171–172.

64. M.J. Daunton, op cit, p298.

65. J.R. Jordan, op cit, p35

66. Ibid, p100.

67. J.K. Young, op cit, p556 passim.

68. Ibid, p582.

69. Ibid, p581.

70. Ibid, p709.

71. J.R. Jordan, op cit, p129.

72. M. Swenarton, op cit, p115.

73. J.K. Young, op cit, p706.

74. Ibid, p581.

75. J. McKee, op cit, p21.

76. Ibid, p22.

77. J.R. Jordan, op cit, pp132–133.

78. Sir E. D. Simon, *The Anti-Slum Campaign* (1933), pp11–13.

79. M. Swenarton, op cit, p193.

80. M. Bowley, op cit, p16.

81. J. Burnett, *A Social History of Housing* (1978), P227.

82. Ibid.

83. Ian S. Wood, *John Wheatley* (1990), p139, quoting Charles Masterman.

84. Ibid, p39.

85. Ibid, p41.

86. M. Bowley, op cit, pp40–43.

87. Douglas Niven, *The Development of Housing in Scotland* (1979), p28.

88. J. McKee, op cit, p118 and a convincing table on p117.

89. M. Bowley, op cit, p264.

90. Annual Reports, The Scottish Board of Health, 1924, pp48–49; 1926, p48; Annual Report of the Department of Health for Scotland, 1929, p10.

91. Ibid, 1929.

92. J. Burnet, op cit, p234.

93. Sir E.D. Simon, op cit, p51.

94. Ibid, p23.

95. R.K. Middlemas, *The Clydesiders* (1965), p151.

96. Allan Massie, *Glasgow*, (1989), p90.

Chapter 2

1. See D. Aldcroft, *The Inter-War Economy: Britain 1919–1939.* (1970)

2. Hugh B. Peebles, *Warshipbuilding on the Clyde,* (1987), p3.

3. Stephen Roskill, *Naval Policy Between the Wars,* Vol 1, (1968). Chapter VIII gives a full account of the Washington Conference and its effects and the same author's *Churchill and the Admirals* (1977) discusses Churchill's oppostition to the cruiser programme.

4. H.B. Peebles, op cit, pp186–194.

5. M. Swenarton, op cit, quoting pp1918 Cmd 0191 VII, para 222.

6. Ibid, p128.

7. Alison Ravetz, *Model Estate: Planned Housing at Quarry Hill Leeds,* (1974), p23.

8. R.F.Harrod, *The Life of John Maynard Keynes* (1951), p346, quoting letter to *The Nation,* 24 May, 1924,

9. Harold Macmillan, *Winds of Change 1914–1939* (1966), p209.

10. SRO DD6/243 Memorandum and Articles of Association of the Scottish National Housing Company; and Richard Rodger, (ed) *Scottish Housing in the Twentieth Century* (1989), essay by David Witham, p97.

11. SRO DD6/542.

12. A.E. Holmans, *Housing Policy in Britain* (1987), pp60–61 on interest rates.

13. Ibid, p295.

14. B. Lenman, op cit, pp216–217. See John R. Hume and Michael S. Moss *Beardmore: The History of a Scottish Industrial Giant* (1979), p5; and p179 for the effect of the 1921 Washington Treaty on naval shipbuilding.

15. Ibid, p192; W.J. Reader, *Architect of Air Power* (The Life of the first Viscount Weir of Eastwood 1877–1959) (1968), p117.

16. Ibid, pp117–126; also Rodger, (ed) op cit, pp136–137, essay by Nicholas J. Morgan.

17. John S. Gibson, *The Thistle and the Crown: A History of the Scottish Office* (1985), pp70–72; Colin Coote, *A Companion of Honour: The Story of Walter Elliot* (1965), p93.

18. J.Gibson, op cit, p70.

19. *Glasgow Herald,* 1 October, 1925.

20. SRO DD6/245.

21. J. Gibson, op cit, p70.

22. Ibid, p71.

23. SRO DD6/246. Memo submitted to Cabinet by Secretary of State.

24. SRO DD6/ 245.

25. SRO DD6/ 243.

26. SRO DD6/ 246.

27. SRO DD6/251. Minute of Agreement dated 30 June and 3 July, 1926.

28. Ibid, Letter to Treasury dated 8 July, 1926.

29. SRO DD6/ 243, DD6/ 248; J.R. Hume and M.S. Moss, op cit, p192.

30. SRO DD6/ 245.

31. W.J. Reader, op cit, p126.

32. J. Gibson, op cit, p71.

33. Martin Gilbert, *Winston S. Churchill, Vol V 1922–1939,* p301; letter Churchill to Baldwin, 2 September, 1928.

34. Harold Macmillan, op cit, p177.

35. C. Coote, op cit, p64.

36. Ibid, p88.

37. Ibid, p93.

38. Ibid.

39. A.M. Mackenzie, *Scotland in Modern Times 1720–1939* (1941), p336.

40. R.H. Campbell, op cit, p186.

41. R.D.Crammond, *Housing Policy in Scotland, 1919–1964*, University of Glasgow Social and Economic Studies Research Paper, No 1, p20.

42. Stephen Merrett, *State Housing in Britain* (1979), pp55–56. See also John English, Ruth Madigan and Peter Norman, *Slum Clearance* (1976) pp20–23.

43. Edward Nevin, *The Mechanism of Cheap Money: A Study of British Monetary Policy,* (1955), p295.

44. Ibid, pp294–295.

45. D. Aldcroft, op cit, pp128–129.

46. Ibid, p342.

47. R.H. Campbell, op cit, pp232–233.

48. H. Marshall (with A. Trevelyan) *Slum* (1933), p65.

49. Ibid, pp43–44.

50. Ibid, pp146–148.

51. J. Gibson, op cit, p78.

52. Ibid, pp76–79.

53. A. M. Mackenzie, op cit, p333.

54. M. Bowley, op cit, p265.

55. SRO DD6/ 1131, Paper of 18/ 1/37.

56. 1938 Annual Report of the Department of Health for Scotland Cmd 5968 IX, p20.

57. SRO DD6/ 251.

58. AR 1937–1947.

59. J. McKee, op cit, pp65–66.

60. Ibid – also pp132–133.

61. J. Gibson, op cit, p84.

62. MCM 1937–38, p3.

63. Adams, op cit, pp234–235 and Official Report, 28 June, 1938, vol 337, no 136, col 1679.

64. MCM 1937–38, pp64–65 and AR 1937–47, pp11–12.

65. AR 1937–47, p15.

66. MOEG 1937–47, p3.

67. MCM 1939, p24

68. MCM 1939, p31 and p91.

69. J. Gibson, op cit, pp138–139.

70. MCM 1937–38, p30.

71. Identified in conversation with William L. Taylor, Leader of Labour Group, Glasgow Corporation, 1962–69 and Chairman of SSHA 1978–81. (23 November, 1987).

72. *Forward*, 13 May, 1939.
73. Ibid, 29 April, 1939.
74. AR 1937–47, p10.
75. MCM 1937–38, p105, and MCM 1938–39, pp26–27.
76. *Forward*, 13 May, 1939.
77. Ibid, 8 July, 1939.
78. Ibid, 15 July, 1939.
79. Ibid, 22 July, 1939.
80. MCM 1939, pp89–90.
81. AR 1937–47, p25 and MCM 1940 various places.

Chapter 3

1. Scottish Housing Advisory Committee, *Planning Our New Homes* (1944) Chapter VIII.
2. Henry Meikle, (ed) *Scotland* (1947), p49.
3. *Social Trends*, various eds.
4. See, for example, the interesting essay on housing in P. Addison, *Now the War is Over*, (1985).
5. Ibid, p54.
6. *Glasgow Herald*, 11 October, 1946.
7. Mary E.H. Smith, *Guide to Housing* (1983 ed), p13.
8. Scottish Office, *A Guide to Non-Traditional Housing in Scotland* (1987), p5.
9. See C.R. Attlee, *As it Happened*, (1954), p125 for an assessment of Johnston.
10. Thomas Johnston, *Memories* (1953), p148.
11. J. Gibson, op cit, p102.
12. MCM 1942, p15.
13. Ibid, pp46–50.
14. Ibid, pp78–79.
15. Scottish Housing Advisory Committee, op cit, Appendix 3 (xix)
16. Ibid, p12, para 9.
17. Ibid, Appendix 3.
18. Ibid.
19. Ibid.
20. Ibid.
21. Ibid, p12, para 10.
22. Ibid, p12, para 11.
23. Ibid, p13, paras 20–23.
24. Ibid, p58, para 277.
25. Ibid, pp91–93.
26. MCM 1945, p32.
27. Scottish Housing Advisory Committee, op cit, p50, para 233.
28. Ibid, pp50–51 paras 234–235.
29. Ibid, p96.
30. D. Niven, op cit, p85.

31. Ibid, p74.

32. MR 1943, p6.

33. MR 1944, p83.

34. Ibid, p40.

35. Scottish Housing Advisory Committee, *Distribution of New Houses in Scotland* (1944), Cmd 6552, p23, para 79. (Various drafts are contained SRO DD6/ 1683.)

36. SRO DD6/ 1126 D.H.S. Memo, *Summary of Conclusions and Recommendations* (May 1944), p5. (38 refers to p40, para 143 in the main report).

37. Cmd 6552, p44, para 159.

38. SRO DD6/ 1126 D.H.S. Secretary of State's Memo, Reaction to Cmd 6552, dated 18/ 8/ 44.

39. Cmd 6552, op cit, p9, para 15; and SRO DD6/ 1683, Draft Report, Chapter 3, para 3.

40. Cmd 6552, op cit, p10, para 18.

41. Ibid, p64, para 231.

42. Ibid, p51, para 194.

43. Ibid, p46, para 170.

44. Ibid, pp46–47, para 171.

45. Ibid, p40, para 142.

46. Ibid, pp44–45, paras 160–161.

47. SRO DD6/ 1126, p11, refers to para 161 of the main report.

48. Ibid, refers to p72, para 259 of the main report.

49. Ibid.

50. Ibid.

51. SRO DD6/ 1683, letter dated 28 January, 1944.

52. MR 1943, p137.

53. Ibid, p77.

54. SRO DD12/35 (Typescript) 1944, p7.

55. Ibid, p8.

56. Ibid, pp8–9.

57. Scottish Housing Advisory Committee, *Planning Our New Homes,* op cit, pp10–11, para 5.

58. Ibid, p11, para 6.

59. MCM, 1944, p24.

60. AR 1937–47, pp187–189.

61. MR 1944, p110.

62. Ibid, pp150–151.

63. Ibid, p155.

64. Ibid, pp157–158.

65. See, for example, progress listed MCM 1945, p2 and p62.

66. MR 1944, p82.

67. Ibid, p95.

68. MCM, 1944, p36.

69. Ibid.

70. MCM 1945, p41.

71. Ibid, p46.

72. Ibid, p64.

73. Ibid, pp94–95.

74. *New Statesman,* 18 August, 1945. Annual Vol, p106.

75. MCM 1945, p63.

76. Ibid, p83.

77. MR 1945, p248.

78. MCM 1945, p74.

79. Ibid, p76.

80. Ibid, pp110–111.

81. Ibid, p122.

82. MR 1945, pp286–287, dated 10 November, 1945.

83. *New Statesman,* 17 November, 1945, Annual Vol, pp327–328.

84. Memorandum by E.M. Nicholson, 6 November, 1945 (CAB 124/ 450) quoted in Kenneth O. Morgan, *Labour in Power 1945–1951,* (1984), p164.

85. Memorandum, Jay to Attlee, 2 November, 1945 (PREM 8/ 228) quoted in Morgan, op cit, p165.

86. MCM 1945, pp134–138.

87. SRO DD6/1683, letter dated 28 January, 1944.

88. AR 1937–47, pp187–189; see pp75–76.

89. See pp74–75.

90. Scottish Housing Statistics.

91. Clyde Valley Regional Planning Committee, *The Clyde Valley Regional Plan 1946* (1949 ed) Appendix 15, p372.

92. R.D.Crammond, op cit, p26.

F93. MCM 1945, pp78–79.

94. Thomas Johnston, op cit, p166.

95. Sir Patrick Abercrombie and Robert H. Matthew, *Clyde Valley Regional Plan 1946* (June 1946 ed.) Chapter 12, pp685–697.

96. Ibid, pp23–24.

97. Ibid, p384.

98. Ibid, p370.

99. Ibid, p685.

100. Ibid, pp695–697.

101. See, for example, Scottish Housing Advisory Committee, *Planning Our New Homes,* op cit, p50. Also many references in SSHA papers 1942–46. It was to confront this problem that the Burt Committee was established in 1943.

102. MCM 1942, pp46–50.

103. *New Statesman,* 17 November, 1945, Annual vol, pp327–328.

104. Ibid, 18 August, 1945, Annual vol, p106.

105. Jay to Attlee, 15 October, 1945 (PREM 8/228), quoted in Kenneth O. Morgan, op cit, p165.

106. C.E.B. Brett, *Housing A Divided Community,* (1986), p26.

107. T.C. Smout, *A Century of the Scottish People 1830–1950*, (1986), p274.

108. *New Statesman*, 25 August, 1945, Annual vol pp118–119.

109. *Forward*, 13 January, 1945.

110. Ibid, 27 January, 1945.

111. Interview with David Halley, 25 July, 1988.

112. Ibid.

113. MCM 1945, p46.

114. *Dictionary of National Biography* (Compact Edition) (1975), Vol 2, p2539, biographical note by F. Brockway.

115. *Glasgow Herald*, 30 July, 1944.

116. R.K.Middlemas, *The Clydesiders*, (1965), p280.

117. Interview with David Halley, 25 July, 1988.

118. *Dictionary of National Biography*. See also G. Brown, *Maxton* (1986), p290, for Maxton's reaction to Buchanan's decision to rejoin the Labour Party.

119. Middlemas, op cit, p287.

120. Ibid, p241.

121. MR 1945, pp95–96.

122. Conversation with William Taylor, November 23, 1987.

123. Douglas Niven, op cit, p77.

124. Interview with David Halley, 25 July 1988.

125. Thomas Johnston, op cit, p169.

126. Ian Donnachie, Christopher Harvie and Ian S. Wood, *Forward: Labour Politics in Scotland 1888–1988*, p78; essay by Harvie on Labour 1939–1951.

127. MR 1945, p141.

128. Interview with David Halley, 25 July, 1988.

129. R.D.Crammond, op cit, p26.

130. MCM 1945, pp143–144.

131. AR 1937–1947, pp272–273.

132. MCM 1946, pp35–36.

133. Ibid, p54.

134. Ibid, 59.

135. Ibid, p71; pp77–78; and interview with David Halley, 25 July, 1988.

136. MCM 1946, p89.

137. AR 1937–1947, pp363–364.

138. MCM 1947, p17.

139. Ibid and p30.

140. Kenneth O. Morgan, op cit, p336.

141. MCM 1947, p17.

142. MR 1947, pp133–144.

143. Ibid, p162.

144. AR 1948–1955, pp3–4.

145. Ibid, p4.

146. P. Addison, op cit, p57.

147. Kenneth O. Morgan, op cit, p334.

148. Ibid, p356.

149. Christopher Harvie, *No Gods and Precious Few Heroes; Scotland 1914–1980*, (1981), p107.

Chapter 4

1. MCM 1947, p62.

2. See, for example, MCM 1948, p48 – minutes of meeting with Robertson.

3. MR 1947, p208.

4. MCM 1947, pp60–61

5. AR 1948–1955, pp3–4

6. Ibid, pp121–122.

7. Ibid

8. R. Smith, *East Kilbride: the biography of a Scottish new town, 1947–1973,* for an interesting discussion of the origins of the new town. See especially p19.

9. Ibid, p15.

10. *Glasgow Herald,* 24 February, 1936; 26 April, 1937.

11. R. Smith, op cit, pp19–20.

12. *Glasgow Herald,* 19 November, 1946.

13. See R. Smith, p21 for a discussion of the Bruce Plan: also Andrew Gibb, *Glasgow: The Making of a City,* (1983), p169.

14. R. Smith, p21.

15. Correlli Barnett, *The Lost Victory: British Dreams, British Realities 1945–1950,* (1995).

16. See, for example, Andrew Gibb, op cit; Miles Horesy, op cit; or Michael Keating, *The City That Refused To Die – Glasgow: the politics of urban regeneration,* (1988).

17. See MCM 1948, p13; MCM 1949 p3, p29, p43, p49; MCM 1950, p1, p13.

18. MCM 1950, p1.

19. M. Horsey, op cit, p38.

20. A. Gibb, op cit, p168.

21. See, for example, Jessie H. Begg, *Tom Notman: The Beloved Pastor,* (1953). My mother's account of the life of her father gives a vivid incidental description of the vibrant lives of his Church of Scotland congregations in Gallowgate, Cowcaddens and St Mary's Govan in the inter-war years.

22. Kenneth O. Morgan, op cit, p401.

23. A.E. Holmans, op cit, p141.

24. MCM 1949, p54.

25. Scottish Special Housing Association (Alexander Watson) *Demonstration Houses; Sighthill, Edinburgh,* (1987) for a description of the various buildings.

26. R.H.Macintosh, *The No-Fines Story,* (undated). The neglect of no-fines immediately after the war and the return to the method are topics discussed in Tom Begg, *50 Special Years,* (1987); see p143, pp152–158, and pp169–172.

27. See Lord Butler, *The Art of the Possible,* (1971), pp154–155, for an account of the eccentric way in which this target was set.

28. MCM 1951, pp58–59.

29. MCM 1952, p36.

30. MCM 1951, p27, p47, and MCM 1953, p4.

31. MCM 1953, pp14–15, p20.

32. Scottish Office, *A Guide to Non-traditional Housing in Scotland* (1987).

33. MCM 1955, p3.

34. AR 1948–1955, p7, p28, p13; MCM 1946, pp44–45, p54; MCM 1947, p68.

35. MCM 1948, p2; MCM 1950, p3, p23, p28, p49.

36. SRO DD6/ 1225, Memorandum 13 November, 1951 and pp1–3.

  SRO DD6/ 1225, Memorandum ? November, 1951; and Memorandum Fiddes to Steel, 24 November, 1951.

37. SRO DD6/1225, Note for Minister of State, April 1952.

38. M. Horsey, op cit, p20.

39. R.D.Crammond, op cit, Chapter IV for a full discussion of this subject.

40. D.H.S. circular 7/1962, 12 February, 1962.

41. Official Report, Scottish Grand Committee, 4 July, 1961, columns 16 and 17.

42. John S. Gibson, op cit, p137.

43. R.D.Crammond, op cit, p78.

44. MCM 1957, p17, p55; AR 1956–1961, pp69–70, p180; MCM 1958 p3, p20.

45. MCM 1958, pp30–31.

46. Compare AR 1956–1961, p136 with p219.

47. MCM 1960, p27 and p63.

48. Annual Digests No 11, 1958, pp34–35; No 12 1959, p31; No 13, 1960, p16 and No 14, 1961, p32.

49. R.H.Macintosh, op cit, p16.

50. See for example MCM 1949, p3 and MCM 1950, p1 for an indication of the views of the Chief Architect of the Department of Health for Scotland and the Association's Chief Technical Officer and Assistant General Manager.

51. Scottish Special Housing Association (Charles McKean), *A Mirror of Scottish Housing*, (1984), p18.

52. *Social Trends* (various eds.)

53. *Social Trends*, No 5 (1974) Table 90, p132; Table 161, p180.

54. Mary E. H. Smith, *Guide to Housing*, (1983), p16 and p20.

55. I.H.Adams, op cit, p228.

56. MCM 1956, p33; MCM 1957, p59; MCM 1958, p62.

57. MR 1963, pp6–10.

58. MCM 1954, p50.

59. MCM 1955, p38.

60. See, for example, MCM 1955, p25, p38; and MCM 1956, p5.

61. MCM 1959, p1, p14, p33, p57, p76; MCM 1960, p1.

62. AR 1948–1955, p412 and p497; MCM 1952, p24.

63. MCM 1950, pp15–16.

64. M. Horsey, op cit, p35.

65. M. Keating, op cit, p23.

66. Ibid. Also M. Horsey, pp39–43.

67. M. Keating, p23.

68. A. Gibb, op cit, p164 and p170.

69. M. Horsey, op cit, pp45–58. See also the magnificent volume by M. Glendinning and S. Methesius, *Tower Block: Modern Public Housing in England, Scotland, Wales and Northern Ireland* (1994), chapter 25, for a fascinating account of the Gibson/Cross era in Glasgow.

70. Ibid, p49.

71. MCM 1960, p70.

72. MCM 1964, p54, p61. Tom Begg, *50 Special Years*, pp191–200.

73. A. Gibb, op cit, p171; Tom Begg, Appendix C, p285 for full list of SSHA multi-storey buildings built in greater Glasgow.

74. MCM 1960, p8.

75. D. Niven, op cit, p76.

76. Ibid, p77. M. Glendinning and S. Methesius, op cit, chapters 24 and 25 for an account of 'package deals'.

77. MCM 1959, pp20–21.

78. MCM 1966, p13, p44; MCM 1967 pp14–16; AR 1962–1967, pp315–316; AR 1968–1975, p25,p37.

79. See Tom Begg, op cit, p204 passim for an account of the 'Economic Expansion' programme.

80. MCM 1966, p53.

81. MCM 1968, p79,p84, p111; MCM 1969 p31 and p137 for the reaction of the SSHA to the news of the Ronan Point disaster.

82. An account of this visit is contained in the Scottish Homes private distribution paper, Tom Begg, *Housing: An International Perspective* (1993).

83. F. Worsdall, op cit, p148.

84. M. Keating, op cit, p116, (table supplied by Glasgow District Council Housing Department).

85. A. Gibb, op cit, p164, (graph constructed from Glasgow District Council Housing Management Department Annual Reports of 1968, p16 and 1979 pp12 and 15).

86. Ibid, p170.

87. Ibid, p150.

88. M. Keating, op cit, p27.

89. G. Gordon, *Perspectives of the Scottish City,* (1985), essay by Michael Pacione, *Renewal, Redevelopment and Rehabilitation in Scottish Cities, 1945–1981.*, p284, quoting Glasgow District Council (1978).

90. I. H. Adams, op cit, p231.

91. Ibid, p182.

92. Whitfield Partnership, *First Report on Strategy,* (Dec 1988) pp5–7.

93. Ibid, p4, Fig 2, Summary of Facts.

94. Bertrand Renaud, *Housing in Socialist Societies,* (World Bank) (1990).

95. Ibid, p8.

96. Tom Begg, *Housing: An International Perspective,* op cit, p17.

97. Ibid, p31.

98. Duncan Maclennan, *Housing and Urban Regeneration in Scotland 1974–1994: From Here to Eternity?* (Information Paper for Danish Parliamentary Delegation, (1994).

Chapter 5

1. *Regional Trends* (1985), p60, Table 3.1.

2. Green Paper, *Scottish Housing* Cmd 6852, (1977), pp4–5.

3. *Regional Trends,* op cit, Table 3.3, p61.

4. Mary E.H. Smith, *Guide to Housing,* (1989 ed.), essay by Duncan Maclennan, *Housing in Scotland,* p677.

5. Paul Balchin, *Housing Policy: An Introduction,* pp60–61.

6. Mary E. H. Smith, (1989), op cit, p681.

7. P. Balchin, op cit p26.

8. MCM 1970, p95; MCM 1971, p45, p114; MCM 1972, p49.

9. MCM 1972, pp57–58.

10. Ibid, p105.

11. MR 1978 (vol 2), p311.

12. MCM 1973, p115, p117; Tom Begg, *50 Special Years,* p220.

13. *Scottish Housing,* Cmd 6852, op cit, p13; pp69–70.

14. J.B. Cullingworth, *Essays on Housing Policy* (1979), pp41–42.

15. Ibid, p107.

16. The Scottish Office, *Statistical Bulletin; Housing Series,* including (HSG/1994/9), p6.

17. Scottish Homes, (Karen Watt and Yvonne Summers) *Housing in Scotland: The National Context for Strategic Planning* (1995), p11.

18. MCM 1979, pp27–28, p58; MCM 1980, p75.

19. Scottish Homes, *Housing in Scotland* (1995) op cit, p5.

20. Ibid, pp13–14.

21. S.S.H.A. (Charles McKean) (1984) op cit, p24.

22. Figures supplied by Scottish Homes, Housing Management Directorate.

23. S.S.H.A. *A Future for Faifley: A Strategy for a Problem Estate,* (1986).

24. Figures supplied by Scottish Homes, Housing Management Directorate.

25. M. Keating, op cit, p114.

26. Ibid, p27.

27. A. Gibb, op cit, p166.

28. MCM 1968, p14, p60; S.S.H.A. *A Chronicle of Forty Years 1937–1977,* p22.

29. AR 1968–1975, pp4–5, p28.

30. Duncan Maclennan, (1994), op cit, p11.

31. Ibid, pp12–14.

32. Ibid, p15.

33. MCM 1976, p30.

34. I.H. Adams, op cit, p233.

35. A. Gibb, op cit, p175.

36. M. Keating, op cit, p98.

37. M. Horsey, op cit, p65.

38. See Tom Begg, *50 Special Years*, Appendix B, p284; Appendix E, pp287–290.

39. Duncan Maclennan, (1994), op cit, pp15–17.

Chapter 6

1. Christopher Harvie, (1981), op cit.

2. M. Keating, op cit, p139.

3. Ibid.

4. *Inquiry into Housing in Glasgow* ('Grieve Report') (1986).

5. Douglas Niven, op cit, p127.

6. Scottish Development Department, *Scottish Special Housing Association, Policy Review* (1986), p1.

7. Scottish Development Department *Housing: The Government's Prposals for Scotland* (November 1987), p1.

8. The author enjoyed many discussions with Sir James Mellon, but structured interviews took place on 23/8/94 and 14/10/94.

9. A good indication of his views is contained in Sir James Mellon, *A Flexible Housing System for the Global Market*, (The Hume Lecture 1994), Hume Occasional Paper No 45 (1994).

10. Structured interviews took place with Peter McKinlay on 1/11/94 and on 9/11/94, but again, these merely augmented many hours of formal and informal discussions.

11. A clear account of these matters is contained in Margaret Thatcher, *The Downing Street Years* (1993), pp699–726.

12. Scottish Homes, *Housing in Scotland* (1995), p24; Housing Finance, *The Quarterly Economics Journal of the Council of Mortgage Lenders.* No 18, (1993): R. Williams, *Owner Occupation in Scotland* (Working Papers, Scottish Homes) (1994).

13. Scottish Homes, Information Paper, (November 1994).

14. Ibid, p2

15. Scottish Homes, Board Paper, *Scottish Homes Future Relationship with Housing Associations and Co-operatives* (September 1994), p5.

16. Ibid.

17. Tom Begg (1993), *Housing: An International Perspective*, op cit, gives a full account of the study tours.

18. A full examination of the outcome within the 'Rural Demonstration Areas' is contained in – Scottish Homes, *Monitoring and Evaluation of Scottish Homes' Rural Demonstration Areas*, Research Report no 34, Aberdeen University/ C.R. Planning, (1994); and summarised in *Precis No 6*.

19. Scottish Homes, *Annual Report 1991–1992*, p19.

20. See for example, article by Margaret Vaughan, *Glasgow Herald* (14/02/95).

21. Figures supplied by Scottish Homes Housing Management Directorate.

22. Scottish Homes, *Housing in Scotland*, (1995) op cit, pp23–25, quoting Business Strategies Ltd., *Regional Planning Services* (1994) and (1995).

23. Ibid, pp7–9, quoting G. Young, *The Private Rented Sector*, Working Papers, Scottish Homes, 1994; and R Best et al, *Consensus and Action: The Future of Private Renting*, 1992.

24. For an examination of Housing Companies see Joseph Rowntree Foundation, *Local Housing Companies: New Opportunities for Council Housing*, (Housing Research Findings No. 82, March 1993).

25. Scottish Homes, *Housing In Scotland*, (1995) op cit p13.
Colour Plates: See Caroline MacGregor, 'Gribloch: The Evolution of the Architectural and Interior Design of a 1930s Scottish Country House', in *Architectural Heritage V* (1995), for an interesting account of the design and construction of Gribloch house.

Commentary

1. See M. Glendinning and S. Methusius, op cit p159, p179 and p239 for interesting comments on the failure of Conservative ministers in the 1950s and early 1960s.

2. Ibid, pp320–321 for a perceptive view of *Cathy Come Home*, and of the initial outlook of Shelter. "Shelter flatly demanded that much more new public housing should be built;" and campaigned for lower rents and higher government subsidies.

Index

Commissioner for the Special
Areas, 41–46
Conservative Party, 22, 56, 81,
117, 121, 125, 126, 130, 169,
170, 180, 186, 218
Coote, C., 35, 36
Corpach, 123
'Council of State', (Council on
Post-War Problems), 56, 57, 85
Coventry, 129
Cowdenbeath, 12
Cowieson, Messrs, 34
Cross, L.W.S., 141
Crow, G., 107
Cullingworth, Prof J.B., 170, 171
Cumbernauld, 112, 117, 135, 138,
140

Dalziel, James, 100, 101
Davidson, W.C., 91
Danderhall, 99
Denmark, 189, 200, 210
Dollan, Sir Patrick, 51
Douglas, 45
Douglas, Sir William, 43
Douglas-Hamilton, Lord James,
192, 203
Douglas-Hamilton, Lord Nigel, 44
Dumbarton, 76, 205
Dumfries, 26
Dumfriesshire, 86
Dundee, 2, 6–8, 16, 19, 21, 33, 34,
40, 52, 76–80, 119, 124, 144,
147, 155, 156, 167, 182, 187,
219
Ardler, 156
Dryburgh, 136, 138, 144
Fintry, 130, 131
Greenmarket, 16
Logie, 21, 219
Whitfield, 65, 156, 157, 158,
174, 187, 208, 216, 218,
(colour plate)
Dunfermline, 31

East Kilbride, 112, 113, 114, 119,
130, 135
Edinburgh, 2, 3, 7, 34, 38, 52, 59,
69, 75, 110, 154, 155, 167, 169,
187, 198, 213
Bingham, 119
Corporation, (District
Council), 40, 64, 65, 110,
119, 154, 155, 190
Corstorphine, 39
Craigmillar, 40, 119, 154
Craigs, 39, (colour plate)
Duddingston, 39
Gracemount, 154
Hyvot, 154, 164
Hillpark, (colour plate), 213
Moredun, 109, 110, 119, 154
Morrison Circus, (colour plate)

Muirhouse, 154, 155
Niddrie, 40, 119, 154, 198, 199
Old Town, 6
Oxgangs, 154
Pilton, 40, 119, 154, 155
Sighthill, 119
Sighthill Experimental Site, 59,
64, 68, 69, 78–80, 98, 104,
121, 122, 169
Sutherland Street, 173
West Granton, 65, 154, 156, 158
Wester Hailes, 65, 155, 158,
163, 174, 187, 208, 218
Elliot, Sir Walter, 32–36, 40,
41–44, 47, 56, 57, 85, 94,
Environment Department, 188
Erskine, 174–177
Esher, Lord, 152

Faifley, 130, 131, 174, 176, 177
Fairfields, 30
Falkirk, 149
Fallin, 46, 80
Fife, 86, 112, 125
Finlay, S.A., 101
Forman, John, 75, 81, 83, 84, 91,
94
Fort William, 135
Forth, 45
Forward, 49–53, 90
Fyfe, Andrew, 191

Gaitskill, H., 104
Galbraith, Commander (Lord
Strathclyde), 122, 126, 136
Galston, 76
Garrion Housing Co-operative,
211
George VI, 45
Germany, 19, 114, 115, 130, 190,
194, 210
Gibb, Andrew, 152
Gibson, David, 141
Gibson, John S., 47, 56, 128
Gilmour, Sir John, 32
Glasgow, 1–13, 21, 24, 32, 38, 40,
44, 49, 55, 63, 65, 72, 76, 79,
84–184 passim, 202, 218, 219
Anderston Cross, 141
Arden, 130
Balornock, 93, 124
Barlanark, 116, 154
Blackhill, 40, 63
Bridgeton, 181
Broomhill, 142, 143
Cadder Road, 124
Cambuslang, 34
Cardonald, 34, 136
Carntyne, 25, 45
Castlemilk, 65, 113, 117, 119,
153, 154, 158, 159, 163, 174,
187, 216, (colour plate)
City Improvement Trust, 4, 5

Comprehensive Development
Areas (CDA's), 141, 150,
151, 152, 178, 181
Corporation, (District Council)
5, 24, 25, 28, 49–54, 82, 85,
93, 94, 96, 113–117, 125,
128, 140–143, 174, 177, 180,
186
Cowcaddens, 32, 141
Craigton, 21
Cranhill, 116
Dalmarnock, 181
Darnley, 117, 140
Drumchapel, 65, 117, 119, 154,
158, 163, 174
Easterhouse, 65, 117, 154, 158,
174, 190
Elderpark, 142
Gallowgate, (colour plate)
Garngad, 34, 35
Garthamlock, 116, 154
Gorbals, 32, 35, 81, 92, 134,
140, 141, 143, (colour plates)
Govan, 12, 141, 152, 179
Govanhill, 26
High Street, 5
Hillington, 54
Hutchesontown, 65, 140, 141,
143
Kinning Park, 142
Knightswood, 25, 141, (colour
plate)
Maryhill, 143, 182–184
Mosspark, 21
Nitshill, 117
Partick, 11, 152, (colour plate)
Pollock, 116, 117, 154
Pollockshaws, 141
Possil, 40, 63
Priesthill, 117
Prospecthill, 109
Red Road, 149
Riddrie, 21
Robroyston, 34
Ruchazie, 116
Shettleston, 34, 181
Shields Road, 142
Sighthill, 142, 144
Springboig, 34
Springburn, 142, 152
Summerston, 140
Toryglen, 116, 124, 136, 137
Townhead, 141
Woodside, 141
Wyndford, 143, 145
Glasgow Eastern Area Renewal
(GEAR) Project, 181–184, 186
Glasgow Herald (*The Herald*), 32
Glasgow West Housing
Association, (colour plate)
Glenrothes, 113, 114, (colour
plate)
Grangemouth, 135, 146, 203